GW00982603

HISTORY OF
Japanese Thought

From the author's preface: '...A number of excellent Western works have already been published on the history of Japanese philosophy. One thinks, for example, of the late TSUCHIDA KYOSON's *Contemporary Thought of Japan and China* (London: Williams and Norgate Ltd.), which appeared about forty years ago, and Father Gino K. PIOVESANA's *Recent Japanese Philosophical Thought, 1862-1962: A Survey* (Tokyo: Enderle Bookstore), published in 1963. Others might also be mentioned. Of all of them, however, it must be noted that they understand Japanese philosophy to have started with the Meiji Restoration and with the entrance of Western culture into Japan. My point of view, however, is fundamentally different, for I am of the opinion that even prior to the Meiji Restoration there was a long history of philosophy in Japan...'

The late Professor HAJIME NAKAMURA, one of the most distinguished and internationally known philosophers and Buddhist scholars in Japan, was Professor Emeritus at the University of Tokyo and Director of the Eastern Institute in Tokyo. He is the author of countless articles and books in both Japanese and English and the author of *Ways of Thinking of Eastern Peoples: India – Tibet – Japan* also published by Kegan Paul.

www.keganpaul.com

THE KEGAN PAUL JAPAN LIBRARY

HISTORY OF
Japanese Thought

592-1868

Japanese Philosophy
before Western culture entered Japan

Hajime Nakamura

KEGAN PAUL
London • New York • Bahrain

First published in English in Tokyo, 1967

This edition first published in 2002 by
Kegan Paul Limited
UK: P.O. Box 256, London WC1B 3SW, England
Tel: 020 7580 5511 Fax: 020 7436 0899
E-Mail: books@keganpaul.com
Internet: http://www.keganpaul.com
USA: 61 West 62nd Street, New York, NY 10023
Tel: (212) 459 0600 Fax: (212) 459 36780
Internet: http://www.columbia.edu/cu/cup
BAHRAIN: bahrain@keganpaul.com

Distributed by:
John Wiley & Sons
Southern Cross Trading Estate
1 Oldlands Way, Bognor Regis
West Sussex, PO22 9SA, England
Tel: (01243) 779 777 Fax: (01243) 820 250

Columbia University Press
61 West 62nd Street, New York, NY 10023
Tel: (212) 459 0600 Fax: (212) 459 36780
Internet: http://www.columbia.edu/cu/cup

© Kegan Paul, 2002

Printed in Great Britain, IBT Global London

ISBN: 0-7103-0650-4

British Library Cataloguing in Publication Data
A catalogue record for this book is available from the British Library.

Library of Congress Cataloging-in-Publication Data
Applied for.

A number of excellent Western works have already been published on the history of Japanese philosophy. One thinks, for example, of the late TSUCHIDA Kyōson's *Contemporary Thought of Japan and China* (London: Williams and Norgate Ltd.), which appeared about forty years ago, and of Father Gino K. PIOVESANA's *Recent Japanese Philosophical Thought, 1862–1962: A Survey* (Tōkyō: Enderle Bookstore), published in 1963. Others might also be mentioned. Of all of them, however, it must be noted that they understand Japanese philosophy to have started with the Meiji Restoration and with the entrance of Western culture into Japan. My point of view, however, is fundamentally different, for I am of the opinion that even prior to the Meiji Restoration there was a long history of philosophy in Japan.

If compared with Greece, India, or China, Japanese philosophy got a late start, but if compared with the various countries of Europe, it was not far behind. The present book is an attempt to trace, in historical perspective, the problems considered in the history of philosophy in Japan.

My particular field of interest is the study of Indian thought, and it is only occasionally, as time permits, that I undertake a study of Japanese Buddhism. But as I am interested in comparative philosophy, and believe that it will become increasingly important in future, I have allowed myself the liberty of writing this brief account of philosophy in pre-modern Japan. Readers of this account will discover, I believe, that Japanese philosophers grappled with the same kinds of problems as did philosophers in the West, in India, and in China, and that the history of Japanese philosophical thought follows much the same course of development as that found elsewhere.

The greater part of the book I wrote originally in English. Chapter IV, however, on the "Controversy between Buddhism and Christianity," and Chapter VI, on "Modern Trends—Specific Problems of the Tokugawa Period," were translated by Mr. ABE Yoshiya and Father William JOHNSTON in proportions indicated in the text.

To all these people I want to take this opportunity to express my profound gratitude.

NAKAMURA Hajime

Editorial Notes

1. Romanization: The Hepburn system with minor modifications has been employed in the romanizations of Japanese words.
2. Personal names: In accordance with the Japanese practice, the family names precede the given names.

CHAPTER I

THE IDEAL OF A UNIVERSAS STATE
AND ITS PHILOSOPHICAS BASIS
—Prince Shotoku and his Successors—

1. The Universal State

Japan became a centralized state under Prince Shōtoku (574–622 A.D.) who, though never elevated to the position of emperor himself, has always been regarded by the Japanese people as a symbol of the state of Japan. His portrait and depictions of famous buildings erected during his regency appear on various postage stamps and on currency issued by the Japanese Government. Even today he lives enshrined in the respect and affection of his countrymen. His spirit can be taken as the basis for the subsequent development of Japanese thought.

Prince Shōtoku was Crown Prince under, and a nephew of, the Empress Suiko (r. 592–628 A.D.), and he held the reins of government as Prince Regent for thirty years (592–622). He is generally regarded as a great statesman of eminent virtues.

The term "universal stat e"as used in this study refers to a society established by a ruler who believed in the existence and validity of universal laws that should be realized regardless of differences between periods, peoples, and places. States that can be so designated came into existence at certain periods in human history when heretofore mutually hostile tribes belonging to the same cultural sphere renounced their antagonisms and formed a single political and military entity. Following political and military unification, a number of changes took place:

(1) A strong ruler emerged who governed the whole area as a single unit and firmly established his own dynasty.

(2) The need for an integrating ideology, which could not be developed while the tribes were in conflict, began to be felt.

(3) The concepts and ideology, or at least the spiritual basis for such an ideology, were provided by a universal world religion.

(4) The ideology or basic concepts of this religion were expressed to the public in the form of official pronouncements or edicts.

Political and cultural phenomena corresponding to this conception of the "univlrsal state" appeared at given periods in the histories of various countries of antiquity. The emperor Ashoka or Asoka (3rd century B.C.) of India, Prince Shōtoku of Japan, and King Songtsan Gampo (also transliterated Srong bTSan sGam Po or Srong-tsan-gam-po; 617–651 A.D.),[1] the first Buddhist king of Tibet, are three examples of rulers who created firm foundations for their respective states and cultures. In South Asia monarchs of commensurate historical significance appeared later in history, among them King Anawrâhta (1044–1077) of Burma and King Jayavarman VII (1181–1215) of Cambodia. While not belonging to the same periods chronologically, these rulers can be understood as belonging to essentially similar stages in the development of civilization.

In the case of China it is difficult to discover a ruler whose historical significance corresponds to that of the leaders previously mentioned. Emperor Wu-ti (r. 502–549 A.D.) of the Liang dynasty or Emperor Wen (r. 581–604 A.D.) of the Sui dynasty[2] might be so considered, especially the latter, who united the whole of China after a long civil war and immediately restored Buddhism, which had been suppressed by his predecessors.

In the milieu of the Asian rulers the universal religion that undergirded the universal state was Buddhism. In the West it was Christianity, and the rulers there who may be thought of as counterparts to these Eastern rulers were Constantine the Great (r. 306–337 A.D.) and Charlemagne (r. 800–814). The Eastern and Western situations, however, were quite different. Their difference was engendered both by the divergence between Eastern and Western cultures and modes of thinking and by the varying natures of the societies in which they arose. It is in recognition of this difference that Prince Shōtoku, founder of the universal state in

Japan and promoter of Japanese culture, should be viewed and appraised.

According to generally accepted tradition, Buddhism was introduced into China in 67 A.D. during the reign of the Emperor Ming-ti of the Later Han dynasty. Of Buddhism's two principal forms, the Hīnayāna and the Mahāyāna, it was the latter that flourished there. In 552 A.D. it was introduced into Japan from Korea when Syöng-Myöng, king of Paekche, a kingdom in southwest Korea during the Three Kingdoms period, sent a mission to the emperor of Japan with presents consisting of "an image of Śakyamuni Buddha in gold and copper, several flags and umbrellas, and a number of sūtras."[3]

The presents and their accompanying message from Paekche engaged the serious attention of the Japanese Court. The Emperor Kimmei (r. 539–571), it was said, was overjoyed, but he thought it prudent to consult his ministers, some of whom argued that Japan should follow the example of other civilized countries by adopting the new religion, while others declared that the native gods might be offended if such respect were shown to "a foreign deity." The two parties quarreled, but the former at length won out.

It was not till the reign of the Empress Suiko (r. 592–628), however, that Buddhism came to the fore in Japan. The outstanding figure during that period was Prince Shōtoku, ppone of the best and most benevolent of all the rulers of Japan and the real founder of Buddhism in Japan.

In those days the country was convulsed by feuding warlords or hereditary local chieftains, each of whom was a law to himself and held the people under him in fief. Shōtoku suppressed these local warlords and set the stage for their abolition, which was brought about after his death in accordance with the Taika Reforms proclaimed by imperial edict in 646. Hereditarily autochthonous and autonomous local rulers were done away with, and their holdings, including "their people and slaves," were confiscated by the state.

In 604 Prince Shōtoku issued what is usually referred to as the "Seventeen-Article Constitution."[5] This was Japan's first legislation, and it is expressive of the original and creative development of Japanese thought in those days, being based chiefly on the spirit of Buddhism and making adaptive use of ideas from China and India. It was, so to speak, the Magna Charta of the nation.

Sometimes identified as "The Law in Seventeen Clauses," the Constitution is generally considered to have been written by Prince Shōtoku himself. Some historians dispute Shōtoku's authorship, but the fact that its main ideas represent Shōtoku's own thinking is beyond dispute.

An important characteristic of the Seventeen-Article Constitution is that its principles were expressed more in the form of moral injunctions than of strictly legal stipulations. Containing no explicit legal regulations, it was intended, rather, to state the fundamentals of ethics and religion and to function as a guide and sanction for laws enacted in later years.

Reflecting Shōtoku's political vision of a centralized bureaucratic state, the ideals embodied in the Constitution were brought to more explicit expression in the Taika Reforms of 646. At that time, some forty years after the promulgation of the Constitution and some twenty-four years after the Prince's death, a significant reshaping of Japanese society was begun. Scholars have confirmed the close connection that exists between the spirit of the Constitution and the political regime that was established in accordance with the Taika Reforms and that achieved the unification of Japan.

As between Shōtoku's Constitution, on the one hand, and Songtsan Gampo's Law and Ashoka's edicts, on the other, a significant difference exists. The latter two were intended for the common people. Songtsan Gampo's Law set forth ethical teachings for the general populace, and Ashoka's edicts, though in some cases directed to the elite, were generally meant for the masses. Shōtoku's Constitution, however, prescribed the "Ways of the Public," that is, normative mental and moral attitudes relative to participation in the concerns of the state. It was designed for officialdom. It provided guidance for the conduct of officials of the imperial government, possibly revealing thereby how much such guidance was needed. This difference between Shōtoku's Constitution and the official pronouncements made by Songtsan Gampo and Ashoka suggests that even at the outset of the centralized state, bureaucracy was already strong in Japan. The supremacy of bureaucrats in the subsequent history of the country may be thought of as foreshadowed in this fact.

Since a centralized or universal state could be created only by subduing and welding together tribes that had been in continuous conflict, it is hardly surprising that the Seventeen-Article Constitution stressed "concord" as the first principle of community and of cooperative organization.[6] Shōtoku advocated "harmony" in human relations beginning with the very first article of his Constitution.

Concord is to be esteemed above all else; make it your first duty to avoid discord. People are prone to partisanship, for few persons are really enlightened. Hence there are those who do not obey their lords and parents, and they come into conflict with their neighbors. But when those above and those below are harmonious and friendly, there is concord in the discussion of affairs, and things become harmonious with the truth. Then what is there that cannot be accomplished? (Article I)[7]

This theme of harmony or concord (in Japanese, 和 wa[8] is characteristic not only of Article I but of the Constitution as a whole. Some scholars maintain that this conception was adopted from Confucianism inasmuch as the word wa appears in the Analects of Confucius. As used in the Analects, however, wa denotes propriety or decorum appropriate to one's status.(Concord was not the subject of discussion. Prince Shōtoku, however, advocated this virtue as the chief principle for the regulation of human behavior.[9] His attitude derived from the Buddhist conception of benevolence, which needs to be distinguished clearly from the Confucian conception of propriety.

Moreover, Shōtoku proposed a definite way of achieving harmony: the ability to refrain from anger in the discussion of whatever business is at hand can only be realized through a profound consciousness of our relatedness in being "simply ordinary men." Men are apt to be bigotted and partial. Within a community or between communities, conflicts easily occur. Such conflicts should be overcome and concord realized so that a harmonious society may be formed. In every article of the Constitution concord is set forth as the ideal to be striven for: between lord and subject, between superior and inferior, among people in general, and within each individual.

It is to be noted, however, that the goal aimed at is concord and not mere obedience. Shōtoku did not teach that people were simply to follow or obey but that discussion should be carried on in an atmosphere of concord or harmony so that right views would ensue. Earnest discussion was most heartily desired. On the other hand, demeanor or language disruptive of concord was to be eschewed.[10] Shōtoku's conception, namely, that avoidance of acrimony in debate is possible only through self-reflection[11] concerning the fact that all people are related in being quite ordinary men, clearly appears in the following:

> Let us cease from wrath and refrain from angry looks. Nor let us be resentful simply because others oppose us. Every person has a mind of his own; each heart has its own leanings. We may regard as wrong what others hold as right; others may regard as wrong what we hold as right. We are not unquestionably sages, nor are they assuredly fools. Both are simply ordinary men. Who is wise enough to judge which of us is good or bad? For we are all wise and foolish by turns, like a ring that has no end. Therefore, though others may give way to anger, let us on the contrary dread our own faults, and though we may be sure that we are in the right, let us act in harmony with others. (Article X)[12]

Discussed without anger in an atmosphere of harmony, problems were to be solved spontaneously and almost of themselves. Interpersonal and group decisions could be truly effected only where concord prevailed. Where it did not, individual would stand at odds with individual, and group with group, in fruitless confrontation.

Prince Shōtoku saw that his people needed a religion to govern their actions and inspire their leaders to humble self-reflection. Buddhism was the religion chosen, and its Three Treasures—the Buddha, the Law, and the Order—were acknowledged as providing the ultimate ideal of all living beings and the ultimate foundation of human life in all countries. "Sincerely revere the Three Treasures" became the theme of the second article of the Constitution, and Emperor Shōmu, in later years (r. 724–749), gave to Japanese tradition the well-known expression "servant of the Three Treasures."

The ideas implicit in Article II of the Constitution are quite important. First among them is the idea that few men are thoroughly bad, that they may be taught to follow Buddhism or the Truth that grounds the universe. This is an idea characteristic of Eastern thought that stands in contrast to certain Western notions. The idea of eternal damnation was alien to Buddha.

A second distinguishing idea is that of the universal Law or Truth as "the final refuge of every kind of generated being and the supreme object of faith in all countries." "What man in what age," Shōtoku asked, "can fail to reverence this Law?" In his view the Law was "the norm" of all living beings, the Buddha was in actuality "the Law embodied," and the embodied Law, "being united with Reason," became the *samgha* or Buddhist Order. According to Shōtoku, therefore, everything converged in the one fundamental principle called the "Law."

In 594 Shōtoku's aunt, the reigning Empress Suiko, issued an edict giving imperial support to the promotion of the Three Treasures. Following that edict, ministers of the Court vied with one another in building Buddhist temples. Thus Buddhism took root, grew, and blossomed. A new epoch in the cultural history of Japan had begun.[13]

It seems likely that other Asian rulers who adopted Buddhism did so for much the same reason as did Shōtoku. The idea of Law or *dharma* that the Buddhist emperor Ashoka chose to espouse in India, however, was not confined to Buddhism alone but was thought of as valid for all religions, though transcending the horizons of the religions of his time. While Ashoka gave support and imperial patronage to the Buddhist religion in particular, Buddhism was only one among many religions— including Brahmanism, Jainism, and the heterodox sect of the Ājivikas —that received his protection. Among Asian rulers, including Prince Shōtoku, Ashoka is distinguished by his catholicity.

Nonetheless, the difference between Shōtoku and Ashoka is not so great as it may seem. Shōtoku knew only one philosophical system that taught universal laws, namely, Buddhism. It was only natural, therefore, that he termed Buddhism "the ultimate ideal of all living beings and the ultimate foundation of human life in all countries." Ashoka, on the other hand, was obliged to recognize the existence of diverse religious claims to universality, for in India in the third century B.C. numerous religious systems were already highly developed, and not a few of them claimed to speak on behalf of universal truth. As between Ashoka and Shōtoku, however, there existed no fundamental difference of principle. Alike, they championed Buddhism, the quintessence of which consists in acknowledging the universal laws taught by all religions and philosophies. Alike, they strove to found a universal state upon what they considered to be the Truth of the universe.

2. Administration of the Universal State

Universal states like those inaugurated by Ashoka, Shōtoku, and Songtsan Gampo were formed in conjunction with the abolition of the hereditary privileges of clan heads and the displacement of political leadership based upon a clan-type social order. Powerful clan rulers were able to preserve political power only upon condition that they become officials of the newly established centralized state.[14]

In the case of Japan, Shōtoku established a form of imperial bureaucratic organization that differed radically from that of earlier periods. This restructured organization, designated the Twelve Court Ranks (kan'i jūni kai), went into effect in 603 A.D.[15] Formerly, the higher Court ranks had been filled only by persons of high social status and had been transmitted hereditarily. Under the new regime, Court appointment and promotion depended upon ability. Merit, not distinction of birth, was the new criterion.

Since the officials functioned, as it were, as the pillars of the centralized state, Shōtoku addressed himself directly to them in his Seventeen-Article Constitution. The first requirement of the universal state was the firm establishment of exemplary ethical behavior among its officials. Thus, for example, the spirit of honoring the good and hating the bad was inculcated. Shōtoku taught:

Punish the vicious and reward the virtuous. This is a rule of excellence and antiquity. Do not, therefore, allow the good deeds of any person to remain concealed, nor the bad deeds of any that you see to go uncorrected. Flatterers and deceivers are like a fatal missile for the overthrow of the state, or a sharp sword for the destruction of the people. Likewise, sycophants are fond of expatiating to their superiors on the errors of inferiors; to their inferiors they censure the faults of the superiors. Such men are neither loyal to their lord nor benevolent toward the people. All this is the source from which grave civil disturbances arise. (Article VI)[16]

As for ideas regarding the kinds of punishments to be meted out, Shōtoku advocated the use of reformative or remedial measures in case of light crimes, but severe punishment in case of grave crimes. He put it thus: "Light crimes should be judged in accordance with our power to reform the offender, but those who commit grave crimes should be delivered up for severe punishment."[17] Shōtoku did not shrink from the use of force, but his concern for moral improvement was paramount.

This moral concern is equally evident in the following admonition to prompt and impartial judgements.

In hearing the cases of common people judges should banish avaricious desires and forget their own interests. Deal impartially with the suits brought by the people. Of the cases to be tried, there are a thousand a day. If in one day there are so many, in the course of several years there will be immense numbers of suits to be settled. Nowadays cious desires and forget their own interests. Deal impartially with the suits brought by the people. Of the cases to be tried, there are a thousand a day. If in one day there are so many, in the course of several years there will be immense numbers of suits to be settled. Nowadays it is alleged that some judges seek their own profit and attend to cases after having taken bribes. This has given rise to the saying: "The lawsuits of the rich are like rocks thrown into water, whereas the lawsuits of the poor are like water thrown upon a rock." Under these circumstances the poor will not know where to betake themselves. Such a state of affairs, if true, signifies a deficiency in the duty of the officials. (Article V)[18]

Shōtoku made the standards held up for officials even more stringent. Officials, said he, should be men of integrity. A good regime does not necessarily guarantee the security and welfare of the country if the persons in charge of its administration are wicked.

Each person is responsible for a certain aspect of the business of the Government. Let not the spheres of duty be confused. When wise and capable persons are entrusted with high offices, a unanimous voice of pleased approval will be heard; but when wicked persons hold high offices, disasters and disturbances will be multiplied. In this world there are few who are endowed with innate wisdom; the goal of sainthood is attained only after long self-discipline. All matters of state, whether great or small, will surely be well administered if the right persons are in the right positions; in all periods, whether critical or peaceful, all affairs will be amenably settled if wise men are secured. In this way the state will be lasting, and the realm will be free from danger. Therefore the wise sovereigns of ancient times sought good men for high offices, and not high offices for favored men. (Article VII)

This teaching, set forth over a thousand years ago, is perhaps not unworthy of consideration even in advanced modern societies of the present day.

It is noteworthy that Shōtoku cautioned officials against jealousy, a hindrance to the wholesome development of community and society.[19]

All officials, high and low, should beware of jealousy. If you are jealous of others, others in turn will be jealous of you, and a vicious circle will be perpetuated. If we find that others excel us in intelligence, we are not pleased; if we find that they surpass us in ability, we become envious. Truly wise persons are seldom seen in this world—possibly one wise man in five centuries, but hardly one sage in ten. Yet unless wise men and sages are secured, how shall the country be well governed? (Article XIV)[20]

Setting forth a number of precepts as guides for the attitudes and behavior of leaders and officials, Shōtoku denounced despotism or arbitrary one-man rule, stressing instead the necessity for discussion with others.

> Decisions concerning important matters should not be made by one person alone. They should be discussed with many others. Small matters are of less importance, and it is unnecessary to consult many persons about them. But in the case of weighty matters, when there is some fear that they might go away, you should arrange things in consultation with many persons, so as to arrive at the right conclusion. (Article XVII)

This idea can be taken as the embryonic beginning of Japanese democratic thought. It has a correlate in Article I, which prescribed that discussion should be carried on in the spirit of concord. The principle thus enunciated was embodied in an imperial edict following the Taika Reforms. This edict stigmatized arbitrary rule by a sovereign—or dictatorship, as we call it today—saying: "Affairs should not be instituted by a single ruler."

Where did this idea of resistance to dictatorship derive from? The ancient way of ruling represented in Japanese mythology is not by the fiat of a monarch or "Lord of All" but by a conference on the shore of a river. If the opinions of the participants had been disregarded, the conference could hardly have been successful. It seems plausible to assume, therefore, that Shōtoku inherited and developed this idea from early Shintō. On the other hand, it is also possible that the rules of the Buddhist Order influenced the thought of the Prince Regent. These rules are set forth in detail in scriptures known to Shōtoku, and they include the rule of majority decision. The fact that consultation with others was not explicitly encouraged by Ashoka or by Songtsan-Gampo is also worthy of note. This idea or spirit of consultation with others was preserved until political power passed from the emperors to the shogunates of feudal Japan. The Japanese emperor system developed as something other than dictatorship.

Despite the stress laid on group involvement in the decision-making process, however, on Shōtoku's view primacy clearly belonged to the emperor. His attitude, unique when contrasted with that of Ashoka and Songtsan-Gampo, is expressed in the following article:

> When you recieve the commands of the Sovereign, you should hear them with reverence. The lord is like heaven, the subjects like the earth. When the heaven above and the earth below are united in performing their duties faithfully in their respective positions, we see the world ruled in perfect order as in the harmonious rotation of the four seasons. If the earth should attempt to supplant the heaven, all would fall to ruin. Therefore, when the lord speaks, let his subjects listen and obey; when the superior acts, let the inferiors comply. Consequently, when you receive the orders of the Sovereign, be attentive in carrying them out faithfully. If you fail in this, ruin will be the natural consequence. (Article III)[21]

What was emphasized by Shōtoku in this connection was the relation between the lord or emperor, the officials, and the common people in this centralized state. Officials were to rule the common people in compliance with the orders of the emperor.

The basic foundation for the administration of the universal state was propriety or, more broadly, ethical principle. If superiors were ethically wanting, the common people could not be ruled; if the common people were likewise deficient, innumerable crimes and delinquent acts would ensue, no matter how assiduous the superiors. Propriety or ethical principle, accordingly, was to be the basis governing officials' attitudes and behavior in their administration of the state.

The relationship between the emperor, the officials, and the people was patterned after the model of ancient China as formulated by Han Confucianism. This model was, however, planted in Japanese soil, and it appears to have been closely connected with the abolition of clan power intrinsic to the Taika Reforms.

Esteem for the prestige of the emperor is an idea that appears conspicuously in the Constitution.

> Provincial governors and district administrators are not to levy taxes on their respective peoples. In a country there should not be two lords; the people should not have two masters. The Sovereign is the

sole master of the people of the whole country. The officials appointed
to administer local affairs are all his subjects. How can they levy arbitrary taxes on the people in the manner of the Government?
(Article XII)
This article may be interpreted as articulating the principle of centralized
administration in the territory under the Imperial Court, and as adum-
brating the subsequent nation-wide abolition of clan ownership of land
and people. The power of regional and local rulers was going to diminish. The saying "In a country there should not be two lords: the people
should not have two masters" expresses an idea that is not uniquely but
conspicuously Japanese and presages the absolutism that later characterized the Japanese imperial institution.

On a broader canvas, it appears that when the prestige of tribal chieftains is transferred to a state ruler who has adopted a universal religion,
there arises a tendency for that ruler to be regarded as a manifestation of
a demigod. Thus in the case of Shōtoku there arose a legend, later transmitted to China, that he was a reincarnation of Eshi (in Chinese, Hui-ssu,
515–577), a Zen master and the second patriarch of the Chinese T'ien-
t'ai Sect.[22] More popular was the belief that he was an incarnation of
Avalokiteśvara Bodhisattva, commonly known in Japan as Kannon.
This belief was given literary form in a poem written some centuries
later by Shinran (1173–1262), founder of the Jōdo Shinshū or True Sect
of the Pure Land:

> Bodhisat' Avalokita
> Disclosed himself as Prince Shōtoku.
> He was kind—a father to us—
> And with us walked as a mother too.[23]

In a similar way King Songtsan-Gampo is worshipped in Tibet as one
of the incarnations of Avalokiteśvara Bodhisattva.[24] With regard to
India and China, however, parallels can be found neither in the various
legends concerning Ashoka nor in the records pertaining to the emperor
Wen. As for Western rulers, the emergence of such legends was of
course precluded by the teachings of Christianity.

Why is it, then, that among the countries cited, a leged of this kind took shape in Japan and Tibet alone? It may be surmised that the birth of such a legend in these two countries has connections with the relatively high prestige there attributed to rulers and with the fact that Buddhism first developed there solely in combination with rulership prestige. In Tibet religious prestige and secular prestige went hand in hand, while in Japan the prestige, religious and secular, ascribed to Shōtoku has not faded even to the present day. A more general statement relative to Japan might be that recognition of the fact that a legend of this kind arose is basic to an accurate understanding of Japanese ways of thinking.

3. Cultural and Humanitarian Policies

Asian rulers of universal states, aspiring to realize universal laws through political measures appropriate to their particular situations, were disposed to favor international contacts. In Shōtoku's time relations between Japan and Korea were relatively brisk. Shōtoku sent envoys to Korea and welcomed Koreans to Japan, many settling down and becoming naturalized citizens. Two Korean scholars, Eji and Esō, are presumed to have been Shōtoku's tutors in Buddhism. Relations between Japan and China were also maintained, envoys being exchanged from time to time.[25]

In order to propagate the universal religion they had adopted, these rulers took several steps: (1) they built many temples and monasteries, (2) they allowed applicants to take orders and gave political and economic protection to monks and nuns, (3) they donated lands to temples and monasteries, and (4) they procured scriptures and statues from other lands. Shōtoku engaged in all these activities. Besides establishing numerous monasteries, in 607 he founded Hōryū-ji Temple, now the oldest wooden architecture in use in the world. From about that time, Buddhism, under the aegis of imperial patronage, began to flourish in Japan.

Shōtoku's literary activity was considerable, and he was apparently well acquainted with the Chinese classics. At the request of the Empress, he lectured on three Chinese-language Mahāyāna sūtras and later wrote commentaries on them.[26] Among Japanese classical writings, these commentaries are the oldest works in existence. It is easy to overlook the significance of the fact that the oldest existing classical writings of Japanese literature happen to be commentaries on Buddhist sūtras developed by the man who was then the actual, though not titular, ruler of Japan. When contrasted with the spread of Christianity in the West, or of Buddhism in South Asia, this development appears to stand without a parallel. That Shōtoku was personally committed to the propagation of Buddhism and that he was highly erudite is doubtless true, and in that respect numerous parallels can be found, but the scene of a ruler giving lectures on the scriptures has no counterpart in, for example, the history of Christianity in the Roman Empire. Though it is clear that Shōtoku considered himself competent to give religious lectures, a self-estimate of this kind would not of itself have led to a similar scene in the West, where sermons or religious lectures were ordinarily delivered only by ordained persons. Even less would such a development have been likely in South Asia, where it was customary for kings to worship monks with every indication of profound respect but for the monks to sit stolidly without the slightest response. An immense number of Buddhist writings were composed in ancient India, but within this corpus no authoritative work by a king has been preserved. In fact relatively few Buddhist books were written by laymen. In Japan, however, not only did the lay ruler Shōtoku wrote books of a technically religious nature, but these books have been preserved and continue to exercise an important influence even today. It is more than likely that the Chinese practice of an emperor's lecturing on Buddhist scriptures was carried over into the Japanese context, but whereas such lectures had little effect in China, the commentaries of Shōtoku, developed from his lectures, have been of decisive significance for Japanese Buddhism. Some scholars contend, as in the case of the Constitution, that Shōtoku's three commentaries are spurious. Yet even if that hypothesis should prove correct, the fact that they were later ascribed to Shōtoku is undeniable. This ascription reflects more than a mere misreading of historical evidence. It suggests and symbolizes the circumstance that those religions which have flourished in Japan have done so only by allying themselves with the prestige of the imperial house.

The desire to realize the teachings of a universal religion in the political
sphere led the rulers of universal states to treat people with affection and
compassion. Thus Shōtoku expressed his concern for the people in word
manifestly informed by Buddhist concepts:

"As the disease of infatuation among the common people is endless,
equally endless are the compassionate measures taken by the bodhisattvas. . . . Common people are less fortunate than others; we teach
them to do meritorious deeds [i.e., deeds that accord with Buddhist
principles]. . . . Ethical properties are what can save people from poverty and affliction, so Buddhas save existent beings in their various
conditions by means of the Four All-Embracing Virtues, the Four
Virtues of Infinite Greatness, and the Six Perfections."[27]

His Constitution, as has been observed, laid stress on the welfare of the
people: sympathy for commoners in their law suits, antipathy for those
who are "neither loyal to their lord nor benevolent toward the people,"
and in connection with strengthening the authority of the central government, a prohibition upon local administrators' levying taxes on their
people. It may be suggested, therefore, that here the common people
came to play a significant role in the consciousness of the ruling class.
That role should not be exaggerated, but neither should it be ignored.
Inasmuch as it continued to exercise influence in subsequent history, it
can be thought of as the starting point of a trend with an affinity for the
gradual development of democracy.

It is also noteworthy that these Asian rulers who professed a universal
religion engaged in humanitarian activities based on a philanthropic
spirit. Shōtoku, for example, founded Shitennō-ji Temple in 587 in what
is now the city of Ōsaka, and this temple was renowned as a creative
enterprise for the relief of suffering. The temple was laid out in four main
divisions: *Kyōden-in,* the great central hall or religious sanctuary proper,
used for training in Buddhist discipline and in aesthetic and scholarly
pursuits; *Hiden-in,* a hall where the poor could obtain relief; *Ryōbyō-in,*
a hospital or clinic where the sick could receive treatment without
charge;[28] and *Seyaku-in,* a dispensary where medicinal herbs were collected, refined, and distributed free of charge. It is not clear whether he

established an animal hospital there, but judging by the name, the Kyōden-in—which means "Institution based on Respect for Existent Beings"—was aimed at promoting the happiness and welfare of all living beings, human and animal alike. Moreover, according to the *Nihongi*, Shōtoku and other members of the imperial family as well as officials of the Court used to set aside fixed days for the purpose of gathering medicinal herbs,[29] and his Court is known to have shown special consideration to the lonely, the destitute, and the aged. The Prince himself, one legend has it, gave some of his own food and clothing to a starving man he came upon at Kataoka Hill.[30] It seems clear, therefore, that Shōtoku's adoption of Buddhism as the universal foundation for a centralized Japanese state had important consequences not only for the spread of Buddhism in Japan but also for the social and political welfare of the Japanese people.

4. Philosophical Thought

The most extensive exposition of Shōtoku's philosophical thought is to be found in his commentaries on the three sūtras mentioned earlier. We propose, therefore, to consider a cluster of philosophically significant concepts as they come into view in an analysis of these commentaries.

Dialectic

One observation that results from a consideration of Shōtoku's procedure is that in his discussions he makes use of a dialectical mode of reasoning. We find him saying, for example:

> The ultimate law of all things is voidness. Hence they are said to be non-ens. Ens is not really ens. But why then should non-ens be non-ens? Accordingly, non-ens is said to be not non-ens. . . . [The meaning of] ens and non-ens is not definite. Nevertheless both are born of causal relationships.[31]

In this case his reasoning is dialectical in the sense that one view is made to neutralize another in the interest of a more fundamental affirmation.

A somewhat different type of dialectic occurs in this comment upon a statement by Yuima:

When is one qualified for enlightenment: in a previous life, in a future life, or in the present life? If a previous life be recommended, then it must be remembered that that life has already passed away. Hence no causal basis that would qualify one for enlightenment now exists. If a future life be urged upon us, we must note that that life has not yet arrived. Thus in this case too there exists no causal basis of qualification for enlightenment. And even in the case of the present life, we must bear in mind that this life is momentary and transient. It is not abiding. Therefore even here there is no causal basis that would qualify one [permanently for enlightenment].[32]

The purport of this line of argument is to make clear the point that existent beings already qualify for enlightenment and that there is no necessity for qualifying action on the part of Buddhas or bodhisattvas. This kind of dialectic, which disposes of inadequate views through a process of *reductio ad absurdum* without explicit enunciation or demonstration of a positive counter-thesis, was also used by Nāgārjuna (Jps. MɪB Ryūju; lived c. 150–250 A.D.),[33] one of the most important philosophers of Mahāyāna Buddhism, and has analogies with the dialectic of Zeno.

Theory of Cause and Effect

Shōtoku set forth a unique theory of cause and effect. According to his conception, the relations between cause and effect are of four kinds:

There are four kinds of cause and effect relationships. The first is *homogeneous*. In this case a cause produces an effect of the same nature as itself. For example, he who first cultivates the practice of uprightness and sincerity does not later do wicked things [but sincere and upright things]. Second, a cause may bring about a result of *heterogeneous* nature. For example, a good action leads to happiness and a bad action to suffering. [Good and bad are moral concepts, whereas happiness and suffering are feelings.] Third, a cause may stand in a *contingent* relation to an effect. Thus, for example, giving food, clothing, etc. to those in need may be a contingent cause in relation to which the practice of religious discipline is an effect. [The former is neither homogeneous nor heterogeneous in relation to the effect but is helpful in causing the effect.] Fourth, cause and effect may be thought of as *similar*. In this case one of a number of heterogeneous causes is singled out [as the main cause]. For example, non-killing may result in a long life.[34]

This conception of cause and effect relationships is quite different from those traditionally set forth in the long history of Buddhist philosophy in Asian countries.[35] How much more it differs from that propounded by Aristotle!

The Absolute

As is generally expounded in Mahāyāna Buddhism, Prince Shōtoku envisages the absolute to be Voidness (*śūnyatā*); and following the thought of the Yuima Sūtra, he called it 'non-duality,' owing to the fact that Voidness is neither being nor non-being.

"The insight of the Bodhisattva penetrates into being, but he never loses sight of Voidness; abiding in Voidness, he accomplishes all works. (For him) Voidness means being, and being means Voidness. He does not stay one-sidedly in either being or non-being, but synthesizes both in non-duality (*advayatā*)."[36]

It is the source from which the penetrating knowledge appears.

"The object of penetrating knowledge (*jñeya*) means, rendered into Chinese, the Mother of Wisdom, which has as its object the ultimate truth (*paramārtha-satya*). Voidness is the source from which wisdom originates; therefore, it is called Mother. Since Voidness is unamde, wisdom originating therefrom is unfettered. . . . (The same wisdom) embraces all objects; in illuminating all the varieties of existences it embraces all the objeits."[37]

Prince Shōtoku inherited the idea of the eternal Buddha from the Lotus Sūtra. The Lotus Sūtra of Mahāyāfia gives a popular belief that Buddha was born in Kapilavastu, attained enlightenment, taught the law and died in Kusinagara. However, this physical narration with Buddha's birth, life, teaching and death are simply a quasi-fiction which was invented for proselyting his teaching. The essence or real body of his teaching is the eternal being. The Mahāyāna substitutes for the historical

Buddha the eternal Buddha. According to the doctrine, Buddha's existence in the earthly form is not his true and proper mode of being. In the Lotus Sūtra[38] Buddha gives a series of passages on this subject:

"In an inconceivable and immeasurable distance in Aeons, I reached superior enlightenment and never ceased to teach the law."

"I show the place of extinction. I reveal to all beings a means of enlightenment, albeit I do not become extinct by that time. In this place I continue preaching the law."

"There I rule myself as well as all beings. But men of perverted minds, in their delusion, do not see me standing thereby."

"Believing in the complete extinction of my body, they pray in different manners to the relics, but me they see not."

"Then I was not completely extinct. It was but a device of mine; repeatedly am I born in the world of the living."

"Such is the glorious power of my wisdom that knows no limit, and the duration of my life is as long as an endless period."

Here we find an Eastern version of Docetism. These verses were regarded by the Nichiren sect of Japan as representing the supreme and essential teaching of Buddhism. But unlike Christian Docetism and Gnostics, the eternal Buddha in Mahāyāna becomes incarnate repeatedly to save suffering people.

In China and Japan the problem of whether God is the maker of heaven and earth was not discussed very seriously. This line of thinking was also accepted by Prince Shōtoku who, however, tried to change the traditional idea of the Essential Body (dharmakāya) of Buddha.

In the philosophy of the Mahāyāna Buddhism the noumenal body was regarded as ineffable, being located beyond the phenomenal sphere. But Prince Shōtoku considered it to be in the phenomenal sphere.

"When the essence of Buddha is concealed, it is called the Perfect-One Store (tathāgata-garbha). When it is manifested, it is called the noumenal body (dharmakāya). Being concealed and being manifested are different in fact, but in their true unity, they are not different in essence."[39]

The absolute should not be sought for in the transcendental sphere.

"The eternal body of noumenon is called the Treasure of Buddha. As this body manifests norms for living beings, it is to be the Treasure of Norms (dharma). Also, this noumenal body being in harmonious relation to principles of actions, it is to be the Treasure of Brotherhood."[40] In Indian and Chinese Buddhism, it is often said that the essential body of Buddha transcends the distinction of the good and bad. But here the good alone is ascribed to the essential body.

"The noumenal body of Buddha has all sorts of the good as its potentials for realizing it."[41]

"The realm of Buddha is equipped with all kinds of virtues."[42]

"The noumenal body is the essence of all virtues."[43] Buddhas are always on the side of the good.

"If Buddhas protect us always in the past, in the future and in the present, doing good is not interrupted."[44]

The basis of human existence is called "perfect-one-store" (tathāgata-garbha). Following the traditional philosophy of the voidness of Mahā-yāna, the Shōman Sūtra defines it as "without origination and destruction". For Prince Shōtoku "without origination" and "without destruction" signified "continuous existence of human soul in this world.[45] From this total negation of origination or creation and destruction or perishing emerges the idea of perfect-one-storeness. It is a store of all changing phenomena which are in reality contained in the store of the Perfect One or Buddha. The transmigrating soul continues to exist without perishing, embraced in the store of this Perfect One, which is the basis of human existence not only after man has been delivered from defilements, but also even while man is still in defilements.[46]

Prince Shōtoku distinguishes hon (source, origin) from shaku (appearance, manifestation). Only that which has its source principium (beginning) can manifest itself in appearance; and that which does not manifest itself in appearance cannot give evidence of its source.[47]

Nirvāna lies not in calm and secluded domain, but in actual life of practice. "The accomplished Nirvāna implies an immeasurable selflessness and activity.[48] In traditional Buddhist philosophy the accomplished Nirvāna (nirupadhi-śesa-nirvāna) is considered to be complete extinction of the self, but Prince Shōtoku tries to find it in the process of religious practice. In other words, the ideal status of human being is in the realization of the unity with ultimate truth in daily life. Shōtoku emphasizɪs the unity of today,[49] i.e. the unity in temporal existence. Truth is exemplified in living persons who conceives the ideal of Yuima or Shōman.

"Yuima was a great sage who had reached the height of perfect Enlightenment. Fundamentally speaking, his person is identified with Ultimate Truth (*tathatā*). But in appearance, his being is identified with all different existences. He exceeded in virtues among the sages. He went beyond the boundaries of human attachment. . . . His mind was not trammeled by affairs of state and family; yet being moved by unintermittent compassion, he worked for the benefit of others. He showed himself living the life of a householder in the town of Vaisāli."[50] [51]

This-Worldliness

The phenomenalistic way of thinking that asserts reality itself is emergent and in flux has been traditionally conspicuous among the Japanese. This emergent and fluid way of thinking is compatible with the inclination of thinking that emphasizes particular human nexuses, which is another way of thinking traditionally conspicuous among the Japanese. These two factors are combined to bring about emphasis upon activities within a concrete human nexus.

It is a well-known fact that primitive Shintoism was closely tied up with agricultural rituals in agrarian villages, and that Shintoist gods have been symbolized, even up to these days, as gods of production.

Coming into contact with foreign cultures and getting acquainted with Chinese religions, the Japanese adopted and absorbed Confucianism in particular, which teaches the way of conduct within a concrete human nexus. The thoughts of Loa-tzu and Chuan-tzu are inclined to a life of seclusion in which one escapes from particular human nexuses and seeks tranquility in solitude for oneself. Such was not to the taste of the Japanese at large. In contrast, Confucianism is essentially a doctrine whose this-worldliness makes it sometimes hard to call a religion. In principally determines rules of conduct according to a system of human relationships. In this respect, Confucianism did not conflict with the existing Japanese thought patterns at the time of its introduction.

In the case of Buddhism, however, there arose some problems. Buddhism declared itself to be a teaching of the other-worldliness. According to the Buddhist philosophy, the positive state of "the-other-worldliness" is arrived at after one has trascended "this world." The central figures in Buddhist orders have all been monks and nuns who have freed themselves not only from their families but from any specific human nexus. They were not allowed to be involved in any economic activities. It is likely that in those days there existed some social reasons that necessiated a great many people becoming monks.

The topographical characteristics of Japan, vastly different from India, required men to serve their fellows within a specific human nexus. The doctrine of early Buddhism together with traditional conservative Buddhism which inherited the former teachings were despised and rejected under the name of Hinayana, and Mahāyāna Buddhism was particularly favored and adopted. Mahāyāna Buddhism was a popular religion that came to the fore in the Christian era, and some schools of Mahāyāna Buddhism, if not all, advocated the comprehending of absolute truth *within secular life*. In accepting Buddhism, the Japanese selectid in particular the branch of that nature. And even in accepting doctrines originally devoid of such a nature, they deliberately bestowed it upon them. The stereotyped phrase, "Japan is the country where Mahāyāna Buddhism is in practice,"[52] can be understood solely in reference to those basic facts.

The attitude of accepting Buddhism is clearly shown in the case of Prince Shōtoku. His "Commentaries upon Three Sutras" are those upon "the Shōman Sutra," "the Yuima Sutra" and "the Hokke Sutra." The selection of these three Sutra out of a multitude was entirely based upon the Japanese way of thinking. "The Shōman Sutra" (= *Srimāladevisimhānada-sūtra*) was preached, in compliance to Buddha's command, by Madame Shōman (Srimālā "Glorious Garland"), who was queen and a lay believer. The "Yuima Sutra" (*Vimalakirtinrdesa-sūtra*) has a dramatic composition, in which Yuima (= Vimalakiriti, "Spotless Fame"), a lay believer, gives a sermon to *priests and ascetics,* reversing the usual order. This commends the grasping of truth in secular life. And according to the "Hokke Sutra" (= *Saddharmapundarika-sutra,* "Lotus Sutra"), all laymen who faithfully follow any of the teachings of Buddha are expected to be redeemed. The Crown Prince himself all through his life remained a lay believer. It is said that he called himself "Shōman, the Child of a Buddha."[53] The intention of Prince Shōtoku was to emphasize the necessity for realizing Buddhist ideals within concrete human situations.[54]

All through the "Commentaries" Shōtoku seeks absolute significance within each practical act of every-day life. He asserts: "Reality is no more than today's occurance of cause and effeat."[55] Such interpetation has something in common with the doctrine of the Tientai and Fa-hien sects, but the paricular expression "today's" makes it distinctly Japanese. Since it attaches great importance to action, for those who have gone through Buddhist reflection, this world of impurities and sufferings in itself turns out to be a place of blessings. "Since I wish to enlighten mankind. I regard life and death as a garden."[56] In his view nirvāna has already been attained. "If one understands that defilements are essentially viod and that there is nothing to be discarded, then one attains nirvāna by himself. If you think that after having discarded defilements one can get into nirvāna, then there is caused a judgment with attachment. How can you call the situation nirvāna?"[57]

Many Buddhist teachers taught that the human body is foul and disgusting. Such an attitude was wrong according to Shōtoku. "One should teach that the body decays easily, but not that one should be disgusted with it!" Buddhist teachers of Asian countries taught that a person should despise his own body and spend his life as a homeless recluse. Prince Shōtoku taught to the contrary.[58] Prince Shōtoku criticized the other-worldly practice of Concervative Buddhists. "Hināyāna ascetics, hating the distractive world, escape into mountains and forests to practice careful disciplining of mind and body. . . . If one still thinks that various objects exist, and cannot give up the assumption, how can he rid his mind of such distractions, even if he stays in mountains and forests?"[59]

Moral Values

Prince Shōtoku esteemed actions and deeds in practice, about the name 'Queen Glorious Garland (Shōman Śrimālā) he said: "In the world one adorns one's own physical body with seven jewels, but she adorns her Essential Body with various deeds."[60] In traditional Mahāyāna philosophy the Essential Body (*dharmakāya*) was considered to be formless and ineffable. Shōtoku, however, contrary to the tradition on the continent of Asia, located it in practical actions in the phenomenal world. Attracted strongly by this ideal, the Prince identified himself with the virtuous queen, sometimes calling himself "Glorious Garland, Buddha's Child."[61] The title Shōtoku, which means "Holy-Virtuous," is also mentioned in his Commentary on the Shōman. This title applied to the Prince is often thought to be posthumous; but more probably, his contemporaries called him by it.

It is the accumulation of good deeds practiced in the worlds of life and death that eventually admit a person into Buddhahood. "Uncountable ten thousands of good deeds equally lead up to becoming a Buddha."[62] It is significant that the ultimate state of religion is not bestowed upon men by divine entities that transcend them, but is realized through practical behavior within the human nefus. "Becoming a Buddha originates in ten thousand good deeds."[63]

According to Prince Shōtoku, all moral values depend upon the mind of man. "Mind is the origin of all virtues. As mind is pure now, how can it be that all virtues originated in it are impure?"[64] Virtue, it seems, was equated by Shōtoku with the good; and "the appearance of good and bad depends on one's self, not on others."[65] Said the Prince, esteeming righteousness, also: "Right mind is the beginning of all deeds."[66]

Shōtoku valued the significance of individuals highly, and in his commentaries made trust in persons preliminary to the teaching of precepts.[67] Not only should ordinary people be respected,[68] he said, but any virtuous person should be regarded as "one's own child."[69]

In the Shōman Sūtra upon which Shōtoku wrote a commentary, Queen Shōman vows to devote her life to the cause of perfecting all living beings, her allegience being represented in the Ten Commitments[70] and the Three Great Vows[71] which are moral and altruistic in character. It is likely that the Prince regarded compassion or love in the genuine sense of the word as the basic human value.[72] But compassion must transcend earthly relations. "Compassion should be without attachment. If there should be attachment, teaching would be defiled; some would become disgusted with the mundane world, and some would encounter hindrances to guiding living beings."[73]

Charity to the poor was commended. "The Buddhas are those who should be most respected. Beggars are those who should be most loved."[74]

Esteem of Activity

Mahāyāna Buddhism stressed altruistic deeds. Prince Shōtoku put special emphasis upon them and considered that Buddhas and Bodhisattvas *should* serve all living beings. That is the Reason he occasionally distorted phrases in the Buddhist scriptures.[75] The advice "to sit always in religious meditation" given in the Lotus Sūtra, for example, was revised by Shōtoku. "Do not approach a person who always sits in religious meditation,"[76] he wrote, meaning that unbroken sitting in meditation prevents a man from doing good deeds.

Buddhist morals were also metamorphosed. The Ifdians considered alms-giving, a virtue of principal importance for Buddhists, as something to be strictly observed. Men who in order to devote themselves generously to serving other beings, either human or animal,[77] abandoned their country, their caste, their right and children, even their own bodies, were extolled in most Buddhist scriptures. Such a life of renouncing everything and possessing nothing was the ideal of Indian ascetics. It was not, however, suitable for the more pragmatic Japanese; and Prince Shōtoku, accordingly, restricted the meaning of "alms-giving" to "the abandonment of properties other than one's own body."[78]

Shōtoku permitted the acquisition of wealth—"Pure life means to obtain riches in accordance with the law."[79] And in his writings traces even of utilitarianism can be noticed. Benefit[80] was considered to be a cause of nirvāna.[81] The Prince went so far as to alter the meanings of several sentences in Buddhist scripture to make them reflect his own utilitarian penchants. In the *Spotless Fame Sūtra,* for example, is the sentence: "In the threefold way the Wheel of the Teaching was set forth." For all the Buddhist world, "the threefold way" traditionally meant that each of the Four Noble Truths should be (1) revealed, (2) practiced, and (3) evidenced personally.[82] Shōtoku, however, explained it as meaning "first, to indicate; second, to teach; third, to *benefit.*" For him, the final good of the teaching of the Four Noble Truths was utilitarian. But although his interpretation bordered on being pragmatic, the "benefit" he remarked was not necessarily to be realized materially.[83] It could be garnered in social activity, a concept that has helped mould the character of Japanese thought since Shōtoku's time and contributed significantly to Japan's emergence as a modern nation so much sooner in history than any of her Asian neighbors.

In respect with this, we should keep in mind that the Japanese put emphasis upon social activities. It is one of the features of the Japanese ways of thinking and it can be traced back even to the thought of Prince Shōtoku.

"We shall discuss the problem of the country. Due to the effects of their moral qualities (*karman*), there are different marks of purity or stain in every country in accordance with the respective characters, good or bad, of the living beings constituting their citizenry. Thus, an ordinary being is affiliated with his own realm or country according to his karma. But a perfect sage is in full communion with Ultimate Truth (*tathatā*) in his enlightenment, and is permanently beyond the differentiation of names or marks, having nothing to do with this or that, give or take. His personality is identified with the Great Void (transcendence), and his mind pervades the whole universe; then how should he limit his marks? How should he assign to himself a specific realm? Yet perpetually moved by all-embracing compassion, he edifies every living being each according to its capacities, and works in every realm where there are living beings. Therefore the text says: The Buddha-realm (or -country) sustained by a Buddha-to-be is constituted by the kinds of living beings (to be edified).[84]

Applied to actual politics, this means that the ideal ruler who is the embodiment of the virtues of the Bodhisattva (Buddha-to-be) should be beyond all the differences of dispositions and interests of the people and yet care for them all, not for the sake of their individual interests but for their ultimate welfare in brotherly fellowship and spiritual communion. The ruler leads the people by his ideal aims and the people follow him in full realization that his high aims are derived from the Ultimate Truth. Spiritual values can be realized in the state only through the apprehension of the highest cause.

Tolerance

Tolerance was a feature of the thought of Prince Shōtoku. He did not forbid and opress Shintoism, the native faith of our race. This primitive religion was placed in its proper sphere of action and alive under the leadership of Buddhism. And this fact is due to the fundamental characteristic of Buddhism. Taking into consideration such an attitude we shall be able to understand why such an edict was proclaimed in the reign of Prince Shōtoku (607 A.D.) as follows: "In my reign, why shall we be negligent of practising the worship of Shintoist gods. All my officials should worship them sincerely."

The rational basis for such a spirit of tolerance and conciliation is to be sought in the tendency, conspicuous among the Japanese, to recognize absolute significance in everything phenomenal. It leads to the acceptance of the raison d'etre of any view held by men, and ends up with the adjustment to any view with a spirit of tolerance and conciliation.

Thus it may safely be said that the spirit of Prince Shōtoku was very tolerant and broad-minded.[85]

In general, there has been a conspicuous tendency of such a spirit of tolerance and conciliation in Japan. It will also be due to the way of thinking to recognize the absolute significance in everything phenomenal.

Such a way of thinking appeared from the earliest days of introduction of Buddhism into Japan. According to Prince Shōtoku, the Lotus Sūtra, supposed to express the ultimate purport of Buddhism, preaches the doctrine of the One Great Vehicle and advocates the theory that "any one of thousands of the good leads to the attainment of Enlightenment."[86] According to the Prince, there is no innate difference between the saint and the most stupid.[87] Everyone of then is primarily and equally a child of the Buddha. Prince Shōtoku regarded the secular moral teaching as the elementary gates to enter Buddhism.

He said, "Even heretics are your teachers."[88] Pagans and Heretics were tolerated.[89] In the eyes of Prince Shōtoku there was no heretic.

He uses expressions of "heretical doctrines" and "pagan religions," but those expressions are borrowed rather from the traditional Indian terminology. He does not mean by them the doctrines of Lao-tzu and Chuang-tzu or Confucianism. His interpretation of Buddhism is characterized by its all-inclusive nature. Only through taking into consideration such a philosophical background, one is able to understand the moral idea of the Prince when he says, "Harmony is to be honored."[90] It was surely this spirit that made possible the emergence of Japan as a unified cultural state.

Prince Shōtoku's philosophical standpoint is represented by expressions like "The One Great Vehicle" or "The Pure One Great Vehicle," which are supposed to have originated from the *Lotus-sūtra*.

When we compare this fact with that in the West, we find a fundamental difference. Christianity gradually came to the fore in spite of various persecutions. Finally freedom of faith was assured by Emperor Constantin in the edict of Milan in the year 313, and Christianity obtained the position of the state religion on the occasion of the unification of the state by Emperor Theodosius in the year 394. Emperor Justinian of the Eastern Roman Empire forbad, in the year 529, to worship heathen gods except the Christian God. Heathen gods were not tolerated.

And we find that there has been in those facts the progress of coming into existence of the difference between the way of thinking of Eastern peoples to view any different idea or religion with a spirit of tolerance and the Western way of thinking to forbid or opress any other religion one by one.

Pacifism

There has been made a criticism against Prince Shōtoku by a scholar that his compassionate attitude was not a thoroughgoing one, for he wages a war on big clans after his conversion and he showed no repentance for his youthful faults in his advanced age. This comment may get to the point to some extent. This might be regarded as a criticism against Japanese Buddhism in general.

But a monarch who was "All-Compassion" is nothing but an outcome of phantasy which has no instance in actual life. A king, in so far as he is a king, wields power, resorts to force. Even the most compassionate Ashoka or Wen-ti was not an exception. Historians explain that the conversion of Constantine took place in order to take the command of his soldiers converted to Christianity. To have power involves necessarily bad.

But there was one distinction that many monarchs in the world had no consciousness of sin, showed no self-reflection, whereas the monarchs who professed the universal religions anew had some consciousness of sin, and showed self-reflection, or awe of the bad. This is something valuable. With this a new page in the history of mankind was opened.

The thought of pasifism or non-resistence is found in the attitude of Yamashiro-no-Oine, the son of Prince Shōtoku. He was attacked by the army of Soga-no-Iruka. He fled with his people, and tarried on a mountain. His chief subordinate advised him to flee towards the Eastern provinces, and, having raised troops, to come back and fight. The prince answered:—"If we did as you say, we should certainly succeed. In my heart, however, I desire for ten years not to impose a burden on the people. For the sake of one person only, why should I distress the ten thousand subjects? Moreover, I do not wish it to be said by after generations that for my sake anyone has mourned the loss of a father or mother. Is it only when one has conquered in battle that he is called a hero? Is he not also a hero who has made firm his country at the expense of his own life?" The prince sent his chief subordinate to the commanders of the enemy with his message, saying:—"If I had raised an army, and attacked Iruka, I should certainly have conquered. But for the sake of one person, I was unwilling to destroy the people. Therefore I deliver up myself to Iruka." Finally he and the younger members of his family, with his consorts, strangled themselves at the same time, and died together.[91]

In one of the pictures on the four sides of the basis of the Small Shrine "Tamamushi-no-zushi" preserved up to the present at the Hōryūji Temple, there is represented the scene of a saint who is giving his body to rear a hungry tiger. It is likely that the ideal of this story was exemplified in the legend of Prince Yamashiro-no-Oine.

Notes

1 The date suggested for King Songtsan Gampo is based on evidence presented in my work *Shoki no Vedanta Tetsugaku* ["Early Vedanta Philosophy"] (Tōkyō: Iwanami Shoten, 1950), pp. 105 ff. Dr. ROERICH places him at c. 650 A.D. Cf. George N. ROERICH, *The Blue Annals*, Part I (Calcutta: Royal Asiatic Society of Bengal) 1949), pp. iii, 49.

2 "The Sui founder presented himself to the populace as a universal monarch, a pious believer and a munificent patron of the church (mahādānapati). Early in his reign he proclaimed the religious ideology for the military campaigns on which he was about to embark:

'With the armed might of a Cakravartin king, We spread the ideals of the ultimately enlightened one. With a hundred victories in a hundred battles, We promote the practice of the ten Buddhist virtues. Therefore We regard the weapons of war as having become like the offerings of incense and flowers presented to Buddha, and the fields of this world as becoming forever identical with the Buddha-land.' " Arthur F. WRIGHT, *Buddhism in Chinese History* (Stanford, California: Stanford University Press, 1959).

3 *Nihongi: Chronicles of Japan from the Earliest Times to A.D. 697*, transl. by W. G. ASTON (London: George Allen and Unwin Ltd., 1896), Part Two, p. 65 (adapted).

4 Charles ELIOT, *Japanese Buddhism* (London: Routledge and Kegan Paul Ltd., 1935), p. 204.

5 Songtsan Gampo proclaimed his "Sixteen-Article Law" at nearly the same time Shōtoku issued his Seventeen-Article Constitution, and even earlier, the emperor Ashoka published many Rock Edicts and Pillar Edicts proclaiming an indeterminate number of precepts. The characteristic common to all three sets of injunctions is that they are presented in the form of moral precepts and that they differ in substance from positive laws.

The Tibetans were especially conscious of this point. According to them, the Sixteen-Article Law was a human law (*mi-chos*) and as such different from the law of the gods (*lha-chos*). Cf. MIBU Taishun, "Buddhist Thought in Tibetan Law," *Journal of Indian and Buddhist Studies*, Vol. V, No. 2 (   ), pp. 414–418. The former was an ethical law, whereas the latter was a religious. An itemized list of the contents of the Sixteen-Article Law is given in the *Matriculation Course of Classical Tibetan* by bLama Mingyur rDo-rJe and E. Denison Ross (Calcutta: , 1911), p. 7. The ethical and the religious laws, taken together, constituted the System of Laws (*chos-lugs*). Ashoka comprehended both under the single term "Just Law" (*dharma*).

On the basis of such fundamental laws, positive laws were formulated. The Tibetans called them "Laws of Ruling" (*rgyal-khrims*). Songtsan Gampo is said "to have instituted laws to punish murder, theft and adultery" (ROERICH, *The Blue Annals*, I, 20 b5). Such laws correspond to the positive laws and ordinances instituted in Japan beginning with the Taika Reforms.

The laws in effect in India during the early Maurya period just before the time of Ashoka appear to have been incorporated into the *Artha Śāstra* ["Treatise on Material Gain"] of Kautilya. Due to later interpolations in the work, however, it is very difficult to identify which laws were actually formulated in the early Maurya period.

6 The first article of the Sixteen-Article Law, as it was set forth in the *Chronicle of Tibet*, indirectly advocated concord by saying: "Whosoever quarrels is punished severely." Ashoka likewise stressed the spirit of concord (*samavāya*).

7 A slightly different version reads:

Harmony is to be valued, and an avoidance of wanton opposition to be honoured. All men are influenced by class-feelings, and there are few who are intelligent. Hence there are some who disobey their lords and fathers, or who maintain feuds with neighbouring villages. But when those above and those below are harmonious and friendly, things spontaneously and of themselves harmonize into truth. Then what is there which cannot be accomplished!

Adapted from the *Nihongi*, Part Two, p. 129.

8 *Analects*, I, 12: "In practising the rules of propriety, a natural ease is to be prized." Here "a natural ease" is the translation of the Chinese word *wa*. *Confucian Analects: Dr. Legge's Version*, edited with notes by OGAERI Yoshio (Tōkyō: Bunki Shoten, 1950), p. 4.

9 In the Chinese versions of Buddhist scriptures such words as *wakei* ("harmony and respect") or *wagō* ("harmony and concord") are frequently used.

10 Cf. Pillar Edict III as cited in D. R. BHANDARKAR, *Aśoka*, 3rd ed. (Calcutta: University of Calcutta, 1955), p. 302. (See following note.)

11 Ashoka likewise asserted the necessity of self-reflection: "(A person) seeth the good deed only, (saying unto himself:) 'This good deed has been done by me.' In no wise doth he see (his)ssin, (saying unto himself:) 'This sin have I committed,' or 'This, indeed, is a depravity.' But this certainly is difficult to scrutinise. Nevertheless, it should certainly be looked into thus: these (passions), indeed, lead to depravity, such as violence, cruelty, anger, conceit, envy, and by reason thereof may I not cause my fall." Pillar Edict III, as translated by D. R. BHANDARKAR, *Aśoka*, p. 302.

12 Cf. the version given in the *Nihongi*, Part Two, p. 131.

13 In the thirtieth year of the Empress Suiko, in the middle of the night of February 22, (April 11, if converted from the lunar to the solar calendar), 622 A.D., Prince Shōtoku died at the age of forty-nine. During the same month he was interred in the Imperial Mausoleum of Mt. Shinaga. (This event coincided roughly with the time of the *hijra* or Hegira, Muhammad's flight from Mecca to Medina.) Eifuku-ji Temple on Mt. Shinaga was erected in conjunction with his interment. It is said that the Empress Suiko herself ordered this temple to be built so that Buddhist masses might be said at the mausoleum perpetually.

14 This development can be observed both in the case of Emperor Wen of the Sui dynasty and in the case of Shōtoku. In India a parallel innovation seems to have been initiated by Chandragupta (c. 317–293 B.C.), the first Maurya emperor and the grandfather of Ashoka.

15 Similar measures appear to have been instituted under Chandragupta due to the advice of his minister Kautilya. The political theory of Kautilya is set forth in the above-mentioned *Kautiliya Artha Śāstra*.

16 A comparable spirit can be discerned in Ashoka. He lamented the fact that the good is difficult but the bad easy:

"The good is difficult to perform. He who initiates the good does something difficult to perform. So I have sought to do. If my sons, grandsons, and my descendants after them, until the aeon of destruction, follow in my steps, they will do what is meritorious, but in this matter he who abandons even a portion of the good will do ill. Verily, sin is easy to commit."

Adapted from the translation of Pillar Edict V contained in Bhandarkar, Aśoka, p. 270.

17 Shōtoku's Shōmangyō-gisho, ed. by HANAYAMA Shinshō (Tōkyō: Iwanami Shoten, 1948), p. 34.

18 Ashoka likewise instructed his officials that they should seek the happiness and welfare of the people, and that for that purpose they should observe the utterances of dharma, the ordinances and instructions of dharma. He too advocated forbearance and lightness of punishment. Cf. Rock Edict XIII.

19 Other rulers of universal states in Asia did the same. Cf. Ashoka's Pillar Edict III and the thirteenth article of Songtsan-Gampo's Law.

20 A phenomenon conspicuous in Japan, and unique, perhaps, in its intensity, is that people are often jealous of each other and try to hold down those who might otherwise be successful. A scholar of jurisprudence who was raised in Europe and naturalized in America and who has a good command of Japanese once told me: "Americans are rather weak when it comes to jealousy, whereas Europeans envy others. If anyone is successful in Europe, he is spoken ill of or found fault with. But that is nothing compared to Japan. It is terrible among the Japanese!" A Japanese acquaintance who had worked for many years in New York once remarked: "In Japan people are censorious! I don't like it. People backbite. In New York I can relax. Nobody there runs to others with criticisms about me." Such personal experiences by people who know what it is like to live in Japan and in other cultures as well have a common focus. If jealousy is part of the Japanese make-up, it can be traced as far back as the age of Shōtoku.

21 The determination to have his edicts observed by the common people was very strong in the case of Ashoka also. His purpose in having edicts inscribed on stone pillars that he erected, or on the polished surfaces of rocks, was that they should be read by the common people. Thus Ashoka wrote: "Since I was consecrated twelve years ago, I have caused dharma edicts to be inscribed for the welfare and happiness of the people, so that without violation thereof, they might in various ways attain to growth in dharma" (Pillar Edict VI). Needless to say, those who could read and understand the edicts must have been limited to the contemporary ruling and intellectual classes. However, those influenced by the edicts must have amounted to a considerable number. Moreover, Ashoka urged people to propagate the dharma. "People should propagate (the teaching) in appropriate ways to their own relatives" (Yerragudi Edict). He saw to it that the edicts were recited on fixed days and thus aimed to preserve their freshness as guides for conduct. "This document should be heard on the Tishya day every quarter; and indeed, on every festive occasion between Tishya days it may be heard by as few as one (official). By acting thus, endeavour to fulfil (my instructions)" (Separate Kalinga Edict I, slightly adapted from Bhandarkar, Aśoka, p. 329). In the case of Ashoka, however, the idea of emphasizing the prestige of the ruler in his capacity as sovereign is not noticeable. His words were to be esteemed, rather, for the reason that they expressed universal laws. Again, in the Sixteen-Article Law of Songtsan-Gampo, loyalty to the monarch is not inculcated even by implication.

22 Itō Keidō, "A legend that Prince Shōtoku was a re-incarnation of Nangaku Eshi and Tōsan-Daishi" in his *Studies on Dōgen*, Vol. I, pp. 319–332.

23 Adapted from the "Hymns in Praise of Prince Shōtoku" as translated in *The Shinshu Seiten: The Holy Scripture of Shinshu* (Honolulu: The Honpa Hongwanji Mission of Hawaii, 1955), p. 247.

24 Thus, e.g., Lobsang Phuntsok Lhalungpa in Kenneth W. Morgan (ed.), *The Path of the Buddha: Buddhism Interpreted by Buddhists* (N.Y.: The Ronald Press Company, 1956), p. 239.

25 See, e.g., the *Nihongi*, Part Two, pp. 136–141, 145–146.

26 The three scriptures were: (1) the *Saddharma-pundarika-sūtra*, known in Japanese as the *Myōhō-renge-kyō* or *Hoke-kyō*, in English as the *Lotus Sūtra*; (2) the *Vimalakirti-nirdeśa-sūtra*, referred to in Japanese as the *Yuima-gyō* and in English as the *Discourse on Ultimate Truth* by Vimalakirti; and (3) the *Śrimālā-devi-simhanāda-sūtra*, ordinarily called the *Shōman-gyō* in Japanese, while in English it has been referred to as the *Book of the Ernest Resolve* by Śrimālā. The three commentaries Shōtoku wrote on these sūtras comprise seven volumes collectively entitled the *Jōgū-gyosei-sho*. Cf. Eliot, *Japanese Buddhism*, p. 205.

27 The "Four All-Embracing Virtues" (Skt. *catvāri samgraha-vastūni*, Jps. *shishōbō*) is a portfolio term having reference to the four ways by which bodhisattvas lead existent beings to enlightenment. These ways are: (1) to do good to others through teaching the true way and through donating material necessities, (2) to use words motivated by love, (3) to seek others' benefit through thought, word, and deed, and (4) to assume the form of the being to be helped and to work diligently alongside that one.

The "Four Virtues of Infinite Greatness" (Skt. *catvāri apramānāni*, Jps. *shi-muryō-shin*) are: (1) infinite goodwill to others, (2) infinite compassion for the sufferings of others, (3) infinite joy in others' happiness, and (4) infinite impartiality, even to the extent of abandoning attachment to the above virtues and being impartial even to enemies.

The "Six Perfections" (Skt. *sat pāramitāh*, Jps. *ropparamitsu*) are: (1) almsgiving, (2) keeping the ethical precepts, (3) persevering despite persecution and suffering, (4) assiduousness in keeping the other five perfections, (5) meditation, and (6) the wisdom of realizing the ultimate reality that lies behind existence.

28 Cf. Ashoka's Fourteen Rock Edicts, II, as cited in Bhandarkar, *Aśoka*, p. 261.

29 With regard to the "hunting of medicinal herbs" and the establishing of dispensaries, cf. again Ashoka's Fourteen Rock Edicts, II, in Bhandarkar's *Aśoka*, p. 261.

30 *Nihongi*, Part Two, pp. 144–145.

31 According to the Hōryūji Edition of the *Yuima-gyō-gisho*, edited by SAEKI Jōin, 1937, Vol. I, p. 16a, the text of the passage is:

實法舉體即空. 故言不有. 有既非有. 無何所無.
故言亦不無.... 有無無定. 故但藉因緣而生.

Ens and Voidness are further discussed in Vol. III, p. 55a.

32 *Yuima-gyō-gisho*, Vol. I, p. 39b.

33 Cf., e.g., the *Mādhyamika Kārikās of Nāgārjuna*, ed. by L. de la V. POUSSIN in the Bibliotheca Buddhica, Vol. IV (1913), esp. Chapter II. This kind of dialectic was also applied in the *Vimalakirtinirdeśa-sūtra* itself. Cf., further, the *Yuima-gyō-gisho*, Vol. II, p. 39a (菩薩品第四) and Vol. III, p. 19b　　　(前際不來, 後際不法, 今則不住. 見阿閦佛國品第十二).

34 The original text of this passage as cited in the *Yuima-gyō-gisho*, Vol. I, p. 26a, is as follows:

因有四種.
一　同性相生. 謂之習因. 如初修直心. 還能不謟之類是.
二　異類相生. 謂之報因. 如善惡生苦樂之類是.
三　相資因. 如行施爲因即生持戒之類是.
四　相似因. 就報因中押出一因. 如不殺生復得長壽之類是.
M. Anesaki, in his *Prince Shōtoku: The Sage Statesman and his Mahāsattva Ideal* (Tōkyō: Shōtoku Taishi Hōsankai, 1948), p. 123 n., translated these four kinds of causes literally as: (1) 習因 *shū-in* or cumulative, (2) 報因 *hō-in* or compensatory, (3) 相資因 *sōshitsu-in* or reciprocal, and (4) 相似因 *sōji-in* or corresponding.

35 See, e.g., Th. Stcherbatsky, *Buddhist Logic*, Vol. I ('s-Gravenhage: Mouton and Co., reprint of 1958), pp. 9, 119–145; Edward J. Thomas, *History of Buddhist Thought*, Second ed. (London: Routledge and Kegan Paul Ltd., 1951), pp. 58–70, 219–220; T. R. V. Murti, *The Central Philosophy of Buddhism: A Study of the Mādhyamika System* (London: George Allen and Unwin Ltd., 1955), pp. 130–143, 165–178.

36 *Yuimakyō Gisho*, vol. 2, A, p. 55a.

37 *Shōmangyō Gisho*, p. 8a.

38 *Saddharmapundarika-sūtra* XV, vv. 1–18. Cf. SBE. vol. XXI, pp. 307–309.

39 *Shōmangyō Gisho*, chapter VIII, p. 58b.

40 常任法身佛寶. 此法身爲物軌則. 自爲法寶. 又此法身則能與理合. 亦爲僧寶.
Shōmangyō Gisho, p. 50b.
We cite the *Shōmangyō Gisho* from the Hōryūji Edition (昭和會本. 勝鬘経義疏). Edited by Jōin Saheki. 3rd ed. May 1943.

41 法者法身. 萬善爲種　*Shōmangyō Gisho*, p.

42 佛地萬德圓備.

43 法身是萬德之正體.　*Shōmangyō Gisho*, p. 6b.

44 若三世常護者. 即作善. 無息.　ibid., p. 9a.

45 今日無作一滅.

46 無作一滅即如來藏. 生死神明依如來藏. 相續不滅. 非但 出惑方爲物依. 從在惑中已爲依也.　*Shōmangyō Gisho*, p. 64b.

47 何即非本無以垂迹. 非迹無以顯本.　*Shōmangyō Gisho*, p. 7a.

48 無餘涅槃即兼無量滅道.　*Shōmangyō Gisho*, p. 61a.

49 今日一体.　*Shōmangyō Gisho*, pp. 49–50.

50 Vaiśāle was a business center in ancient India.

51 p.1. a *Yuimakyō Gisho*,

52 According to a legend, when Shinran visited the mausoleum of Prince Shōtoku at the age of nineteen, the Prince appeared to him in a dream and conferred upon him a verse in which the phrase "Japan is the country where Mahāyāna Buddhism is in practice" occurred. (Goten Ryōku: *Takada Shinran Seitōden*, vol. I. in *Shinshū Zensho* Shindenbu, p. 337. Cf. Hōkū: *Jōgō Taishi Shūiri*, in *Dainihon Bukkyō Zensho*, vol. 112, p. 142.

53 Shōson Miyamoto: *Chūdō-shisō oyobi sono Hattatsu*, Kyoto, Hōzōkan, 1944. pp. 888, 889.

54 Prince Shōtoku often paraphrase the term *bodhisattva* with the word 義士 (man of principle). (Shinshō Hanayama: *Shūmangyō Gisho no Kenkyū*, Tokyo Iwanami-shoten, 1944, pp. 432, 433.) His adopting man of principle (義士) instead of *bodhisattva* (大士, 開士) the usual translation, seems to give testimony to the fact that he wanted to emphasize the necessity for the practice of *bodhisattvas* to be realized in concrete human nexuses.

55 Shinshō Hanayama: *"Hokke Gisho no Kenkyū"*, p. 469. Tokyo, the Oriental Library, 1933.

56 *Yuimakyō Gisho*, in *Dainihon Bukkyō Zensho*, p. 141.

57 *Yuimakyō Gisho*, vol. 2, p. 3b.

58 *Yuimakyō Gisho*, vol. 3, p. 4b.

59 *Yuimakyō Gisho*, vol. 2, p. 2b.

60 勝鬘者．世以七寶嚴其肉身．而今以萬行嚴其法身．故云勝鬘．
Shōmagyō Gisho, p. 1a.

61 Busshi Shōman. 佛子勝鬘

62 *Hokke Gisho*, in Dainihon Bukkyō Zensho, p. 4b.

63 Ibid., p. 28a. Similar expressions are found here and there. Cf. ibid., pp. 5a, 34a, 28a,
HANAYAMA: *Hokke Gisho no Kenkyū*, pp. 469, 489.

64 心爲萬德元本．今心既淨．則生一切衆德那得不淨．
Yuimakyō Gisho, vol. 1, p. 29b.

65 *Yuimakyō Gisho*, vol. 3, p. 22a.

66 直心乃是萬行之始． *Yuimakyō Gisho*, vol. 1, p. 29b.

67 一………證．人是可信．二………證法是可信．人能弘法故先證．
法由人弘故後證． *Shōmangyō, Gisho*, p. 2b.

68 *Yuimakyō Gisho*, vol. 3A, p. 16a.

69 我子之稱．不別自他．唯在於善．今勝鬘既爲爲己子．且有明德．應聞勝道．
故亦自稱我子也． *Shōmangyō Gisho*, p. 3b-4a.

70 十大受

71 三大願

72 Compassion or love is discussed in detail, *Yuimakyō Gisho*, vol. 3A, p. 35f.

73 不以愛見悲．若有愛見．即化道爲漏．亦於生死有厭足
且化物有礙． *Shōmangyō Gisho*, p. 12a.

74 *Yuimakyō Gisho*, vol. 2, p. 59a.

75 The phrase 得一切衆生殊勝供養 was interpreted "to make (**B**uddhas and Bodhisattvas) worship all living beings of distinction". It would be needless to say that it is a twisted
interpretation. He introduced here an altruistic idea. (Cf. HANAYAMA: Shomangyō Gisho
no Kenkyū, pp. 434-437.)

76 HANAYAMA: Hokke Gisho no Kenkyū, pp. 386, 387.

77 The famous story of abandonment of Prince Vessantara (*Jataka* No. 547), for example, is a good illustration.

78 Shinshō HANAYAMA: Shomangyō Gisho no Kenkyū, p. 432.

79 如法得財爲淨命 *Yuimakyō Gisho*, vol. 2, p. 57a.

80 利

81 *Yuimakyō Gisho*, vol. 2, p. 31b.

82 示勸證

83 「三轉法輪於大于」者．即謂四諦教．三輪者．
一是．二教．三利也． *Yuimakyō Gisho*, vol. 1, p. 17a.

84 *Yuimakyō Gisho*, vol. 1, p. 21b.

85 Due to this characteristic of Buddhism, neither Prince Shōtoku nor King Songtsan-
Gampo, not to mention Ashoka, suppressed indigenous faiths native to his respective
people, although they both esteemed and reverenced Buddhism. That is why Shintoism
in Japan, and the Bon religion in Tibet have been preserved, as their respective religion, up
to the present. In Burma the faith of Nats is prevalent even now among common people.

86 Shinshō HANAYAMA: *Hokke-gisho no Kenkyū*, p. 664f.

87 Ibid., p. 117f.

88 *Yuimanyō Gisho,* vol. 2, p. 17a.

89 *Yuimakyō Gisho,* vol. 2, p. 14b.

90 Shinshō HANAYAMA: *op. cit.,* p. 460.

91 Kazunori (Takeo) MOCHIZUKI: *A Treatise on Prince Shōtoku.* Tokyo, Shin-Kyōiku-Kenkyū-Kai, 1958, pp. 10–11.

CHAPTER II

PHILOSOPHICAL IDEAS OF THE NARA AND HEIAN PERIODS

1. Introductory Remarks

Philosophical ideas were maintained and discussed by the Six Sects of Nara and Tendai and Shingon sects which appeared at the beginning of the Heian period.

The Six Sects of the Nara Period

In the Nara period (701–794 A.D.) six sects were introduced from China into Japan.

(1) The Risshū or Ritsu sect. Its main principles are the observation of strict monastic discipline and, above all, the correct transmission of the holy orders. The monks of this sect strictly adhere to the descipline of Conservative Buddhism flourishing in South Asiatic Countries.

(2) The Kusha sect is a school of Conservative Buddhism. It is based upon the *Kusha-ron* (*Abhidharmakosa*) composed by Vasubandhu (about 320–400 A.D.).

(3) The Jōjitsu sect is based upon the *Jōjitsu-ron* (*Satyasiddhisāstra*) written by Harivarman (A.D. 250–350). This is a school of Conservative Buddhism, which has been adapted to the doctrine of the "Void" to some extent.

(4) The Sanron sect is derived from the Mādhyamika school in India. It stresses the doctrine of the "Void." The word *Sanron* literally means "The Three Treatises," i.e., The *Madhyamakasāstra*, the *Dvādasamukha-sāstra* of Nāgārjuna, and the *Śata-sāstra* of Āryadeva. This school is based upon these Three Treatises.

(5) The Hossō sect is a kind of Buddhist idealism. It is derived from the Yogācāra school in India. It regards everything at the manifestation of the fundamental Mind-principle underlying all phenomena.

(6) The Kegon sect is based on the *Kegon* or *Avatamasaka sūtra*. The principal object of worship in this sect is Vairrocana Buddha.

These six sects might be called scholastic because their sphere of influence was limited to the monks and did not extend to the common people.

At the beginning of the Heian period (794–1192 A.D.) the Tendai and Shingon sects came to Japan.

The Two Major Sects of the Heian Period

(1) *The Tendai Sect*

The Tendai sect was introduced into Japan by Saichō (767–822 A.D.), Master Dengyō (Dengyō Daishi) being his honorary name, entered a monastery at an early age, and was ordained at eighteen (785 A.D.). As the ecclesiastical life of Nara was uncongenial to him, he left the city and lived at first in solitude on Mount Hiei, near his birthplace, and gradually collected a group of companions and built a small monastery.

In 804 he was sent by the Emperor to China to discover the best form of Buddhism. He studied the school of T'ien-T'ai (Tendai) at its headquarters, and also the Shingon and the Zen schools. He returned next year laden with books and knowledge. The humble monastery founded by him grew up later into a priestly city of some three thousand temples.

The tendai sect is based on the Hokke-kyo or *Lotus-sūtra*. Conforming to this, this sect teaches that all men can become Buddhas and urges them to attempt to do so.

The most remarkable characteristic of Tendai is its comprehensive and and encyclopaedic character. It finds a place for all scriptures, regarding them as a progressive revelation, gradually disclosed by the Buddha during his life, as he found that the intelligence of his listeners ripened.

According to our common sense, it seems that parts depend on one another and all depend on the whole. But the so-called complete or perfect teaching (En-gyō) of this sect goes beyond this. It sees that the whole and the parts are identical. The Whole Cosmos and all the Buddhas are present in a grain of sand or on the point of a hair. A celebrated maxim says: One thought is the three thousand spheres (that is, the whole universe) and the three thousand spheres are but one thought. That is to say, the relations involved in the simplest thought are so numerous that they imply the existense of the whole universe, our perceptions and thoughts being identical with absolute reality. This leads to the doctrine of ontology. There are three forms of existence: the void, the temporary, and the middle. That is, all things which exist depend on their relations. If we try to isolate them and to conceive of them as entering into no relations, they become unthinkable and in fact non-existent.

But as temporary formative parts of the whole they do exist and the whole could not realize its true nature if it did not manifest itself in particulars. So in that sense all things exist as phenomenal beings. Things exist or do not exist according to our view of their relations to it, but the middle exists absolutely. Phenomena and the one absolute truth are, if rightly regarded, synonymous. When the significance of each of the three is properly cognized, this is the enlightenment as obtained by the Buddha himself.

(2) *The Shingon Sect*

The Shingon Sect is the third largest religious organization in Japan, ranking after Shin-shū and Sōtō sects and possesses about twelve thousand temples.

Kūkai (774–835 A.D.) or Master Kōbō (Kōbō Daishi), was the first man to make Shingon well known in Japan. He went to China for study, where he spent two years (804–6) in studying Shingon under Hui-Kuo, the celebrated abbot of the Ch'ing-Lung temple at Ch'ang-An. He is also said to have applied himself to Sanskrit under the guidance of an Indian monk called Prājna, and is believed to have introduced into Japan the slightly altered form of the Sanskrit letters called Shittan (siddham), which is written in vertical columns and much used in Shingon books. Prājna is believed to have cooperated with Nestorian priests in making translations. Kūkai, in this way, may have come into contact with Christians.

Kūkai returned to Japan in 806 and was well received by the Emperor. He founded the great monastery of Kōyasan in the province of Kii. He died at Kōyasan in 835 A.D. There has been prevalent a mystical view about him. He died at the Kongōbu-ji Temple of Mt. Kōya on March 21st of the 2nd year of Showa. But the believers in Shingon sect say he just entered meditation awaiting the time of descent of Maitreya the Buddha, and Kūkai did not die. He is as yet alive. So, at a fixed time, a properly qualified high priest comes and changes Kūkai's gown in the inner sanctuary, where Kūkai is supposed to be still staying in meditation. What is the condition of Kūkai the great teacher of Buddhism now? It is a great secret that must not be discussed among the laity.

In all the annals and legends of Japanese Buddhism there is no more celebrated name than his, and whether as saint, miracle-worker, writer, painter or sculptor, he is familiar to the most learned, and the most ignorant, of his countrymen. The equivalent of the phrase "Homer sometimes nods" in Japanese is "Kōbō mo fude no ayamari"; or "Even Kōbō sometimes makes a slip of the pen."

Shingon means "true word," that is, a sacred spell (or mantra) and this sect is mingled with magical elements.

About 700 A.D. Indian Buddhism had become a very mixed creed and may have incorporated many Iranian and Central Asiatic elements. This form of Buddhism is called Esoteric Buddhism. (Vajrayāna)

The common people of Japan of those days wanted a religion which was impregnated with magic. That is why the Shingon sect was highly welcomed in Japan.

In Shingon there are definite secret doctrines which can be communicated orally. He who has not yet been initiated cannot claim to understand the explanations.

The initiated is sprinkled with holy water, and there is, in this respect, some similarity with Christian baptism. The ceremony of initiation is called Kwanchō (or Kwanjō), a translation of the Sanskrit abhiseka, or sprinkling, sometimes rendered in English by the most misleading expression, "baptism."

It is true that part of the ceremony generally consists in the religious aspersion by water, but it is not at all a rite performed on children or others, when they first become members of the sect, but a form of initiation into the higher mysteries, and granted only as an exceptional privilege.

Voidness

The philosophy of Voidness (śūnyatā) in Japan was represented by the Sanron sect which concentrated in studying the works of Nārgārjuna and Āryadeva. It is believed that Eji, a preceptor of Prince Shōtoku, who came from Korea, was a master in the Sanron philosophy. It was Ekan who came also from Korea to the Imperial court in 625 A.D. that introduced the sect. The philosophy of this sect was studied in major monasteries of Nara, although scholarship was not flourishing.

The Mahāyāna mystics taught the theory of the 'Void.' Mahāyāna Buddhism found in the theory of relational origination the basis for the void, emptiness, śūnyata.[1] "Sunya" means swollen. Anything swollen is void inside. The little circle which we nowadays know as zero, was called "void" (śūnya) in Sanskrit. This was originally an Indian invention which was introduced into the West through the Arabs about 1150 A.D. The Mahāyāna philosophers, especially those of the Mādhyamika school, advocated as follows: there is no real existence; all things are but appearance and are in truth empty, "devoid" of their own essence. Even non-existence is not reality; everything occurs conditioned by everything else. Voidness or emptiness is not nothingness nor annihilation, but that which stands right in the middle between affirmation and negation, existence and non-existence, eternity and annihilation. So 'Voidness' means 'relationality' of all things.

A scriptural passage of a Mahāyāna sūtra runs as follows: "Just as, in the vast ethereal sphere, stars and darkness, light and mirage, dew, foam, lightning and clouds emerge, become visible, and vanish again, like the features of a dream—so everything endowed with an individual shape is to be regarded."[2]

The doctrine of the Void (śūnyata) is not nihilism. On the contrary, Mahāyāna Buddhists asserted that it is the true basis for the foundation of ethical values. There is nothing in the Void, but everything comes out of it. Cf. mirror. the Void is all-inclusive; having no opposite, there is nothing which it excludes or opposes. It is living void, because all forms come out of it, and whoever realizes the void is filled with life and power and the Bodhisattva's love (karuna) for all beings. Love is the moral equivalent of all-inclusiveness, which is nothing but the "Void." The fundamental basis upon which everything occurs is the "Void." So, knowing the "Void" means omniscience. The Void resembles a crystal ball, which is visible to our eyes only because of what it reflects. Hold it up before a flower, and there within it is a flower. Hold it up before the empty sky, and there seems to be nothing in it, but only because it is reflecting the emptiness of the sky. Its true nature remains unknown. As the crystal ball reflects images, the manifold phenomena appears spontaneously within the Void. When we realize the 'Void' good-acts come out spontaneously.[3]

The Mādhyamika philosophers denied change in the phenomenal world, and set forth the theory of ineffability of the truth. Nāgārjuna, the great Mahāyāna philosopher, asserted at the beginning of his work(as follows:

"The Buddha has proclaimed the principle of Dependent Origination (Relationality), the principle that nothing (in the universe) can disappear, nor can (anything new) arise, nothing has an end, nor is there anything eternal, nothing is identical with itself, nor is there anything differentiated (in itself), there is no motion, neither towards us, nor from us."[4] Here the word "relationality" means the same as the "void." One has come to know that fundamentally nothing whatsoever is happening to the true essence of one's nature,[5] nothing to give cause for either distress or joy. He denied change itself.

On this standpoint negation itself should be negated. Denial of denial is required.[6] Nāgārjuna says, "If something non-relational (not 'void')

did really exist, we would then likewise admit the existence of the relational, but there is absolutely nothing non-relational, how then can
we admit the existence of the relational (or the truth of 'void')."[7]

The philosophy of 'Voidness' has no fixed dogma.

"If I have theses (of my own to prove),
I may commit mistakes just for the sake (of proving)
But I have none. I cannot be accused
(Of being inconsistent)."[8]

Āryadeva said:

"If I neither admit a thing's reality,
Nor unreality, nor both (at once),
Then, to confute me
A long time will be needed."[9]

The Mādhyamika philosophers had the conviction that their standpoint will not be refuted.

It has not yet been made clear to what extent Japanese scholar-monks
developed the philosophy beyond the San-lun sect of China. Anyhow,
the Japanese Sanron scholars left us voluminous works such as the
Chūron-shoki by Anchō (763–814), which is a voluminous subcommen-
tary in 8 vols., 16 parts on the *Madhyamaka-sāstra* of Nāgārjuna. Even
in the history of Chinese thought we don't come across such a huge work
on the *Madhyamaka-sāstra*. This work is not a systematical tratise, but in
between lines of comment we find sophisticated argumentations also.

In Japan the doctrinal study of the Sanron sect developed beyond the
scope of the three fundamental texts of this sect; it included more than
fifty Chinese Buddhist texts which presented both "theoretical" and
"practical" sides of the Mādhyamika standpoint of the philosophy of
Voidness. But it was overcome by other systems and it disappeared
finally.

(2) Interrelational Existence

The right knowledge of the truth of interdependent causation, as was
set forth in early Buddhism, lead to a recognition of the interdependent
relations of various aspects of actual human existence. This thought was

especially emphasized by the Kegon sect of China and Japan.

According to the concept of Interdependent Origination of Mahāyāna, all existences and phenomena are interrelated. Even a flower is closely connected with all the universe; a flower itself has no separate existence in the metaphysical sense. One cannot sever himself from the past. This can be said of everything in the universe. The tiny violet droops its fairy head just so much, and no more, it is balanced by the universe. It is a violet, not an oak, because it is the outcome of the interrelational existence of an endless series of the past existence.

The interconnection between one individual and the whole universe was especially stressed by the *Buddhāvatamsaka-sūtra,* and the Hua-yen sect in China and the Kegon sect in Japan. The *Buddhāvatamsaka-sūtra* says: "Within one pore of the body all living beings are accommodated"[10] or "All things appear in one pore."[11] "The visible body of a Buddha teaches the ocean of merits of all Buddhas."[12] This theory was expressed throughout all Mahāyāna-sutras, especially in the *Buddhāvatamsaka-sūtra,* in India.

The Hua-yen philosophy of China sets forth the theory of interrelation from the spatial viewpoint in the fourfold manner as follows:

(1) One is in one;

(2) One is in all:

(3) All is in one;

(4) All are in all.

From the viewpoint of time the following formula is set forth:

(1) When one is taken in by all, one enters into all;

(2) When all is taken-in by one, all enters into one;

(3) When one is taken in by one, one enters into one;

(4) When all is taken-in by all, all enters into all.

All things in the universe are brought into existence according to the above-mentioned formula at the same time.[13]

The Hua-yen philosophy interprets the universe thus viewed to be motivated by one Great Compassionate Soul. And the relationship among individual persons is governed by the theory of independence under the surveillance of this one Great Compassionate Soul. According to the legend Ryōnin (1072–1132), the founder of the *Yuzū Nembutsu* ("Circulation" of *Nembutsu*) teaching of Japan once witnessed Amida Buddha. He dedicated a poem to Amida:

"One person is all persons; all persons are one person; one meritorious
deed is all meritorious deeds; all meritorious deeds are one meritorious
deed. This is a deliverance to the Pure Land by the grace of Amida."

Namely, the merit gained by an invocation of Amida is circulated and transferred to all sentient beings, so that the *Nembutsu* of one believer procures salvation for all others.

Later Dōgen (1200–1253) also advocated one's unification with others:
"The self and others should be benefitted at the same time."[14]

This theory of the unity if the self and others is quite different from the emanation theory of some western mystic thinkers such as that of Plotinus and Neoplatonists. To describe their theory, they resorted imaginary figures of celestial bodies and angles. The Eastern mystics employ metaphor of a mirror. The parable often used in the Kegon philosophy is as follows:

"Set up points of the compass including the zenith and the nadir in
front of you. When you place a lamp at the center, you notice each
one of the ten mirrors reflecting the light; when you pick up one of ten,
you will see that it also reflects all the rest of the ten reflecting the light
including that of the one you picked up. Each one of the nine is inherent in the one and the one in each one of the nine."[15]

A term mirror-knowledge (*adarsajnana*) was given in Buddhist Idealism (*yogacara*) to express this theory of unity.

According to this theory, the way to deliver oneself from suffering is nothing other than the perfect realization of the truth of interdependent relationship. This truth is generally expressed by the formula:

"When *this* exists, *that* occurs; when *this* does not exist, *that* does not
exist; when *this* is destroyed, *that* is destroyed."

This truth is also observed in the two-fold conception of stepping up and down the twelve links in the chain of causation.

Thus the true realization of the truth, as was set forth in Buddhism, must lead to a recognition of the interdependent relations of various aspects of actual human existence because, as expounded by Mahāyānists, the truth of interdependent relationship lies in the principle of negation of the very existence of things that are transient and void—since they, being interdependent, do not exist independently and separately. As far as the truth of interdependent relationship is thus interpreted, suffering is the inevitable consequence of one's attachment to the existence of things and of one's claiming their unvarying continuity in defiance of the truth. If, on the contrary, one realizes the truth as it is and knows the vanity of the existence of things, one should not undergo suffering caused by the experience of decay, disease and eath.

It is in this sense that Sakyamuni freed himself from suffering by thoroughly realizing this truth of interdependent relationship.

4. The Absolute

Words, Categories

In Mahāyāna Buddhism we find also a theory of, so to speak, trinity. According to this theory, Buddha is envisaged under the following three aspects which are essentially one.

(1) The essential body (dharmakāya, *hosshin* in Japanese), which is the pure and differentiated one. It is tautology of the "Void".

(2) The enjoying body (sambhogakāya, *hōjin* in Japanese), which is the perfect figure of Buddha who enjoys the results of his religious practices in the past. It is a Buddha as an ideal and accomplished personality which is provided with every kind of virtue.

(3) The body of transformation (nirmāna-kaya, *ōjin* in Japanese), by which the Buddha works for the good of all creatures.

Among these the second in particular became the object of worship among the followers of Mahāyāna Buddhism. And the concept of "the Essential Lelf" became the pivot of Buddhist philosophy and it culminated in the Shgon (Vajrayāna). The main idea of Shingon is cosmotheism, which is somewhat different from pantheism. The whole universe is regarded as body of the supreme Buddha Vairocana, being composed of six elements: earth, water fire, air, ether, and consciousness.

Farms of the Buddha

In parallel with this, a trinity was conceived. It consists of Amitayus, Avalokitesvara and Mahasthamaprapta (i.e. "the one who has attained great strength"). Assimilated by Buddhims, Avalokitesvara was called a great Bodhisattva, so great that he is nearly as perfect as Buddha. Mahāyāna Buddhists regarded the absolute Buddha as the "void" which transcends being and non-being. This idea of the Three Bodies of Buddha was especially inherited and discussed by the Tendai sect in Japan.[16]

On the other hand, Kūkai propounded the theory of the Four Bodies of Buddha:[17]

1) Essential Body (*jishōshin, svābhāvika-kāya*) or the body of Buddha which is an ultimate existance.

2) Enjoyment Body (*hōjin, sambhoga-kāva*) or a body of reward as a result of his long practice and vows as a *bodhisattva*.

3) Body of Transformation (*keshin, nirmāna-kāya*) or a body of his activity for the benefit of all creatures, i.e. historical person of Buddha.

4) Homogeneous Body (*torushin*). This is the body of Buddha who takes the appearance of human or celestial beings or of animals.[18]

On the other hand, the Japanese Tendai philosophy inherited the theory of Ten Categories from Master T'ien-t'ai of China. They are: form, essence (nature), substance, cause, force, activity, circumstance, effect, reward (result), ultimate aim.[19]

5. Affirmation of the World

The basic doctrines of Buddhism was reinterpreted by Japanese Buddhist thinkers who put more accent on the life in this world. According to the views of Indian Buddhist believers, all living beings repeat their life-cycles in an infinite process of transmigration of the soul; and a life in this world is but an infinitesmal period within this eternal circulation of life. Buddhism, however, as first interpreted by Chinese philosophers who emphasized more this-worldliness of life, which was succeeded and developed by Japanese Buddhists. Several sects of Japanese Buddhism emphasize the belief that even ordinary men are able to become Buddhas, should they attain enlightenment in this wdrld (*sokushin jobutsu*).

According to Saichō's comments on various doctrines of Buddhism, Hinayāna Buddhism is a circuitous teaching, since it advocates the practice of religion through countless lives in an immensely long span of time. Some Mahāyāna sects hold that religious practice should be carried out all through this long periods of life and such teaching was not much accepted by the Japanese populace of Saichō's time. Mahāyāna in general directs the way in which even ordinary man can become a Buddha in a limited time (*a direct way*). And it is the doctrine of the Lotus Sūtra that gives the fullest expression to this idea (The Great Straight Way).[20] Saichō used the phrase, *Sokushin Jōbutsu* (becoming Buddha alive in human body).[21] But in the theory of *Sokushin Jōbutsu* taught by Saichō (767–822), the doctrine of this-worldliness was not thoroughly developped. It was Japanese Tendai scholars who later pushed the idea of this-world Buddhahood, for the Tendai doctrine in China did not allow a man to become a Buddha in his life time. Even if he did achieve Buddhahood, it was supposed to be the consequence of ascetic practices achieved through many lives, so that one could become a Buddha only on reaching the threshold of true religion. Around hundred years later after Saichō a Tendai scholar An'nen (ca. 884) began to preach not only that one could become Buddha in this world, but also that one could do so through ascetic practice during one's life, and would be permitted to be a Buddha realized alive in human body.[22]

In the system of Japanese Shingon philosophy which doctrine of this-worldliness was plainly expressed by Kūkai (774–835), substance consists of six elements which are earth, water, fire, wind, space and consciousness; in short, matters (comprising the first five elements) and mind (i.e. consciousness). The five elements cannot exist without the consciousness, and the consciousness likewise cannot be without the five elements.[23] The six elements can be examined from two different aspects, viz. the noumenal (undifferentiated) or unconditional aspect and the conditional or phenomenal aspect. The former refers to the eternal, unchanging substance; the latter, the everchanging reality, which corresponds to the *natura naturans;* and latter, *natura naturata,* of the Medieval Western philosophy.

The essence lives in absolute truth (the world of the Law, *dharmadhātu, hokkai*), and they are so perfectly interrelated as never to obstruct (or contradict) one another. It follows that mankind and Buddhas are identical in their essence. Kūkai preached that should one follow this reasoning, formation of figures with one's hands, recitation of incantations, or concentration of one's mind (the three actions of man's body, mouth and mind), would be identified with those of Buddha.

Three Mysteries

For the religious practice the Shingon philosophy ascribes mystical meanings to specific syllables. For example, the mystical syllable *Hūm* is not only the symbol, but is itself the living breath which is itself the living substance penetrating the cosmos. This eternal living substance is called the *original principle of Three Mysteries* or *Three Mysteries of the Original Existence* or again *Three Bodies of the Original Existence*,[24] because the three mysteries are the esoteric actions of doing, speaking and thinking.[25]

One striking difference between Japanese and Chinese Tendai thoughts lies in the fact that the Tendai doctrine of Japan puts emphasis upon *things*, while in China the doctrine of the same sect regards *reason* as most important. *Things* here mean observable specificities or particularities limited in time and space. Shimei (Ssu-min 1060–1128), a Chinese Tendai scholar, preached that the first half (*shakumon*) of the Lotus Sūtra explains the perfect *truth* in conformity with the Law of Reason (perfect reason), while the second half (*honmon*) of the Sūtra exposes the perfect truth in accordance with phenomena (perfect things). For this Chinese priests even this latter expresses eternal Buddha. In contrast, Eshin (942–1017), a Japanese Tendai scholar, while accepting this two-fold interpretation, took the perfect reason for the comprehension of the multiplicity of phenomenal world by virtue of indiscriminatory truth (*sessō kishō*) and the perfect thing for the revelation of the truth through the multiplicity of phenomena.[26]

Based upon this theory, Saichō asserted that both priests and laymen should achieve the same ideal. According to Kūkai, absolute reason should be realized in actuality. Reality is revealed in accordance with things.

The emphasis upon this-worldliness rans parallel to the stress upon all the creative activities of men. In a country like India where the intensity of heat, seasonal rainfall, and the fertility of the soil are combined to bring forth a rich harvest without much agrarian labor to be exerted, the ethics of class distinction rather than that of production is emphasized. That is a reason why alms-giving comes to be considered as most important. In a country like Japan, in contrast, production is of vital importance, hence stress is placed upon the ethics of labor in various professions.

The Lotus Sūtra,[27] the most important of Japanese Buddhist scriptures, was more acceptable to Japanese as giving a theoretical basis for such a social and economic demand.

In this Sūtra it reads: If one preaches with the comprehension of the true purport of the Lotus Sūtra, nothing will contradict the True Aspect of Reality and even in elucidating secular treatises, the words of this-worldly government or the deeds or production, he will do it all in accordance with the True Doctrine.[28]

Everything is true as far as it is taught by those who realized the truth of the Lotus Sūtra. However, the same sentence was interpreted in Japan to mean that all activities even in the fields of politics and economics were to be subjected to the Absolute One. Chōsui Shisen (964–1038) says: "The One Mind, the Eternal Truth, and the aspect of appearance and disappearance are no separate things. That they are one is revealed in that they are three; that they are three is discussed in that they are one. Government and production, therefore, could be in no contradiction to the True Aspect of Reality."[29] This idea of Chōsui came to be understood as an integral part of the doctrines of Lotus Sūtra.[30]

6. Synthesis of Philosophies

A special trend of philosophy which aimed at the synthesis of divergent philosophical currents developed in Japan in early period. Buddhism brought about a huge amount of scriptures in which sundry teaching were given. In some cases they were even contradictory. In ancient China attempts were made to expound and coordinate such different teachings. It culminated in the system of Master T'ien-t'ai who propounded the theory of Five Periods[31] and Eight Kinds of Teaching.[32] According to him, Buddha's different teachings were gradually revealed in the five periods of his life-time and the teaching in the Lotus Sūtra is among others the ultimate and the best. He classified the teachings of Buddha in terms of adjectives: "sudden, gradual, secret, undetermined, collected, developed, distinguished and accomplished"[33] The teaching in the accomplished form should be the most perfect one, which was again made more explicit by the Tendai school.

This doctrine was brought into Japan by Master Dengyō and a more flexible interpretation was given to it by the scholarly monks of Japanese Tendai sect.

The synthesis of sundry philosophies expounded by Master Kōbō was more comprehensive. Dengyō limited himself in the teaching of Buddhist doctrines, whereas Kōbō was more conciliatory and tolerant towards native faiths of Japanese populace. His system involved in it not only Buddhist doctrines but also a considerable amount of pagan thought. According to him, even heathen thoughts can be manifestations of the basic principles of Mahāvairocana Buddha.

Kōbō expounded the doctrine of Ten Stages of human life:[34]

(1) The first stage[35] is that of "common people who are like sheep." Their desire is simply the satisfaction of appetite. They are not capable of differentiating the good and the evil.

(2) The second[36] is called that of "foolish children who practise fasting." They cautiously observe moral precepts in order to prevent society from falling into disorder. Among other religious systems Confucianism will be the one which also emphasizes the importance of morality by observing the five relationships.[37] But it gives no indication of liberating men out of mundane existence.

(3) The third[38] is that of those who practise to become "infant who knows no fears." This idea is illustrated in Taoism. Also the Shingon sect accepted Taoist claims for longevity and magic arts, although those were

regarded as of lower value. The irony of history is that the popular acceptance of Shingon belief was mainly by virtue of these pagan claims which appealed both commoners and nobles in the ancient Imperial court.

(4) and (5) are the stages which are represented by Hinayāna philosophy. The fourth stage[39] is that of those who realize that there is no *ego* and that which is called the *ego* or self is merely a conglomeration of aggregates (*skandhas*). The fifth stage [40]is that of those who endeavor to uproot evil *karma* until all passion and trouble ceases.

(6) With the sixth stage[41] we rise to the realm of Mahāyāna as is shown in Buddhist Idealism (the Hossō sect). Those who have reached this stage take all phenomena for nothing other than the revelation of the stored consciousness or memory and feel an infinite compassion for the salvation of all beings.

(7) The seventh stage[42] is that of the philosophers of voidness. According to them, there is neither becoming nor perishing, neither singularity nor pluralities. This idea of undifferentiation of nothingness is a clear characteristic manifested in the Sanron sect both in China and Japan.

(8) The eighth stage[43] is that of the Tendai school which teaches "one way without action". It means that the ultimate reality is identical with our experience of the phenomenal world, in the assumption that there is no realm of reality apart from mundane world.

(9) The ninth stage[44] is that of the Kegon school. It teaches the truth that there is no separate entity and the truth is realized in the ceaseless function of the universe.

(10) The tenth and highest stage[45] is that of Shingon itself. Now the doors to esoteric truth whose realm is beautifully adorned are open to the practitioners. Through the performance of the mystic rites of Shingon the adepts realize that man and the universe are Mahā-vairocana himself.

This all-comprehensive interpretation of Kūkai is depicted in his philosophical novel which is called *Indications to the Three Teachings*. It is the earliest example of a novel in Japanese literature that has come down to us today. Kūkai (774–835), alias Master Kōbō, discusses in this work the three teachings of Buddhism, Taoism and Confucianism in a form of dialoques. Although he evaluates Buddhism as the highest of the three, he also accepts different modes of beings:

"Living beings are not of the same nature—there are birds which fly high in the sky and fish which sink low in the water. To guide different types of people, we have three teachings of Buddhism, Taoism and Confucianism.[46] Although they vary in depth, they are all teachings of sages. Even if one chooses the first (i.e. Buddhism), he needs not necessarily repudiate loyalty and fiilial piety (of Taoism and Confucianism) by doing so."[47]

Notes

1 The term 'sunyata' was translated as 'relativity' or 'contingency' by STCHRBATSKY. (STCHRBATSKYe Buddhist Nirvāna, passim). Aristotle also took the notion of relativity in a generalized sense. In his *Metaphysica* he treated *Ad aliquid*, not as one among the distinct categories, but as implicated with all the categories. (Cf. G. GROTE: Aristotle ed. Bain, p. 88) He does not maintain that the relative is unreal, but he declares it to be Being (End) in the lowest degree (ibid., p. 85). The question whether Being (End) is itself relative he leaves unsolved. (STCHRBATSKY: op. cit. pp. 42–43) But still the term 'relativity' is misleading. I followed to suggestion by Prof. Philip P. WIENER that it be translated 'relationality.'

2 Vajracchedikā-prajñāpāramitā-sūtra, 32.

3 "A perfectly good will would therefore be equally subject to objective laws (viz. laws of good), but could not be conceived as *obliged* thereby to act lawfully, because of itself from its subjective constitution it can only be determined by the conception of good. Therefore no imperatives hold for the Divine will or in general for a holy will; ought is here out of place, because volition is already of itself necessarily in unison, with the law." KANT's *Metaphysics of Morals*, p. 31 (Abbot's edition).

4 The opening verse of the *Madhyamaka-kārikās*.

5 *Madhyamaka-kārikās*, I, 1. (STCHERBATSKY: BN. p. 93)

6 The question whether Relativity is itself relative is mentioned and declined with the remark that it is absurd by RUSSELL. (*ABC of Relativity*, p. 14)

7 *Madhyamaka-kārikās*, XIII, 7.

8 A verse of the Vigrahavyavartani, cited in Prasannapada, p. 16.

9 *Catuhśataka*, XVI, 25, cited in Prasannapada, p. 16. STCHERBATSKY: op. cit., p. 95.

10 The *Hua-yen sūtra*, vol. 46, p. 245b.

11 *Ibid.*, p. 403c.

12 Sarvaromavivara-asesabuddha-gunasamudra-megha-nigarjana-varna. (Gandavyuha-sūtra, ed. by D. T. SUZUKI and H. IDZUMI, p. 347, 1.24) I translated the word in collation with the Tang version. (Vol. 73, Taisho, p. 38b).

13 Kegon Gokyo-sho etc.

14 *Shōbō-Genzō, Bodaisatta Shishōbō* (Dogen Zenji Zenshū, p. 259).

15 SUZUKI Daisetzu Teitaro, *The Essence of Buddhism*. Kyoto, Hōzōkan, 1948, p. 56.

16 Cf. TAKAKUSU Junjiro: Essentials of Buddhist Philosophy, University of Hawaii
16 Cf. TAKAKUSU: *Essentials of Buddhist Philosophy*, University of Hawaii Press, 1947, p. 141.

17 Sokushin Jōbutsu-gi.

18 Shōji Jissō-gi.

19 This theory of Ten Categories should be studied in comparison with those of Aristotle and aticandra.

20 SHIOIRI Ryōchū, *Dengyō Daishi to Hokkekyō* (Master Dengyō and the Lotus Sūtra) in *Nihon Bukkyō no Rekishi to Rinen* (History and Ideas of Japanese Buddhism) compiled by ONO Seiichiro and HANAYAMA Shinshō, pp. 117ff

21 See *Hokke Shūku* (法華秀句 Excellent Words of the Lotus Sūtra) by Saichō, II; *Dengyō Daishi Zenshū* (Complete Works of Master Dengyō), II, 265–266; 280.

22 *Shokushin J,butsugi Shiki* (即身成佛義私記 Remarks on the Doctrine of Becoming Buddha Alive) in *Tendaishū Sōsho* (Collected writings of the Tendai Sect); *Annen Senshū* (Works of Annen) 7, II, 210. Some passages are translated in my *Ways of Thinking of Eastern People*, p. 364.

23 *Hizō Hōyaku.*

24 These words in the *Bodai Shin-ron* (Treatise on the Bodhi Mind) are said to have been written by Nāgārjuna. Kūkai wrote "Commentaries on Becoming a Buddha Alive in the Human Body."

25 *Unjigi* (吽字義)

26 SHIMAJI Daitō, *Tendai Kyōgaku-shi* (天台教學史 History of Tendai Theology), p. 492.

27 The *Lotus Sūtra* (Hokekyō 法華経, Saddharmapandarika-sūtra).

28 This sentence (in the   法華功德品) is very famous and highly esteemed among Japanese. But the original Sanskrit text runs as follows: "And the sermon he preaches will not fade from his memory. The popular maxims of common life, whether sayings or counsels, he will know how to reconcile with the rules of the law." (The *Saddharmapundarika* or the Lotus of the True Law, translated by H. KERN. Oxford, 1909. SBE. vol. 21, p. 351. Cf. the edition by H. HERN and NANJIO B., St. Petersbourg, Imprimerie de l'Academie Imperiale des Sciences, 1912, Bibliotheca Buddhica 10, p. 372; the edition by WOGIHARA Unrai and TSUCHIDA C., Tokyo, Seigo-Kenkyū-kai, 1934, p. 315). Here we find no word "politics" or "economics".

29 Chōsui's Commentary on the *Sūrangama Sūtra*, Vol. 1a.

30 The spirit is already seen in Prince Shōtoku. But his commentaries on the 法歸功德品 of the Lotus Sūtra does not mention it.

31 五時

32 八教

33 頓, 漸, 秘密, 不定, 藏, 通, 別, 圓

34 十住心

35 This theory was expounded in his Jūjūshinron (十住心論 A Treatise on the Ten Stages) and more detailed accounts are given in his Hizō Hōyaku (秘藏寶鑰 A Jewel Key to the Secret Treasure-house).

36 異生羝羊心, 愚童持齋心

37 Cf. Wilhelm SCHIFFER, Gokai and Gojō, *Monumenta Nipponica*, vol. 3, No. 1, 1940, pp. 281–290.

38 嬰童無畏心

39 唯蘊無我心

40 拔業因種心

41 他緣大乘心

42 覺心不生心

43 一道無間心
44 極無自性心
45 秘密荘厳心
46 *Sangō Shiki* (三教指歸).
47 In the preface to his *Indications to the Three Teachings*. Cf. Y. S. HAKEDA, The Religious Novel of Kūkai, *MonumentamNipponica,* vol. 20, Nos. 3–4, 1965. pp. 283–297.

CHAPTER III

MEDIEVAL THOUGHT

1. Medieval Society of Japan

The period after the introduction of Buddhism until the beginning of
Tokugawa period is usually divided into pre-Nara, Nara, Heian and
Kamakura-Muromachi periods, based on the location of the central
government of each epoch. The Kamakura-Muromachi period (12th
to 16th century) is called Medieval Ages, the period being in between
that of ancient society of court nobles and that of the Tokugawa society
of Shōgun. It is generally characterized that the pre-Medieval period
was an epoch when the Buddhism as a universal or cosmopolitan religion
was introduced in close relationship with the different thinking patterns
of the Continental schools and sects of Asia and was succeeded by four
centuries (9th to 12th century) of transition and digestion which were
called Heian period; whereas the Medieval period was that of the nat-
uralization of the imported religious thoughts. It was an epoch when the
Japanese race developed her own culture under the patronage of the
feudal governments of warriors.[1]

In the latter half of the Heian period there was a gradual uprising of
warrior class who had been hitherto subjugated by the nobility of central
Imperial court. The old regime of Emperors came to a collapse and at the
end of the twelfth century the Kamakura shogunate of warriors was
established. A deploration was heard when the rule of the nobles was
seized by emergent warriors, as an Empress who became a nun in this
transistory epoch lamented:

"I was a daughter of Minister Taira (a clan of warriors) and the mother of the former Emperor. The entire land was once in my control. But now, alas, I have nobody to rely upon. . . . The nun of Nii, the former infant Emperor in her arms, threw herself into the sea. The sight I can never forget. The clamor and shouting of the naval soldiers are still audible. Even the cries and groans in the infernal flame of the Avīci will never surpass this cruel horrible scene!"[2]

The vicissitude of the powers gave a considerable influence among Japanese public of the day. The continual struggle among warriors for power and the feeling of disappointment thereof among the people led them to hanker for religious teachings upon which they could depend. The climate was favorable for the propagation of religious teachings. Thus the many religious doctrines which had been so far Japanized permeated into the nation and gradually their orthodoxy was established.

As in the society of the West, the social structure of Medieval Japan was hierarchical. Strict regulations were provided for creating a stabilized order of subjugation of retainers to their lords, family members and the neighborhood to their patriarchs, children to their father and so forth. For example, a Chinese doctrine[3] which was highly esteemed by Japanese as typical of the feudjl ethics of women reads as follows:

"A woman should obey her father in her youth, her husband after marriage and her son in her old age."[4]

Also in the field of education teachers were respectfully waited upon by their students, as is shown in a following saying:

"When accompanying his master, a disciple should walk three steps behind him, so as not to step on his shade."

The most conspicuous character of the feudal ethics may be the loyalty of the retainers to their lords. An admonition was given to warriors:

"The relationship between lord and retainers is of an utmost importance. Regarding this, one should never waver, even when one may be admonished to follow some other way by Shakyamuni, Confucius or the Effulgent God (i.e. foremost ancestor of Emperors). If one goes astray in this, he will be misled by banal doctrines of Shintoism or Buddhism. Let us be doomed to fall in hell, or let us be punished by gods. We have nothing else to do in mind but to serve our lord whole-heartedly!"[6]

A psalmic passage in the Bible gives a Hebrew devotion to the god of Israel:

> "My heart and my flesh may fall.
> But God is the strength of my heart
> and my portion for ever."[7]

The tone is similar. Simple difference lies in that the place of God in the Psalm was replaced by feudal lord in Japan. This signifies that this feudal ethics of warrior was regarded as something far superior to religious teachings. Loyalty was thus encouraged in defiance of religious author-ity. However, the admonition goes on:

> "We are sure that Buddha and gods
> will approve our attitude."

It looks like that these warrior's precepts needed religious sanction. But it virtually implied a contradiction, because this vulgarized inter-pretation of Shinto and Buddhist doctrines were not entirely in accord-ance with their original teachings. This attitude of currying favor of religious doctrines for warrior's ethics was, however, an obvious feature of feudal thought in Japan. The ultimate expression of taking respon-sibility in case of failures was to commit suicide which was called *seppuku* or *harakiri*.

2. The Supremacy of Religion
Major Sects of Buddhism

Zen Buddhism was introduced from China at the beginning of the Kamakura period (1192–1333) and the sects of Pure Land (*Jōdo*) and of Nichiren (1222–1282) were founded at the same time. Since then, how-ever, new sects were not created until Meiji Restoration in 1868. The major sects of Japanese Buddhism which are still extant are classified as follows:

    a. *Tendai*
    b. *Shingon*
    c. *Zen*

  d. *Jōdo*
  e. *Nichiren*

The *Tendai* and *Shingon* sects were originated in the Heian period, and the *Zen, Jōdo* and *Nichiren* sects came into being in the epoch called Kamakura.

(1) *Jōdo or Pure Land Buddhism*

According to the tradition, the Pure Land Buddhism was originally founded in the first or second century after Christ in India. Its teaching is based on the Larger and Smaller *Sukhāvatí-uyūha-Sūtras* and *Amitāyurdhyāna Sūtra* which were composed in about the second century. They advocate the existence of Western Paradise of Pure Land or *Sukhāvatí* which is called *Jōdo* in Japanese. The believers of Amida's faith were supposed to be born again after death as a reward for their faith and merits they achieved in their life time.

The Saviour is called Amida or *Amitābha* in Sanskrit who is presiding over the Pure Land. The eighteenth of Amida's forty-eight vows reads as follows:

(1) *Pure Realm Buddhism*

Pure Realm Buddhism as such was founded in the first or second century in India. It was based on the larger and smaller Sukhāvatī-vyūha Sūtras and on the Amitāyurdhyāna Sūtra. These speak of the Western Paradise of the Pure Realm (Sukhāvatī, Jōdo in Japanese).

The believers were supposed to be born there after death as the reward for their faith and good works.

The Savior of this School is Amida (Amitābha), and is said to be presiding at present over the Pure Realm. Once in the past he made the series of the famous Forty-Eight Vows, the eighteenth of which reads: "If, after my obtaining Buddhahood, all beings in the ten quarters should desire in sincerity and faith to be born into my country, and if they should not be born by only thinking of me ten times, I will not attain the highest enlightenment."

Now he has become a Buddha; he has fulfilled the Vows. Anyone who worships him in sincerity and faith will not fail to be saved.

(2) *The Nichiren Sect*

Nichiren (1222–1282) was born the son of a fisherman. He studied all schools widely until he decided for himself what was the true way to deliverance. He first entered the Shingon School, and then studied in the Tendai School on Mount Hiei. There, he came to the conclusion that only one scripture was needed, that is "the Lotus Sūtra" (Saddharma-pundarīka-sūtra, the Lotus of the Good Law) and that the deliverance of the country from its sufferings in those days could best be achieved by a vigorous campaign of a return to the Lotus Sūtra and the Sakyamuni Buddha.

He was a born religious demagog, and wandered all over the country, literally banging the drum of his beliefs at all quarters. Because of his rudeness to all other sects and the government, he soon in trouble with the authorities and his life was a long chain of persecutions, with an almost miraculous escape. Extreme religious fervor is most conspicuous among the followers of this sect and some of the common people in later days.

(3) *Zen Buddhism*

As a specific form of Buddhism, Zen is first found in China, being a peculiar Chinese version of the kind of Buddhism which was brought from India by the sage Bodhidharma, in, or about, the year 527. Bodhidharma's Buddhism was a variety of the Mahāyāna School, the Buddhism of Northern India.

Bodhidharma's variety of the Mahāyāna was known as Dhyāna Buddhism, pronounced Ch'an in Chinese and Zen in Japanese, and though the nearest English equivalent of Dhyāna is "contemplation", this term has acquired a static and even dreamy connotation quite foreign to Dhyāna.

Dhyāna, Ch'an, or Zen means immediate insight into the nature of Reality or life. In China, Dhyāna Buddhism was strongly influenced by Taoism and Confusicanism, and, under the guidance of the practical mentality of the Chinese, emerged in the seventh century as the Zen we know today.

In 1911 Eisai (1141–1215) brought it to Japan, where it may be found to this day in its most vital form and where, too, it has had an extremely far-reaching effect upon the national culture.

The Zen Buddhism which was introduced into Japan by Eisai is called the Rinzai sect (the Lin-chi in Chinese), whereas that which was introduced by Dōgen (1200–1253), his disciple, is called the Sōtō sect (the Ts'ao-T'ung in Chinese).

Japanese Buddhism, as divided into the above-mentioned sects, has been the spiritual basis for Japanese culture for centuries to come.

Other-Worldliness

In the days which were the turning-points to the Middle Ages, other-worldly character was conspicuous among people, as in other countries.

Gradually the Japanese came to subscribe to Buddhism which was at first a religion aline to them, and finally they went so far as to believe that conformity to the Buddhist way of celibacy and ritual acts of bodily mortification rendered a higher service to their parents than preservation of the body and perpetuation of the family.

Buddhist masters emphasized terrible aspects of human life. Shantao of China explaining the human predicament in his parable of the White Path, shows man beset on all sides by evil beasts, poisonous vermin and vicious ruffians, symbolizing the sense organs, the consciousnesses, and the various psychic and physical constituents of the ordinary human self. The white path is "comparable to the pure aspiration for rebirth in the Pure Land which arises in the midst of the passions of greed and anger."[9] Lin-chi, the Zen master, emphasized emptiness of this life: "Followers of the Way, do not acknowledge this dream-like illusory world, for sooner or later death will come. . . . Seeking only the barest minimum of food, do with it; spend your time in the shabbiest of garments and go to visit a good teacher." This attitude was inherited by medieval monks.[10]

Monks were enjoined to spend a calm and quiet life, having secluded themselves from the secular activities. Master Tientai of China said:

"There are four things in which people ply. Monks in monasteries should not engage in these things. These four are: first, worldly life; second, worldly customs; third, various techniques, e.g. medicines, fortune-telling, sculpture, painting, chess, calligraphy and sorcery; fourth, sciences, e.g. study on scriptures, discussion and debate."[11] This ideal was inherited by the T'ien-tai sect of China and the Tendai sect of Japan. Even such a man of letters as Monk Kenko[12] in medieval Japan admired such a life.

As an escape from worldly life a peculiar kind of practice appeared in medieval Japan. The worship of local mountain deities in medieval Japan became very much influenced by the popular Buddhism that was founded on the forms of worship of a variety of Shingon Buddhism known as 'shugendo' or 'the Way of the mountain anchorites' or 'yamabushi', a special sect syncretic of Buddhism and Shintoism. Well-known examples were Mt. Katsuragi and Kimbusen in Yamato, Hakusan in Kaga, Futaara-san at Nikko in Shimotsuke, and Gassan, Yudono-san and Haguro-san, the Three Mountains of Dewa. In these places the influence of the yamabushi made itself felt in very early days.

When one wanted to become a recluse or a monk, there must have been conflict with his family or in other human relations. This problem was discussed in Japan as in other countries of both East and West. Somebody asked Master Dōgen: "My mother is very old, and I am the only son. If I should become a recluse, she cannot live for even one day. What shall I do?" The master replied: "If you are surely aspiring for the Way of Buddha, you should take orders, having prepared for the livelihood of your mother. However, if it is difficult, you should take orders immediately. Even if your old mother should starve to death, her merit of letting her only son enter into the Way of Buddha is very great, isn't it? Her merit will cause her to attain enlightenment in an after-life in the future."[13] Otherworldliness was so conspicous in the medieval Japan.

Otherworldliness, when it gets to the extreme, leads one to deny one's own existence. It encourages suicide. Throughout the history of Buddhist China, it was common practice for a monk to burn his thumb, his fingers, or even his whole body, as a form of merit in emulation of the supreme sacrifice of the Bodhisattva Bhaishajyaraja, the King of Medicine, one of the deities of Mahayana Buddhism. Each of the two great Buddhist Biographical Series devoted one section to biographies of Chinese monks who had burned themselves to death, or otherwise committed suicide, as supreme sacrifices. This section is under the heading "Those who gave up their lives". It contains detailed stories of hundreds of such suicides. A monk would announce his date of self-destruction and, on that day, would tie his whole body in oiled cloth, light the fagot pyre and his own body with a torch in his own hand, and go on mumbling the sacred titles of the Buddhas until he was completely overpowered by the flames. Very often such human sacrifices were witnessed by thousands of pious Buddhists whose plaintive wailings would accompany the slow burning of the pious monk. It is little wonder that many people committed suicide in order to be born in the Pure Land among the followers of Shan-tao who taught the doctrine 'loathe this defiled world and desire to be reborn in the Pure Land'. Such a custom was imitated by some Japanese Buddhists in the medieval age. Some burnt themselves, and others set sail on the ocean never to return, for the purpose of reaching the Pure Land (Fuduraku, Potalaka in Sanskrit) of Kwannon Bodhisattva, which was supposed to be located in the southern sea.

Criticism on such an otherworldly tendency of Buddhism was severely made in the Tokugawa period by Confucianists and scholars of National Lore. Finally in the modern age the assertions of this-worldliness became conspicuous.

Establishment of Religious Authority

Religions spread through persons. Common pleple needed spiritual leaders. An attitude of complete devotion to a specific person in medieval Japan was illustrated in the worship of the founders and chief abbots of respective sects.

The admiration of believers towards their spiritual leaders gave rise to sectarian orders.

Religious orders increased their prestige. They were given lands; they were extended special support by feudal lords. The lands owned by religious orders were tax-exempt. Anybody who had fled into the precincts of the orders could not be caught. There was the right of asylum although there is no Japanese equivalent for the world.

In Eastern countries monasticism had existed among Buddhists and Jains several hundred years before the Christian era. However, the Buddhist monasticism which was similar to that in the West occurred in nearly the same period in Zen Buddhism.

The period of preaching by Bodhidharma, the founder of Chinese Zen Buddhism, was 470–532. He inherited the Buddhism of the Cupta period. Until this period, Indian monasteries claimed to accommodate monks "from the four directions". There was no *closedness* among monasteries in general, as can be seen in monasteries of Southern Asia. This way of life was inherited by early Zen Buddhists of China. With Tao-shin (580–651), the fourth patriarch, a remarkable change in the way of life occurred in the Zen order. He resided on the Double Peak Mountain for thirty years, and did not go to any other place, but around him more than five hundred people lived constantly. The living together by a great number of monks became customary since then.

This way of life may be Buddhist transformation of traditional way of life. From the end of the Civil War Period to the Han dynasty Chinese recluses lived together in groups in mountains, and had their own ideal of life. This seems to have been inherited by Zen Buddhists.

The establishment of group life in monasteries by Tao-hsin can be compared to the founding of the first Christian monastery by Pachomius, an Egyptian, in about 315 or 320. In the monasteries derived from Pachomius, the monks did much work, chiefly agricultural, instead of spending the whole of their time in resisting the temptations of the flesh.[14] This is exactly true with the Zen revolution in the life of Buddhist monasteries.

Zen Buddhists in mountains had to work to sustain their livelihood. They came to engage in economical production. It was not for making wares to sell on the market, but only for self-sufficiency, but it was none the less production. Formerly Buddhist monks kept away from production, now their attitude turned to the contrary. Zen priests began to cultivate fields attached to their own temples in order to secure foods permanently, since then. Although Buddhist monasticism existed before him, Buddhist monks did not engage in manual labor. They did not want to be involved in any kind of productive work. They just practiced meditation without working physically. This attitude has been preserved throughout Asiatic countries except China and Japan. It was only from Tao'-hsin's time on that monks came to do all their own work and practiced meditation in calm places, secluded from the secular world. For example, it was forbidden by the Book of Disciplines (Vinaya) in traditional Buddhism for monks to dig in the ground or to cut grasses and trees. (Pacittiya 10 and 11). This provision was common to Jainism. However, early Zen order disregarded this provision. Master Po-chang (720–814) said that to dig in the ground and to cut grasses and trees did not necessarily cause sins. His motto: "If one did not work a day, one should not eat on that day," has become their favorite one. Master Po-chang laid the rule of Zen monasteries in detail, which became the standard of later Zen monasteries. (This might be compared with the rule of St. Benedict.)

In Zen monasteries monks kept gardens, rice-paddies, field, and kitchens. Monks engaged in cultivation and farming. Not only meditation, religious services, and reading, but also such manual labor as sweeping and cooking and receiving guests were required for monks. In Japan Zen temples have been well known especially for cleanness due to manual labor by monks.

In Japan monks of many sects went so far as to engage in such kinds of economic activity as constructing roads, resthouses, hospitals, ponds, harbors, exploitations of fields, and so on. Such kinds of work were encouraged in Japan as rendering service to others, which was claimed to be the essence of Mahāyāna. For laymen all sorts of productive work except slaying animals and selling wines, weapons, and so on, were encouraged.

Throughout the medieval ages the attitude of hostility to pagan literature was held. Some Buddhist masters also, generally speaking, held a similar attitude. Master Dōgen ordered his disciples: "You should give

up useless things such as *belle lettres* and poems. You should solely concentrate on practicing the Way of Buddha".[15] "You should not read
books of the other sects, secular books and so on. If you feel like reading,
collected works of Zen masters are allowed."[16] In medieval Japan the
feudal lords who engaged often in warfare and killed people donated
lands and funds to Buddhist temples for expiation of their sins. As the
end of the Heian period and at the beginning of the Kamakura period
in Japan the established religious orders protected (supported) by the
court and knights became so corrupted that many monks fled from the
orders. Some lived as recluses in forests; other preached their own faiths
as individuals among people. In spite of so many striking parallels and
similarities which existed in the Middle Ages between Japan and the
West, we find remarkable differences. Probably the most important one
is papacy. In Japan heretics were not tried by court or law. Inquisition
or burning at the stake did not occur even once due to religious reasons.
The differences are still of contemporary significance.

Approach to Common People
  With the rise of the standard of living and the gradual expansion of
the scope of freedom among common people in later Middle Ages,
culture began to spread among them, and transformed itself to be acceptable to them. This change appeared in various aspects of culture. In the
field of thought some religious leaders came to give up the classical
Chinese and to adopt the languages of common people.
  This tendency appeared in Japan also at nearly the same period as in
the West, with Buddhist leaders of new movements in the Kamakura
period. The last word of vow by St. Honen was written in 1212 in
Japanese; Master Dōgen, who introduced Sōto Zen into Japan, wrote
his many works in Japaneje. We find a transition from the court poems
of the Heian nobility to the poems and songs by people in general in the
medieval ages of Japan. Novels by the Heian court ladies dealt with the
life of the nobles alone, whereas those in the late medieval ages came to
relate the life of common people. The pictures of scrolls in the Heian
period extolled the life of nobles and glorified huge temples, but early

in the medieval ages some scrolls appeared such as "Playing Scenes of Birds and Animals" (*Chōjū Giga*) ascribed to Bishop Toba, in which the demeanor of priests was sarcastically painted in the figures of birds and animals.

As a step of approach to people, some religious authorities became lenient towards women.

In the Heian period there had been established some holy places or large temples where women were not allowed to come in. Master Dōgen protested to it, saying:[17] "In the country of Japan there is a laughing stock. What is claimed to be a limited holy place or an asylum (place for practice) of Mahāyāna does not allow nuns and women to come in. This bad custom has been existing for many years, and yet people do not know it is a bad thing. . . . Was there any convention in the lifetime of Lord Buddha which nuns and women did not attend? . . . Those would-be holy places, on the other hand, welcome kings, premiers, ministers and officials! What a corruption!"[18]

3. Compassion and Schools of Pure Faith

Having considered religious practices, we shall now turn to some main ideas or doctrines and their developments. We shall now consider how development may be seen in relation to social developments and pressures by noting in two traditions (1) a growing regard for the Common Man, with a corresponding emphasis of Compassion and Love, (2) Cults related to this motif (Bodhisattvas), and (3) developments of the idea of Vicarious Sacrifice.

The Compassion-Love Doctrine

In India when the conservative Buddhist Order became a large organization with huge endowments, the monks did not render much service to the common people. The monks of conservative Buddhism (so-called Hirayana) were apt to be very self-complacent and self-righteous. Being fond of solitude they despised the common people; they did not want to partake of the worries and sufferings of the common lot.

As the protest against such an attitude in India, some religious leaders advocated a new form of Buddhism, which is called Mahāyāna (the Great Vehicle). They were in close contact with the common people and felt their needs. They vehemently attacked the self-complacent and self-righteous attitude of Conservative Buddhists.

In the Greater Vehicle (Mahāyāna) the virtue of compassion[19] was more stressed than in Hinayana. We admit that Compassion motif was not entirely absent in the Conservative Buddhism called Hinayana. But Mahāyānists claimed that Compassion was a chief characteristic of Mahāyāna. "To those whose intelligence is low and whose mind is quiet the Way of Sravaka (Hinayana) is taught to have them get out of suffering. To those whose intelligence is slightly keener and clearer and who hanker for the teaching of the Interdependent Origination the Way of Pratyksbuddha (an ascetic who practices by himself) is preached. To those whose intelligence is excellent and who aspire to benefit living beings out of Great Compassion the Way of Bodhisattva (Mahāyāna) is taught."[20] They said, 'The Buddha-Mind is nothing but Great Compassion.'[21]

The compassion of the Buddha was stressed. The Buddha in the Lotus Sūtra says: "I am the father. All living beings are my children."[22] "In the whole universe there is not a single spot so small as a mustard seed where the Buddha has not surrendered his bodt for the sake of creatures."[23] The compassion of the Buddha comes to everybody equally. It is compared with raining:[24] "That great raincloud, big with water, is wreathed with flashes of lightning and rouses with its thundering calls all creatures." "All those grasses, shrubs, and trees are vivified by the cloud that both refreshes the thirsty earth and waters the herbs." "In the same way . . . I preach with ever the same voice, constantly taking enlightenment as my text. For this is equal for all; no partiality is in it, neither hatred nor affection." "I recreate the whole world like a cloud shedding its water without distinction; I have the same feeling for respectable people as for the low."

The Buddha became more and more magnified and deified. The Buddha was no longer regarded as a man but, so to speak, the living

God,[25] in the eyes of Catholic missionaries who came to Japan about 400 years ago.

In order to show us what Buddha's compassion, a Buddhist counterpart to the parable of the "Prodigal Son" was set forth in the Lotus Sutra. In the Buddhist parable[26] of the Prodigal Son, Buddha is represented as the good, wealthy father, who means well towards his sons, the human beings,—

A rich man has an only son, who roams about in foreign lands for fifty years. While the father grows richer and richer, and has become a great man, the son lives in foreign parts, poor and in reduced circumstances. As a beggar he at last returns to his home, where his father has been yearning for him all the time. The beggar comes to the house of his father, whom, however, he does not recognize in the great man, who, like a king surrounded by a retinue, sits before his mansion. When he sees the pomp and splendor, he flees for fear that he, the ragged beggar, might be ill-treated. His father, however, recognized him at once and sends out servants to bring the beggar in. Trembling and shaking with fear, he is dragged in, and he falls unconscious. Then his father commands that he shall be released. Gladly the beggar gets up, and goes to the poor quarter of the town. Now the rich man thinks out a plan whereby he may win the confidence of his son. He sends workmen to hire him for the humblest work in his house; he sometimes chats with him and gradually becomes intimate with him. In this way twenty years pass, without the father's making himself known. Not until the hour of his death does he cause all his relatives to assemble, and announce that the beggar, who has now become a trusted servant, is his own son; and he makes him the heir to all his wealth. The rich man is Buddha; the son who was lost and is found again, represents the human beings, whom Buddha, as the wise father, gradually draws to himself, and finally appoints as his fortunate heirs.

In this parable Prince Shōtoku, St. Nichiren and others found the illuminative compassion of Buddha.

It is often reported that Buddhism has softened the rough warrior races of Tibet and Mongolia, and nearly effaced all traces of their original brutality. In Japan also, according to the statistical reports, cases of murder or assault are relatively rare in districts where the Buddhist influence is strong.

This attitude of compassion motivates one to esteem highly the natural disposition of man. Japanese Buddhism tends to be most conspicuous in that respect. Even Buddhist ideas were preached with a close reference to matters of love, and sexual love is considered not to be incompatible with religious matter. Zen Buddhism in China does not seem to have much emphasized the idea of compassion. There is not a single reference made to the word "compassion" in the wellknown scriptures of Chinese Zen Buddhism. After Zen Buddhism was brought into Japan, however, it came to emphasize deeds of benevolence.

The spirit of tolerance and compassion of the Buddhist made it impossible to cultivate a deep hatred evento wards sinners. There existed hardly any punishment that was cruel in those days when Buddhism flourished. It was also reported as so by Chinese pilgrims in regards to ancient India under Buddhist influence. It holds true with some of the Buddhist countries in Southern Asia. In Japan also, during the Heian period, capital punishment was never practiced for a period of nearly three hundred and fifty years.

The Role of Bodhisattvas

Along with development of Compassion Motif, in Mahāyāna Buddhism, the worship of Bodhisattvas came into existence. The Bodhisattva was originally the Buddha before Enlightenment. But later anybody who aspires for Enlightenment and renders help willingly to suffering creatures was called a 'bodhisattva'. Bodhisattvas, being so compassionate, were supposed to extend hands of help willingly. The practice of the bodhisattva requires vigor and endeavor. In Tibetan, the word Bodhisattva is translated as Heroic Being (Byanchub sems-dpah). The figure of the Bodhisattva was made the ideal for intellectual leaders at the time of Prince Shōtoku, but it is likely that the Bodhisattva ideal came to spread among common people in the Heian and medieval periods.

The images of Buddhas and Bodhisattva were made and their worship was greatly encouraged. In Mahāyāna Buddhism the worship of images, in addition to the existing worship of stupas, was exceedingly encouraged. "All who caused jewel images to be made and dedicated, adorned with the thirty-two characteristic signs, reached enlightenment. Others who had images of Sugatas (Buddhas) made of the seven precious substances, of copper or brass, have all of them reached enlightenment. Those who ordered beautiful statues of Sugatas to be made of lead, iron, clay or plaster have etc. Those who made images (of the Sugatas) on painted walls, with complete limbs and the hundred holy signs, whether they drew them themselves or had them drawn by others, have &c. Those even, whether men or boys, who during the lesson or in play, by way of amusement, made upon the walls (such),images with the nail or a pieie of wood, have all of them reached enlightenment."[25]

Various kinds of legends and stories extolling Buddhas, Bodhisattvas, and devout believers came into existence in Mahāyāna, and they were introduced into Japan.

Magical elements crept into universal religions. In Mahāyāna, Bodhisattvas were worshipped for their magical power, which brings forth fortune, wealth, the healing of diseases, the dispelling of disasters, etc., and these were the motivating powers to convert common people to Buddhist faith.

Buddhist bodhisattvas are not historical individuals, although they repeatedly are born in this world to help suffering beings.

We may also note that the cult of the goddess of mercy in Mahāyāna lands has certain analogies with the cult of the Virgin in the West. It is especially represented in the worship of the Bodhisattva Avolokitesvara or Kwan-yin in Chinese or Kannon in Japanese, who looks like a mother. Avalokitasvara has been probably the most worshipped divine being in Asian countries. The Virgin Mary was the friend of the souls, and all alike, lord and lady, serf and maid, took refuge under the broad folds of the protecting Mary. The similarities shared with Mary are so very convincing that in the days when Catholics were persecuted due to political reasons in the feudal Japan, Japanese Catholics worshipped the images of Maria secretly under the pretention that they were the images of Buddhist Kannon. They secretly called them "Maria-Kannon'. In spite of obvious similarities, there are remarkable differences. Avalokitesvara was by origin a male person, although his outlook became female. Moreover, whereas Maria was a historical individual, Avalokitasvara was not supposed to be a historical individual, for his real personality was regarded to be eternal. Kannon shares some features with Catholic saints also. "If one happens to fall into the dreadful ocean, the abode of Nagas, marine monsters, and demons, he has but to think of Avalokitesvara, and he shall never sink down in the vast waters"[26] Kannon is probably the most popular Bodhisattva for common people in Japan.

A tradition about the coming Buddha, Maitreya, also came to the fore. Maitreya (etymologically derived from 'mitra', meaning friend), personifies friendliness in terms of etymology. It is said that his legend was to some extent stimulated by Persian eschatology. But it met the spiritual needs of the new age. Maitreya was devotionally worshipped especially in the medieval ages in Japan.

We find a Buddhist Healer and Savior in the figure of the Healing Teacher (Bhaisajyaguruvaidūryaprabhāsa).

Even transcendental Wisdom came to be deified and worshipped as an object of worship in the form of 'the Holy Goddess Wisdom' (Bhagavatī Prajñā-pāramitā) in India and other South-Asian countries, but such an ideal figure was not favored by common people who do not like abstract ideation.

Owing to the up-rising saint-worship in Japan, Buddhists made pilgrimages to the places especially related with the life of the founder of each sect.

they crossed, there lies a small market-town or rural port, which by some is called Greensburgh, but which is more generally and properly known by the name of Tarry Town." (W. Irving: The Sketch Book) In America we find often taxi-drivers driving with an icon of St. Christopher. In Japan taxi-drivers drive with an amulet of Fudō (Acalanātha Vidyārāja) of the Naritasan Temple within their cars, even as American drivers do.

Vicarious Atonement

A Buddhist conception of vicarious atonement was expressed for example by Nagarjuna. In his work Ratnavali he said: "May my merits go to others; may the sufferings of others ripen upon me!"[1]

"To take over the sufferings of others by oneself" was extolled as an ideal of Mahāyāna ascetics. However, we should not overlook a great difference between Christianity and Mahāyāna. In Christianity vicarious atonement is affected by Christ alone, whereas in Buddhism by any bodhisattva.

Northern Buddhists found the ideal image of vicarious atonement especially in Ksitigarbha or Jizō of Japan. The name of Ksitigarbha means "Earth-womb" or "Earth-store-house". The original meaning of the title is not very clear, but it was interpreted to mean that he is lord of the nether world. Some scholars think that the belief in Ksitigarbha first appeared in Central Asia. Legend has it that he has vowed to deliver all creatures from hell. He visits them in their places of suffering to deliver them. In Japan he is the special protector of dead children. When someone died to save others, people in Japan erect an image of Jizō in honor of him, calling it "Lord Jizō in Vicarious Atonement" (Migawari Mizōson). It is said that Jizō will never enter nirvāna, so long as there remains even one person suffering from afflictions, and that he stays in the mundane world with sinners.

As the ideal to take on sufferings of all men; we are reminded of the images of Amitabha in Shinshu Buddhism of Japan, which are always of standing posture to show his readiness to help suffering people.

The idea of vicarious atonement is naturally closely related to a sense of human need, and ideas of sin remedied by compassionate Grace, which will be discussed in the following section.

Deliverance in Pure Land

The consciousness of sin was most conspicuous in Pure Land Buddhism among Japanese Buddhists. This tendency was already harbingered in scriptures of early Pure Land[27] Buddhism. These scriptures were compiled in the age of spiritual unrest probably at the end of Kusana dynasty

in the second century. There the consciousness of spiritual crisis was conspicuous. A scripture says that the teaching was meant for the people in
the degenerated age. "The Buddha taught the Law which all the world
is reluctant to accept, during this corruption of the present kalpa, during
this corruption of belief, during this corruption of life, during this corruption of passions."[28]

The believers of Pure Land Buddhism were supposed to be born there
after death as the reward for their faith and good works. The Savior of
this School is Amida (Sanskrit: *Amitabha*, lit. "Immense Light", and
Amitayus, lit. "Eternal Life"). Pure Realm Buddhists speak of the Western Paradise of the Pure Realm (*Sukhāvati*, in Japanese *Jōdo*). The Pure
Realm of Amitabha is depicted in a gorgeous way. '—The Pure Land is
prosperous, rich, good to live in, and is fertile, and lovely. It is gragrant
with several sweet-smelling scents, rich in manifold flowers and fruits,
adorned with gem trees, and frequented by tribes of manifold sweet-
voiced birds.—'.

The scriptures of Pure Land Buddhism explain that Amitabha Buddha
is now in the Pure Land in the West, beyond numberless Buddha Lands,
where he casts his light in all ten directions and is Preaching to save countless sentient beings. Therefore, Skyamuni taught that we should always
concentrate on Amitabha. The Smaller-Sukhavati Sutra speaks of the
birth by grace:—'Beings are not born in that Buddha country as a reward and result of good works performed in the present life. No, all men
and women who hear and bear in mind for one, two, three, four, five,
six or seven nights the name of Amitabha when they come to die,
Amitabha stands before them in the hour of death, they will depart from
this life with quiet minds, and after death they will be born in paradise.'[29]

The Larger Sukhavati Sūtra tells how Dharmakara (later Amitabha
Buddha), when he was still a Bodhisttva striving to become a Buddha,
had made forty-eight vows to help ordinary people be reborn to his
selfless Pure Land where they could attain Enlightenment by hearing,
believing and rejoicing in the Merit of Amitabha which is above the
natural world, and unthinkable. Now that he has become a Buddha his
vows are fulfilled and the Pure Land of tranquil sustenance (which is

Endless Life and Boundless Light) is established and salvation by the great mercy and the power of Amitabha Vows is undoubtable to men.

The followers of the Pure Realm sects of Buddhism seek Buddha-hook—that is, Enlightenment—through rebirth in Amida Buddha's Pure Land of the Supreme Happiness. Rebirth in the Pure Realm is attained by faith in the power of Amitabha Vows to save all beings. Amitabha's Vows are recorded in the Great Sūtra of the Endless Life, the *Sukhavativ-yuha Sutra*, which claims to be the discourse between Sakyamuni Buddha and Ananda, his disciple. The Sūtra tells us that the monk Dharmakara, the future Amitabha, made forty-eight vows which were to be fulfilled when he became a Buddha. When he became the Buddha Amitabha, these vows became a power which can save human beings regardless of the law of karma.

The doctrine of self-cultivation and the worship of the Buddha, which are both preached in Buddhism, may seem contradictory to each other. However, both have arisen from the same source. According to Buddhist philosophy, we should endeavor to realize our true self in moral and religious sense; this ideal is quite compatible with the worship of the one who has already realized one's true self in a perfect way. In Mahāyāna Buddhism many Buddhas and Bodhisattvas were worshipped. The worship of Amitabha Buddha has particularly played a very important role especially for Chinese and Japanese Buddhism.

The scriptures of this school emphasized the act of concentrating on the name of Amitabha, and Shan-tao of China interpreted it as voicing repeatedly the name of Amitabha in mouth. This practice has been continued since then in China and Japan.

Incidentally, Mahāyāna Buddhists supposed that in the Pure Land there is no human woman, although they admitted the existence of heavenly nymphs (*apsaras*). Amitabha Buddha, before his attaining Buddhahood, made a vow: "If, after I have obtained Enlightenment, women in immeasurable, innumerable, inconceivable, incomparable, immense Buddha-countries on all sides, after having heard my name, should allow carelessness to arise, should not turn their thoughts towards Enlightenment, should, when they are free from birth, not despise their female nature; and if they, being born again, should assume a second female nature, then may I not obtain the highest perfect Enlightenment." (The 34th vow of Dharmākara; i.e. the former Amitābha) The thought that a woman is born a man in after-life is often set forth in Buddhist literature.

Sense of Sin and Need of Divine Grace

There were thinkers who admitted the deep-rootedness of sin in human existence. This character was most conspicuous in Shinran of Japan. Shinran (1173–1263) was the person who carried the idea of Buddha's grace to an extreme conclusion. He became the founder of the Shinshu sect which is the sect most professed by people in the present day. He has often been compared to Luther not only in this respect but also in that he married a nun and spent his life as a married priest. But as he lived in nearly the same period as Thomas Aquinas, which corresponds with the beginning of the Medieval Ages of Japan, it would not be inappropriate to discuss his thought in the framework of Medieval thought.[30]

Shinran reflected: We should realize what calamity is involved in the mere fact of our being alive. All living beings are sinful. We cannot live without committing sins. We are all karmabound. Hōnen, Shinran's master, saw "man with blind eyes, capable of doing nothing."[31] The sins which are always committed by men were glared at by Shinran without covering up.

> "Though I seek my refuge in the true faith of the Pure Land,
> Yet hath not mine heart been truly sincere.
> Deceit and untruth are in my flesh,
> And in my soul is no clear shining."[32]

It is no wonder that those who did not believe the teachings of the Buddha committed various wicked thing. However, even those who had already heard the teachings of Buddhism and were practicing them also were committing sins. This fact was the starting-point of reflection for Shinran. "I am already neither a priest nor a layman. Therefore, my surname should be 'Bald-headed fool' (Gutoku, i.e. outwardly shaven, inwardly secular, polluted.)"[33]

To trace the origin, in Indian Buddhism the concept of sin distinguished from the concept of 'bad' or 'evil' was not clear. The words *akusala* or *papa,* could mean either. Such terms as *agha, kilbisa, enas,* etc. were used from antiquity, and inherited by Buddhists, but it is not likely that they had any important significance in Buddhist theology as being different from evil, one reason being that Buddhism did not presuppose the concept of God. But when Shinran used the term *"zaiaku"* or *"zaisho",* it reflected keener self-reflection of the innate sin of man.

Shinran did not systematize his concept of sin. In his main work (called "Kyogyo-shin-sho")[34] he conveyed the traditional concept of the Ten Sins or Evil Deeds (*Juaku*) and the Five Heinous Sins (*Gogyakuzai*).

The Ten Sins are: 1) to kill, 2) to steal, 3) to seek unlawful lust, 4) to tell lies, 5) to flatter, 6) to slander, 7) to use a double tongue, 8) to be greedy, 9) to become angry, 10) to hold wrong views.

The Five Deadly Sins are: 1) patricide, 2) matricide, 3) killing of *arhans,* 4) causing disorder to Buddhist Brotherhood, 5) Causing blood to come out of the Buddha's body. But his sin-consciousness was deep.

According to Shinran sin is essential to man; we cannot avoid committing sins. It is deeply rooted in human existence. He deplored:

"In their outward seeming, are all men diligent and truth-speaking,

But in their souls are greed, and eager and unjust deceitfulness,

And in their flesh do lying and cunning triumph.

Too strong for me is the evil of my heart. I cannot overcome it.

Therefore is my soul like unto the poison of serpents,

Even my righteous deeds, being mingled with this poison, must be named the deeds of deceitfulness."[35]

Shinran felt he was destine' to hell.[36]

One feature which distinguishes Shinran, who expressed a thought so very similar to Christianity, from Augustine is that he did not entertain the idea of original sin.

Shinran stresses solely salvation of common men by grace of Amitabha Buddha. "Take refuge in the Ultimate Strength, for His pure radiance is above all things. He who perceiveth the Light is set free from the fetters of Karma."[37] "Take refuge in the Mighty Consoler. Wherewoever

His mercy shineth throughout all the worlds, men rejoice in its gladden-ing light."[38] "Without His Compassionate Vow how can we wretched beings be liberated from the fetters of birth-and-death?"[39]

One might say:—We cannot perceive grace of Buddha. Is it not in-visible? Shinran replies:—It is our grave sins that prevent us from notic-ing it. Although we are not aware, we are already embraced by grace of Amitabha.

> "Though we are covered with illusion,
> And cannot see the light of salvation,
> Untired is He who always shines upon me!"[40]

As we live especially in a Corrupted Age, we cannot be saved from the mundane world without relying upon the original vow of Amitabha.

"No hope is there that the men now living in this last, closing age shall escape the fetters of life and death if they refuse the merciful prom-ise of the Blessed One."[41]

Ordinary people are all wicked persons, those where "there is no mercy".[42] Therefore they cannot save themselves by their own power. Mercy is what comes from Buddha.

In Shinran's opinion, it is solely due to the original vow of Amitabha Buddha that so very sinful men are saved. "Shameless though I be and having no truth in my soul, yet by virtue of the Holy Name, the merits of Him are widely spread throughout all directions."[43]

Only through meditating on the reflection that we are sinful, we come to feel compassionate to others. The attitude of compassion can be founded only by grace. "We are wicked and sinful, but through the virtue of faith we try to do good for the welfare and peace of the world—yet not through our own power, but through that of Another (i.e. Amitabha)." All men, whether they are honest or criminal, are, without any distinc-tion, admitted to Amida's Pure Realm. Faith in Amida's grace is the one and only condition of admission. We are equally sinful, and Amida is a being of compassionate love in the genuine form comparable to the highest God, but unlike the Christian God, he is not a judge. There is no conception of punishment by Amida. The Shin sect holds the view that the evil also are rightfully eligible for salvation by Amitabha Buddha.

Shinran brought this idea of Buddha's grace to its extreme conclusion. A saying of Hōnen's goes like this: "Even a bad man will be received in Buddha's Land, but how much more a good man!" Shinran turned this to the reverse—"Even a good man will be received in Buddha's Land, but how much more a bad man!"[44] To elaborate on this, a good man may be able to save himself by his own merit. But it is not to be expected that a bad man can save himself by his own merit; he needs the grace of the Buddha. He has no other means. Now even a good man who does not necessarily need grace can be saved; how much more a bad man who cannot be saved otherwise than by grace. The sinner has only to believe in the Grace of Amitabha, and the Pure Realm would be his. Here faith became the sole requisite to salvation; all of the other Buddhist moral-philosophy was swept away. For Shinran no ceremony was necessary for salvation except genuine faith.

In connection with grace and faith a controversy occurred in religions of grace in different traditions. In Pure Land Buddhism of China and Japan the relation between faith (shin) and work (gyō) was an issue of heated debate. Many leaders thought that both should cooperate. But Shinran firmly said that pure faith alone is enough, and that one should not rely upon work.

In Japan, generally speaking, Buddhist faith was professed in terms of human nexus. Many people were converted for the beautitude of their parents, relatives or masters or feudal lords, etc. But Shinran's professed faith was genuinely individualistic. "I, Shinran, for the sake of filial piety towards my parents, have never, even once, uttered the Nembutsu (invocation to Amida). The reason is that all sentient beings in some birth or life have been my parents or my brothers. We can save all of them when we become Buddhas in the next life."[45] Individualism in the religious sense of the word was very conspicuous in the case of Shinran. Yuien, Shinran's disciple, conveyed the belief of his master as follows: "The Master (Shinran) used, to say, 'When I carefully consider the Vow which Amida brought forth after five kalpas' contemplation, I find that it was solely for me, Shinran alone! So, how gracious is the Original

Vow of Amida who resolved to save me, possessed of many karmic sins!' "[46]

It has been a conspicuous tendency among the Japanese people to esteem master-disciple relationship to form a closely knit group around a master. Shinran denied it defiantly. "It is utterly unreasonable for those who are devoted solely to the Nembutsu (invocation to Amida) to quarrel, saying, 'These are my disciples', or 'Those are others' disciple'. I, Shinran, do not have even one disciple of my own. The reason is, if I should lead others to utter the Nembutsu by my own efforts, I might call them my disciples. But it is truly ridiculous to call them my disciples, when they utter the Nembutsu through the working of Amida Buddha."[47]

But the relationship between the absolute and the individual differed with traditions. Western medieval thinkers always looked upon God with awe. Hindu saints called the individual "the slave of God". However, Japanese Pure Land leaders never used the term 'slave'. (Chinese one, either, do no seem to have used such an appellation.) They called Amida Buddha 'parent' (singular). It implies all the believers are his children. As parents want to bring up their children to the same state as themselves, Amida makes all sinners Buddhas like Amida. There is no discrimination. If there should be any discrimination, Amida's compassion would not be complete.

The Japanese devotion to Amida has been practiced in the repetition of the phrase: Nambu Amidabutsu (Adoration to Amida Buddha). This phrase is called the Title of Six Syllables.

Then how many times have we repeated the title or name of the Highest One. Some devout believers of Japanese Pure Land Buddhism thought that the oftener they repeated the phrase, the more merit one could obtain. There occurred a legend that Saint Hōnen repeated the phrase a million times. On this point, Hōnen's opinion does not seem to be clear. He simply said: "It is very good to believe in the grace of Buddha with the heart, and repeat the name of Buddha with the mouth."[48] Shinran thought that both faith and repetition of the name were required. "Though you have faith, and do not repeat the name of Amida Buddha, it profits you nothing. Though you repeat the name of Amida Buddha, and do not have faith, you will not be able to be born into the Pure Land. Therefore, you should believe in the grace and repeat the name of Amida, and you will undoubtedly be born into the Buddha's Land."[49] But he did not want to separate these two. "Faith and adoration are not two different things but one, for there is no adoration without faith, and no faith without adoration."[50]

The problem of 'eligibility of wicked persons is formed'. Only for the reason that we are wicked persons we are qualified to be saved, some people said. (In this connection we should compare this Western antinomianism.) Among the later followers of Shinran there appeared some people who boastfully said that they were not afraid of committing sins. This allegiance was called 'Pride in the Original Vows (of Amitābha)'.[51]

The teaching of eligibility of wicked persons does not mean to encourage bad actions. Such a thought was forbidden as heresy by the Shinshu sect. Out of pure faith good deeds come out spontaneously.

"Unto us hat our Father given those two spiritual gifts. Of these the first is the Virtue whereby we attain unto His Kingdom, and the second is the Virtue whereby having so attained we return into this world for the salvation of men. By the merit of these two gifts are we initiates of the true faith and of its deeds."

"When we shall have attained unto the faith and the deeds of the Merciful Promise through our Father that is in all things able to give them unto us, birth and death are henceforward as Nirvana. And this is called the Gift of Departure."[52]

The thought that the Compassion of Buddha should be realized in actual deeds was stressed by later Shinshu priests. Kakunyo sang: "Outside our wish to give things to others out of compassion, Where can we find the form of Buddha!" Rennyo (1415–1499) said: "When it rains or when it is terribly hot, let workmen stop work early. This is an outcome of the great compassion of Buddha."[53] Compassion should be realized in daily life, and Buddhism does not exist outside it.

With regard to the feature that the conciousness of human sinfulness was exceedingly strong, Shinran was quite unique in the history of Buddhism. But his concept of sin was still derived from the traditional one.

"Though sin hath no substance in itself, and is but the shadow of our illusion, and soul (lit. the essence of mind) is pure in itself, yet in all this world there is no sincere man."[54]

According to Shinran, Sin is *devoid* of its own reality in itself, and therefore man can be liberated.

Although Shinran expressed confession similar to that of Christian thinkers, he did not entertain the thought of the original sin of the ancestors of mankind. Shinran, on the other hand, did not ascribe the origin of sin to the ancestors of mankind. Here we find a reason why the faith in the Pure Land has been compatible in Japan with ancestoral worship. If one's faith is pure and genuine, one should not rely upon anything else than Him, the absolute, in whom he takes refuge. But common men in the world were beset by various superstitions. This fact was discussed by Buddhist thinkers in the Medieval Ages. Shinran deplored:

"Sad and corrupt is it that the priests and people, following after the superstitions of auspicious times and days, seek sooth-saying and festivals,

And worship the gods of heaven and earth."[55]

It is interesting to notice a similar echo in medieval philosophical Shintoism also. The anonymous writers of the *Shinto Gobusho* (Five Major Works of Shintoism) says: "What pleases the Deity is virtue and sincerity, and not any number of material offerings."[56]

The degeneration of the clergy was a topic of heated debate in those days.

"Being of one accord with the many minds of the heathen,

They bow in worship before devils.

While yet wearing the robe of a Buddhist monk."[57]

Sacerdotalism was still stressed by Shinran, who asserted that a monk, even if he should be degenerated and only outwardly a monk, should not be despised, but respected. "May they yet bring offerings with homage unto the priests, even as you do unto Sariputta and Moggallana (the two great disciples of the Buddha); though they are priests but in name and without discipline, for this is the time of degeneration and of the last days."[58]

This opinion was shared by Master Dōgen[69] also, whose standpoint was quite opposite to that of Shinran. Needless to say of Master Dōgen and other strict masters, even Shinran who made a remarkable step towards secularization of priests, still remained within the range of venerating clergy. This seems to represent a feature of medieval thought. The existence of clergy was first denied by the Islam, and then by the Sikhs in India, and by Quakers in the West. Recently in Japan,[70] such new movements as Non-church movement among Christians or Laymen Buddhism occurred. In this respect Shinran seems to be located on the historical turning point.

4. The Way of Meditation

The Object of Contemplation

On the other hand we find a different type of thought in the Medieval Ages. That is the type of mysticism and meditation. This represents a view of inherent goodness in human nature, opposed to more extreme views of sin.

Meditation was essential to the contemplative life of the Medieval Ages. Zen Buddhists practiced Zen meditation, as the practitioners of the Hindu sects practiced yoga, and Western mystics meditated on God. The places where meditation was practised were monasteries. In the Far East Tao-hsin (580–651) established Zen monasteries for the first time.[71]

The requirements for meditation were more or less the same in various advanced religions. Practitioners need composure of mind, abstinence from sensual enjoyments, and persistence in concentration of mind. They should practice in quietude.

The unique contribution of Zen to higher religion is its method of reaching and presenting the truth. Many different method of instruction have been used by Zen masters.

In the Rinzai sect practioners have to concentrate on enigmatic or paradoxical, non-logical questions called 'koans'.[72] Koans were substantially based upon mondos. A considerable part of Zen literature consists of mondo, of brief dialogues between masters and disciples, which illustrate its peculiar method of instruction, pointing to the truth, the real vow, without interposing ideas and notions about it.

A monk asked Tung-shan, "How do we escape the heat when summer comes and the cold when winter is here?" The master said, "Why don't you go where there is no summer, no winter?" "Where is such a place?" "When the cold season comes, one is thoroughly chilled; when the hot summer is here, one swelter."

There are some koans which logically do not make any sense. Answers do not reply to questions.

"Once a monk asked Tung-shan: 'What is the Buddha?' Tungshan replied: 'Three pounds of flax.' "

Zen has sometimes to attack and smash human concepts quite violently. Thus its technique has often the appearance of spiritual shock-tactics. Paradoxes are used because it is difficult to express pure experience in the form of ordinary, formal logic.

How paradoxical these dialogues are, can be illustrated in the following:

The Zen master Chao-chu was asked, "What is the Tao?"

He replied, "Everyday life is the Tao."

"How," pursued the enquirer, "does one get into harmony with it?"

"If you try to get into harmony with it, you will get away from it."

A rather systematized saying runs as follows:

Like unto space it knows no boundaries;
Yet it is right here with us, ever retaining its serenity and fullness;
It is only when you seek it that you lose it.
You cannot take hold of it, nor can you get rid of it;
While you can do neither, it goes on its own way;
You remain silent and it speaks; you speak and it is silent;

The great gate of charity is wide open with no obstructions whatever before it.[73]

For Zen masters, the best way to express our deepest experiences is by the use of paradoxes which transcend the opposites. For example, these are typical paradoxes[74] to be used for meditation: "Where there is nothing, there is all." "To die the great death is to gain the great life." "Drop into a deep chasm and live again after your death." "We have been separated for a long time and have never been apart. We meet each other throughout the day, and do not meet a moment." "If you abandon superior training you find original Enlightenment in your hand; if you leave original Enlightenment, superior training fills your body." Paradoxes like these bring objective logic to a deadlock and from there it is possible to uncover the vital way of turning around.

Sometimes the *koans* seem to contradict each other. When asked, "What is Buddha?" Ba-so answered, "This mind is Buddha", but on another occasion he said, "This mind is not Buddha". But both assertions are no less than ferry-boats which lead us to the enlightenment.

Some *koans* can be translated into logical expressions.[75] A famous *koan* is this: "Before father and mother were born, what was your true nature?" It can be worded: "Beyond time and space, what is Reality?"

The way of practice in the Sōto Zen is fairly different. Master Dōgen also made meditation the essential practice of meditation. "Why do you encourage others to practice meditation?" The answer: "This is the right gate to the teaching of Buddha."[76] "Meditation is the gate to Comfort and Happiness."[77] However, the Sōtō Zen went still farther than the Rinzai Zen. It rejected even *koans*. Practitioners should not endeavor to concentrate on anything. Master Dōgen said: "In meditation, if mind is distracted, don't try to suppress it. Let it be as it is!"[78] He disliked the term "Zen sect".[79] He claimed to convey the right path of religion. If one limit the Way with the word "Zen sect", one loses the way. Sōtō Zen emphasizes silent sitting and meditating on the illumination or insight received while waiting in silence.

Concerning the object of contemplation we can conclude that in Western and Eastern meditations the way of contemplating the object by practitioners are more or less similar, whereas the Zen way of approach has been diametrically opposed to them.

Intuitive Knowledge of Mystics

Zen Buddhism taught intuitive knowledge of the absolute. A well-known motto of Zen: "Direct pointing to the mind of man"[80] emphasizes that we originally have the Buddhamind and need the actual experience of it. That is, the master points to the Buddha-nature, or Reality itself. Enlightenment takes place in a "timeless moment", i.e. outside time, in eternity, and that it is an act of the Absolute itself, not our own doing. One cannot do anything at all to become enlightened. To expect austerities or meditation to bring forth salvation is like "rubbing a brick to make it into a mirror." "Seeing into one's own nature",[81] another motto of Zen, means that the seeing of this Buddhamind is the same as becoming the Buddha—that you are the Buddha.

This intuition cannot be attained arbitrarily. The true law of the Buddha should be transmitted from mind to mind and from personality to personality.

The Zen motto: "A special transmission outside the classified teachings"[82] means that systems of teachings based upon the Sūtra are not relied upon, and that the true law is transmitted by other means. Therefore, to attain the goal of Zen we must begin by receiving guidance from a true master of Zen who has synthesized understanding and action. Under the guidance of the master—the transmission from mind to mind —Zen practitioners believe deeply in our original Buddhahood and express this through the Zen meditative disciplines which bring out the Buddha and the patriarchs in ourselves. As we learn to bring out the Buddha and patriarchs in ourselves, we must emphasize living experience rather than the words and letters of the Sūtras.

Zen claims a special lineage of transmission of the teaching from Mahākāśyapa, the great disciple of Sakyamuni. Zen people say: When the Buddha conveyed the teaching, all stoop nonplussed save Mahākāśyapa, whose understanding smile brought this recognition from his master: "I have the most precious treasure, spiritual and transcendental,

which this moment I hand over to you, O venerable Mahākāśyapa!"
Tradition asserts that this knowledge was handed down from Mahākāśyapa through a line of patriarchs to Bodhidharma, who brought it to
China, where it continued to be passed from teacher to teacher. Because
this knowledge can never be written down, Zen does not rely on scriptures, even though it may use them as expediencies for edifying people.

It seems to have been an ironical destiny of human beings that intuitive knowledge which should be universal was due to be conveyed
only in specific lineage in different traditions.

Dōgen identified the practice of meditation (zazen) with enlightenment, the innate Buddha-nature, is the a priori basis of the practice which
itself embodies enlightenment in the process of one's endeavor.

Dōgen says: "In Buddhism, practice and enlightenment are one and
the same. Since practice has its basis in enlightenment, the practice even
of the beginner contains the whole of original enlightenment. Thus while
giving directions as to the exercise, the Zen master warns him not to
await enlightenment apart from the exercise, because this exercise points
directly to the original enlightenment, it has no beginning."[83]

The Zen disciple does not seek for some Supreme Being above him,
but rather he finds in himself the Buddha-nature spontaneously as the
foundation of his own existence. "Let the light be reflected so it falls back
and irradiates the self," says Dōgen. "Then mind and body will of
themselves disappear and the original countenance will become manifest."[84]

In this sense meditation should be esteemed as such. "Even though one
should know Meditation as the Buddha Law, yet if he does not comprehend Meditation as Meditation, how then can he know the Buddha
Law as Buddha Law?"[85]

Practical Significance of Meditation

In Zen monasteries meditation was exhorted towards the goal as
follows: Master Po-chang taught to "cling to nothing, crave for nothing".[86] This is what he impressed upon his disciples as being fundamental.
The *koan* of 'nothing' was highly esteemed in later days. "When you

forget the good and the non-good, the wordly life and the religious life and all other things, and permit no thoughts relating to them to arise, and you abandon body and mind—then there is complete freedom. When the mind is like wood or stone, there is nothing to be discriminated."[87]

Enlightenment was often compared to light. Master Wu-men compared enlightenment to 'lightening a religious candle'.[88]

To attain enlightenment means in Zen Buddhism to break down the bondages of our petty, selfish ego. Zen masters called it metaphorically "to break down a lacquer-painted pail" or "the collapse of mind and body".

This ultimate situation is not realized by petty deliberation of man, but by the absolute itself.

This paint seems to be quite dissimilar to the thought of Zen Buddhism, especially of the Lin-chi or Rinzai sect. But we have an echo of this thought in another branch of Zen Buddhism, i.e. the Sōtō sect founded by Master Dōgen.

Dōgen also said: "When you let your body and mind go free (without attachment and worry) and forget them, and entrust yourself to the 'home' of Buddha, then everything will be conducted by Buddha. When you follow the process, you will become free from the sufferings of life and death, and become Buddha."[89]

Justification of moral virtues is possible by the fundamental supposition that we human beings are in our essence good and pure. In Zen Buddhism they say that "living beings are by origin (essentially) Buddhas".[90]

The Absolute in Phenomena

Zen dispelled all kinds of ratiocination on the absolute. The Buddha dwells hidden in all inconspicuous things of daily life. To take them just as they come, that is all that enlightenment amounts to. Zen is spiritual freedom, the liberation of our true nature from the burden of those fixed ideas and feelings about Reality which we accumulate through fear— the fear that life will run away from us. These *mondo* may seem puzzling at the first glance, but in fact there is nothing obscure or hidden about them. The truth which they indicate is, however, of radical simplicity and self-evidence.

"It is so clear that it takes long to see.
You must know that the fire which you are seeking
is the fire in your own lantern,
And that your rice has been cooked from the very beginning."[91]

A Zen poet says:

"*How wondrous, how miraculous, this—*
I draw water and I carry fuel!"
"*In spring, the flowers, and in autumn the moon,*
In summer a refreshing breeze, and in winter the snow.
What else do I have need of?"[92]

Zen masters expressed their teachings with reference to individual cases, casting away the restrictions of general propositions.

In the respect that they resorted to enigmatic questions, Zen and the Tantric religion of India were similar. But, whereas the Tantric religion explained the manifestation of the world as due to the efficacy of the primordial female power (*sakti*), Zen Buddhism did not extoll the creative or sexual power of female deities, being indifferent to metaphysical questions.

The process of the phenomenal world is activity, mighty self-posting, a procreation not under the compulsion of laws or blind impulse but in the creative power and freedom of sublime wonder. Dōgen says, "Being is time, and time is being. Everything in the world is time at each moment. To practice religious disciplines and to attain Enlightenment and to enter into Nirvana are nothing but to ascertain that these events are Being, time, and that all time is all Being."[93] Dōgen's assertion seems to be very radical. He said: "Birth and death is the life of Buddha".[94] Some Chinese Zen masters also defined Buddhahood as 'pure intelligence'. But Dōgen defiantly repudiated such an opinion as heresy, not Buddhist.[95]

The Sōtō sect is traditionally supposed to maintain "the Five Ranks"[96] dialectic propounded by Tung-shan (Tōzan 洞山) (807–869), the Chinese founder of the Sōtō Zen. But in actuality this theory has not been so influential as the teachings by Master Dōgen himself.

5. The Concept of Time and Change

One of the main features of Japanese ways of thinking has been the attitude of the acceptance of actuality in the phenomenal world as the absolute.

The Japanese have had the attitude to lay a greater emphasis upon the intuitive sensible concrete rather than universals and the attitude to lay an emphasis upon the fluid, incipient character of the events. This way of thinking may come to regard the phenomenal world itself as the Absolute and to reject the recognition of the Absolute existing over and above the phenomenal world. What is widely known among post-Meiji philosophers as the "Theory that the phenomenal is actually the real" has a deep root in Japanese tradition.

It was characteristic of the religious views of the ancient Japanese that they believed spirits to reside in all kinds of things. They personified all kinds of spirits other than those of human beings, concerning them all as ancestral gods, tending to view every spirit as noumenon of gods. It is such a turn of thought that gave birth to the Shinto shrines, for in order to perform religious ceremonies the gods and spirits were fixed in certain specified places.

This way of thinking is what runs through the subsequent history of Shintoism down to this day. "Nowhere in a shadow in which a god does not reside. Peaks, ridges, pines, cryptomerias, mountains, rivers, seas, villages, plains, and fields, everywhere there is a god. We can receive the constant and intimate help of these spirits in our tasks, many courtiers are passing".[97] This thought was inherited by later Shintoists.[98]

Buddhist philosophy likewise was received and assimilated on the basis of this way of thinking. Japanese Buddhism emphasized the transience of the phenomenal world. But the Japanese attitude towards this transience is very different from the Indian. The Japanese disposition is to lay a greater emphasis upon sensible, concrete events, intuitively apprehended, than upon universals. It is in direct contrast to the characteristic Indian reaction to the world of change, which is to reject it in favor of an ultimate reality, a transcendent Absolute in which the mind can find refuge from the ceaseless flux of observed phenomena. The Japanese reaction is rather to accept, even to welcome, the fluidity and impermanence of the phenomenal world.

To begin with, the Tendai sect in Japan is not the same as in China. The Tendai scholars in medieval Japan, using the same nomenclature as that used in the continental Buddhism, arrived at a system of thought that is distinctly original. This is what is called Honkaku-Hōmon, which asserts that the aspects of the phenomenal world are the Buddha. The word Honkaku or Enlightenment appears in the Chinese translation of the *Mahāyāna-sraddhotpāda-sāstra* (*Daijyō-kishinron*)[99] which was originally composed in India. In the continent, this word meant the ultimate comprehension of what is beyond the phenomenal world, whereas in Japan the same word was brought down to refer to what is within the phenomenal world. In this way, the chsracteristic feature of the Tendai Buddhism in Japan consists in their laying an emphasis upon things rather than principles. The Japanese Tendai scholars were not very faithful to the original texts of the Chinese Tendai. They sometimes interpreted the original texts in rather unnatural way, their interpretation being based upon the standpoind of the Phenomenal Absolute.[100]

It is natural that the Nichiren sect, which is an outgrowth of the Japanese Tendai, also lays an emphasis upon such a turn of thought, Nichiren asserts that the crux of Budda's thought is revealed in the Jyuryōbon[101] chapter (Duration of life of the Tathāgata) of the Lotus Sūtra, saying, "In the earlier half of the whole sūtra, the ten directions are called the pure land and this place the soiled land, while, (in this Jyuryōbon part), on the contrary, this place is called the main land and the pure land in the ten directions the soiled land where Buddha has made an incarnation".[102] The Nichiren sect states that, while the Tendai sect from China onward takes the standpoint of "Action according to principles", Nichiren emphasized "Action according to things".

The method of thinking that seeks for the Absolute in the Phenomenal World plays an effective role in the assimilation of the Zen sect as well.

The Zen Buddhism in Master Dōgen seems to have been influenced by the Japanese Tendai Buddhism. This fact has often been alluded to by the specialists but has not been fully eoplored. Here I shall point out a few examples which reveal the above-mentioned way of thinking. The Chinese translated "dharmatā"[103] in Sanskrit as "the real aspect of all things". This concept refers to the real aspect of all kinds of phenomena in our experience, and, therefore, is composed of two distinct, contradictory elements, "All things" and "the real aspect". But, the Tendai Buddhism, gave this phrase an interpretation of "All things are the real aspect" and took the viewpoint that the phenomena are the reality. Dōgen gave a different twist to this interpretation and emphasized that "the real aspect are all things". He means to say that the truth which people search for is, in reality, nothing but the real world of our daily experience. Thus he says, "The real aspect are all things. All things are this aspect, this character, this body, this mind, this world, this wind and this rain, this sequence of daily going, living, sitting, and lying down, this series of melancholy, joy, action, and inaction, this stick and wand, this Buddha's smile, this transmission and reception of the doctrine, this study and practice, this evergreen pine and ever unbreakable bamboo".[204]

When one asserts "all things are the real aspect", the predicate being of a larger denotation, the real aspect seems to contain something other than all things. But in the expression "the real aspect are all things", the meaning is that there is nothing that is not exposed to us.[205] For Dōgen, therefore, the fluid aspects of impermanence is in itself the absolute state. The changeable character of the phenomenal world is of absolute significance for Dōgen.

Master Dōgen, the thirteenth-century thinker who is said to have founded the Sōtō-Zen sect, asserts the transience of things as strongly as any Indian Buddhist. "Time flies more swiftly than an arrow and life is more transient than dew. We cannot call back a single day that has passed." But his emphasis is positive, not negative: "A man may live as the slave of the senses for one hundred years but if he lives one day upholding the Good Law, it will favorably influence his coming life for many years." And Dōgen stresses the primacy of the phenomenal world:

"We ought to love and respect this life and this body, since it is through this life and this body that we have the opportunity to practice the Law and make known the power of the Buddha. Accordingly, righteous practice for one day is the Seed of Buddhahood, of the righteous action of All the Buddhas."[206]

What we see and experience is thus recognized as itself the ultimate reality. There is no greater reality, changeless and invisible; there is nothing to be apprehended that is not already exposed to us.[207] For Master Dōgen, impermanence is itself the absolute state, and this impermanence is not to be rejected but to be valued. "Impermanence is the Buddhahood. . . ."[208] The impermanence of grass, trees, and forests is verily the Buddhahood. The impermanence of the person's body and mind is verily the Buddhahood. The impermanence of the country and scenery is verily the Buddhahood."[209]

In other places Dōgen says: "Death and life are the very life of the Buddha," and "There mountains, rivers and earth are all the Seed of Buddhahood." In the Lotus Sūtra, Dōgen finds the same vein of thought: "Concerning the Lotus Sūtra . . . the cry of a monkey is drowned in the sound of a rapid river. [Even] these are preaching this sūtra, this above all "He who attains the purport of this sūtra, says the Master, will discern the preaching of the doctrine even in the voices at an auction sale, for even in the mundane world "our Buddha's voice and form [are] in all the sounds of the rapid river and colors of the ridge."[210]

One is reminded of the words of the Chinese poet Su Tung-p'o: "The voice of the rapids is verily the wide long tongue [of the Buddha]. The color of the mountains is no other than [his] pure chaste body." This way of thinking is Japanese Zen Buddhism. In the words of Master Mujū, "Mountains, rivers, earth, there is not a thing that is not real."[211]

Starting from such a viewpoint, Dōgen gives to some phrases of Indian Buddhist scriptures interpretations that are essentially different from the original meaning. There is a phrase in the *Mahāpari-nirvāna-sūtra*[212] that goes as follows: "He who desires to know the meaning of Buddhahood should survey the time and wait for the occasion to come. If the time comes, the Buddhahood will be revealed of itself." To this concept of Buddhahood as something possible and accessible, Dōgen gives a characteristic twist. He reads the phrase "survey of time"[213] as "make a survey in terms of time", and the phrase "if the time comes" as "the time has already come." His interpretation of the original passage becomes, in this way, something like the following:

Buddhahood is time. He who wants to know Buddhahood may know it by knowing time as it is revealed to us. And as time is something in which we are already immersed, Buddhahood also is not something that is to be sought in the future but is something that is realized where we are.[214]

We see here Dōgen's effort to free himself from the idealistic viewpoint held by some of the Indian Mahāyāna Buddhists. In Dōgen's unique philosophy of time, "all being is time",[215] the ever-changing, incessant temporal flux is identified with ultimate Being itself.

In the words of a Chinese Zen Buddhist, Yaoshan, (751–834) there appears the phrase "at a certain time". Dōgen interprets this phrase unjustifiably as "Being time" and comments as follows: "So-called Being Time means that time already is being and all being is time."[216] Taking this opportunity, Dōgen goes on to his unique philosophy of time. According to his philosophy, the every changing, incessant, flow of time is the ultimate Being.

Again and again Dōgen emphasizes that the true reality is not static but dynamic. "It is heretical doctrine," says he, "to think the mind mobile and the essence of things static. It is a heretical doctrine to think that the essence is crystal clear and the appearance changeable."[217] Again, "It is a heretical doctrine to think that in essence water does not run, and the tree does not pass through vicissitude. The Buddha's way consists in the form that exists and the conditions that exist. The bloom of flowers and the fall of leaves are the conditions that exist. And yet unwise people think that in the world of essence there should be no bloom of flowers and no fall of leaves."[218]

Dōgen criticizes the Chinese Zen Buddhist Ta-hui (1089–1163), who taught that mind and essence are not caught up in the world of birth and death. Accordingly to Dōgen, Ta-hui was wrong in teaching that "the mind is solely perception and conceptualization, and the essence is pure and tranquil."[219] Here again a static way of thinking is rejected, and this rejection makes Dōgen's emphasis very different from anything which Indian or Chinese Buddhism has prepared us for.

In this sense time is accorded neither substantiality nor continuity. Moments of time stand side by side for human existence. Every moment is self-contained. In every moment only the present exists in the real sense of the word. Dōgen says, "You should fix your heart on the exercise only today in this moment, without losing the light of time."[220] The *now* is absolute. The whole of enlightenment is contained in every moment. Therefore, every moment of exercise is of infinite worth. Here we can find a strange coincidence with the philosophy of *today* (now) by Prince Shōtoku.

The way of thinking that recognizes absolute significance in the temporary, phenomenal world seems to be culturally related to the traditional Japanese love of nature. The Japanese love mountains, rivers, flowers, birds, grass and trees, and represent them in the patterns of their kimonos; they are fond of the delicacies of the season, keeping edibles in their natural form as much as possible in cooking. Within the house, flowers are arranged in a vase and dwarf trees are placed in the alcove, flowers and birds are engraved in the transom and painted on the sliding screen, and in the garden miniature mountains, streams and lakes are created. Japanese literature is deeply involved with nature and treats it with warm affection. Typical are the essays in the *Pillow Book* (*Makura no Sōshi*), which describes the beauties of the seasons. The loving concern with the particularities of nature is familiar to us through Japanese art; it is just as marked in Japanese poetry. If the poems on nature were to be removed from the collections of Japanese poems, how many would be left? Haiku, the characteristic Japanese seventeen-syllable short poems, are unthinkable apart from natural objects and the changing seasons, but the differences in attitude are as instructive as the similarities. Here is a poem by Master Dōgen:

> *Flowers are in spring, cuchoos in summer,*
> *In autumn is the moon, and in winter*

The pallid glimmer of snow.

The meaning of the above poem is very close to that of the Chinese verse by Wu-men Hui-k'ai:

A hundred flowers are in spring, in autumn is the moon,
In summer is the cool wind, the snow is in winter;
If nothing is on the mind to afflict a man,
That is his best season.

Similar as the poems are, the Japanese substitution of "cuckoos" for the Chinese "cool wind" has produced an entirely different effect. Both cuckoos and cool wind are sensible phenomena, but while the wind gives the sense of indefinite, remote boundlessness, the cuckoos give an impression that is limited, almost cosy.

An even better example is the poem composed on his deathbed by Ryōkan:

For a memento of my existence
What shall I leave (I need not leave anything)?
Flowers in the spring, cuckoos in the summer
And maple leaves in the autumn.

"Maple leaves" are felt to be far closer to ourselves than "the moon", which Wu-men chose to associate with autumn. Enjoyment of nature is common to both China and Japan, but whereas the Chinese prefer the boundless and distant, the Japanese prefer the simple and compact. Dōgen took a Spartan attitude towards human desires, but he had a tender heart for seasonal beauties:

The peach blossoms begin
To bloom in the breeze of the spring;
Not a shadow of doubt
On the branches and leaves is left.
Though I know that I shall meet
The autumn moon again,
How sleepless I remain
On this moonlit night.

What is the origin of this tendency of the Japanese to grasp the absolute in terms of the world as it exists in time? Probably in the mildness of the weather, the benign character of the landscape, and the rapid and conspicuous change of seasons. Since Nature appears to be relatively benevolent to man he can love it rather than abhor it. Nature, as it changes in time, is thought of as at one with man, not hostile to him. Man feels congenial to his world, he has no grudge against it. This is at least a partial explanation for what is a basic tendency in Japanese thought.

6. The Philosophy of History

As Japan is situated near the continent of China, the Chinese conception of history has been very influential in the past of Japan, and Buddhist conception of history also was introduced into Japan as it had been existing in China. However, the Japanese has kept their traditional ways of thinking which modified the notion of history introduced from abroad.[221]

Whatever its source, this willingness to accept the human beings' situation in time has many manifestations in Japanese philosophy. The Japanese came to produce peculiarly Japanese-style books of history. The Japanese produced a lot of classical works of history. Among them the *Gukan-shō* by Bishop Jichin seems to be foremost in this respect that the notion of reality by Japanese Buddhists is most clearly reflected in the notion of history. He deplored that the age in which he lived was a degenerated one. This critical consciousness was most keenly felt in the Kamakura period. The consciousness that they lived in immoral times was conspicuous among emperors of those days also.[222]

Most of the Buddhist sects in Japan teach that doctrines should always be made "a propos of the time." Later Mahāyāna Buddhism employs the concept of the Three Times, the three periods which follow the demise of Lord Buddha. The first thousand years is called the Period of the Perfect Law, when the religion of the Buddha was genuinely and perfectly practiced. The second thousand years is the Period of the Copied Law, when the religion of the Buddha was practiced only in limiting the practices of the sages and monks of the past. The last period, the Period of the Latter Law, is seen as a time of open degeneration.

These ideas took deep root in Japan. The idea, in particular, of the third, degenerate age penetrated deep into the core of the doctrines of various sects. These admitted that they were in the age of degeneration, but instead of exhorting a return to the Perfect, or even the Copied Law, they claimed that the exigencies of the time should be considered and religious doctrines made suitable to them. The sects even vied in claiming the superiority of their respective sūtras (or doctrines) *because* they were most suited to the corruption of the age. Nichiren, the Buddhist prophet, claimed that one could be saved only by the spiritual power of the Lotus Sūtra, whose gospel he alone was entitled to spread. The corruption of the age is no handicap: "The Adoration of the Lotus of the Perfect Truth shall prevail beyond the coming ages of ten thousand years, nay eternally in the future." It is indeed an advantage.

Is it not true that one hundred years' training in a heavenly paradise does not compare with one day's work in the earthly world, and that all service to the Truth during the two thousand years of the ages of the Perfect Law and the Copied Law is inferior to that done in the one span of time in the age of the Latter Law? All these differences are due, not to Nichiren's own wisdom, but to the virtues inherent in the times. Flowers bloom in the spring, and fruits are ripe in the autumn; it is hot in summer and cold in winter. Is it not time that makes these differences?[223] Nichiren here welcomes the processes of time, even if they bring corruption; he sees them as an opportunity for service to the truth. Time provides the opportunity for a turning point from degeneration to regeneration.

Nichiren laid special emphasis upon the particularity and specificity of the truth of humanity. The Japanese unfriendliness for universals is plain in this passage:

"The learning of just one word or one phrase of the Right Law, if only it accords with the time and the propensity of the learner, would lead him to the attainment of the Way. The mastery of a thousand scriptures and ten thousand theories, if they should not accord with the time and the propensity of the one who masters them, would lead his nowhere."[224]

Nichiren evaluates doctrines by five standards, all specific in character. These are: the teaching of the sūtra, the spiritual endowments of the

learner (what he calls the "propensity"), the country in which the doctrine is practiced, and the temporal order of circumstances affecting the
practice of the doctrine. Saichō, an ancient Buddhist teacher, also regarded the time and the country as important factors, but it was Nichiren who established them as basic principles, presented in a clear and
distinct form. Such a method of evaluation of religious truth in terms of
social and individual particularities, would hardly be found in the Buddhist thought of India or China. It is clear that even where India and
Japan have shared a set of religious assumptions, the characteristic national habits of thought have led to entirely different conceptions both
of Time and of Ultimate Reality.

Man is an existence in history. History is brought into shape when a
state or society is established. The state or society of Japan has been fea-
tured by the Imperial Household of long continuation. A feature of
Japanese historiography is as follows: Japan has been a unified country
located in narrow islands under the rule of the Imperial Household whose
origin cannot be traced. Many Japanese historiographies of the past centered on extolling the prestige of the Imperial Household.

When one looks at the many legends related in the *Kojiki* and the
Nihonshoki, the most ancient annals of Japan, one finds that stories of the
gods are not told for the purpose of demonstrating the greatness of the
divinities believed in by the ancients; on the contrary, it is only for the
purpose of showing the divine character of the Emperor that accounts
are given of the gods which are its basis and of the historical blood relation of these gods.

According to the tales of the gods in the *Kojiki,* after the heavens and
the earth were separated, the two divinities Izanami and Izanagi des-
cended to the island of Onokoro, and then gave birth to the various islands of Ōyashima (i.e. the territory of Japan). After that they have birth
to various other divities; the gods of the wind, of trees and mountains
were born, and at the end the goddess (Izanami) died from burns, because who gave birth to the god of fire. Thereupon, the god (Izanagi)
wanted to meet his spouse, and went to the land of night and saw her.

Then, after returning to this world, when he washed the filth (of the land of death from hemself), from his eyes and nose were born the three divinities Amaterasu-ōmikani, Tsukiyomi-no-mikoto, and Susanō-no-mikoto. It is said that this Amaterasu-ōmikami was the ancestor of the Imperial House.[225] *In this way the legend of the ancestors of the royal house is connected with the legend of the creation of the universe.* This is probably something without parallel among other nations. At least among other civilized people of the East, these two types of legends are separated. Thus, the divine authority of the Imperial House is enhanced by the fact that its lineage is connected with the legend of the creation of heaven and earth.

The early Buddhists of India held a sort of the theory of social contract, according to which the monarch was originally elected from among people for the welfare of people. But the Japanese who accepted Buddhism on a large scale refused nevertheless to adopt its concept of the state which to them appear to run counter to the native ides of "state structure (*kokutai*)". We thus have a writer of history of Japan like Kitabatake Chikafusa who was ready on the one hand to accept Buddhism in general but was eager on the other to emphasize the importance of the Japanese Imperial Family in the following way: The Buddhist theory (of state) is merely an Indian theory; Indian monarchs may have been the descendants of a monarch selected for the people's welfare, but "Our Imperial Family is the only continuous and unending line of family descending from its Heavenly Ancestors".[226] Hirata Atsutane on the other hand discredits the whole Indian theory of the origin of the state as mere explanation of the origin of "Indian chieftains".[227]

Kokan Shiren (1278–1346), writer of a history of Japanese Buddhism, said in the introduction to the work: "Japan is a pure, pure entity".

The basis of the state is rooted in nature. No Chinese dynasty has ever been like this. This is why we praise our country. This 'nature' is the three sacred treasures. The three treasures are the sacred mirror, the sacred sword, and the sacred jewel. These three are all natural, heaven-made products. The fact that our country has one imperial line which reaches far back in time and is unbroken over the ages is surely due to these treasures, which are natural and heaven-made. Therefore, even after countless generations, there is no danger that the throne will be menaced. Surely, these heaven-produced sacred treasures will not become the playthings of another clan or of foreign arms".[228]

The tendency to view the history of Japan only in the light of the prestige of the Imperial Household has completely vanished. This is probably to keep pace with the new development of the world situation. However, to view history as such in the light of actuality as the absolute is of some significance even in the future. This way of thinking is noticed even in the philosophy of the late Nishida, the founder of a modern trend of Japanese philosophy, and it is even compatible with Hegelianism or Marxism, which is very prevalent among contemporary Japanese philosophers and historians.

7. Conclusions

The discussions so far are not enough to cover details of medieval thought. We have roughly pointed to some problems and features which can be noticed in medieval Japan. But they will suffice to evidence that there was a tage of thought which can be roughly called 'medieval'.

In the discussions made so far, it has been made clear that in Buddhism there were at least two types, i.e.:

1) Self-Reliance or Self-Power (or *jiriki* in Japanese)

2) Dependence on Grace or the Other Power (or *Tariki* in Japanese). The former way is self-saving, whereas the latter way represents 'saving by another'. Or even in one branch of a religion we find two types mixed up, although one type is more predominant. We would say that if is misleading to identify any one religion with one type only.

So far we have pointed out some similar ideas and problems of the Medieval Ages of Japan. It is almost impossible to summarize them in short sentences, however, we can understand they are important in the history of Japanese thought and are still of contemporary significance.

Notes

1 It was Emperor Daigo who opened an independent road of Japanese culture from that of China. In the reign of Emperor Uda Japanese embassy was closed. From this time on Japan's own literature began to be composed. Such tendency is also evident in his-toriography. The early four Japanese official chronicles were compiled after the pattern of Chinese history, *Shi-king* of Han period written by Sse Ma CHIEN, but later chronicles such as *Chronicle of Emperor Montoku* (*Montoku Jitsuroku*) and *Chronicle of Three Reigns* (*Sandai Jitsuroku*) differ from the preceding four. There is an evident sign of decrease in taking models of historiography in Chinese chronicles and the descriptions became more Japanese in style. The course was succeeded by the writers of *The Tales of Glorious Days* (*Eiga Monogatari* and *The Great Mirror* (*Okagami*).

2 *Tales of the Heike* (*Heike Monogatari*), Chapter of Ohara Gokō.

3 Both in China and Japan this moral is called the "Three Obeyances." Rf. *The Book of Rites,* Chapter of the Rites for Observing Mourning.

4 Rf. *The Rise and Fall of the Genji and Heike Clans* (*Genpei Seisuiki*), Vol. 47; the *Samantabhadrapranidhānacarya* of the *Buddhāvatamsuka Sūtra.*

6 *Hagakure.* Although this work was compiled in the Tokugawa period, it incorporates the practices of medieval warriors.

7 Psalms, 73 :26.

8 "Harakiri" is a Japanese word coined by Westerner and not used in Japan.

9 *Taisho,* XXXVII, p. 273a.

10 *Taisho,* XLVII, p. 498a.

11 *Mo-ho-chi-kuan,* vol. 4a. (*Taisho,* vol. 46, p. 36a; pp. 42, c-43a). Cf. *Taisho,* vol. 46, p. 265b.

12 *Tsurezuregusa,* paragraph, 75.

13 *Shōbō Genzō Zuimon-ki,* vol. III. *Dōgenzenji Zenshū,* ed. by ŌKUBO Doshu, Tokyo, Shunjusha, 1930, p. 34.

14 *Collected Sayings of Master Po-chang.*

15 *Shōbō Genzō Zuimonki,* vol. 1, in *Dōgen Zenji Zenshū,* p. 7.

16 Ibid., vol. II, in *Dōgen Zenji Zenshū,* p. 18.

17 The chapter of TOKUZUI Raihai in the *Shōbō Genzō* (Dōgen Zenji Zenshū, pp. 44–51).

18 He said such a custom did not exist neither in India nor in China. Ibid., p. 48.

19 The Sanskrit word for "compassion" is *maitri* or *karunā* or *dayā*. Maitri can be translated as 'friendliness' also, because the word derives from the word 'mitra' meaning 'friend'. The word 'karuna' was translated into Chinese with the word meaning 'sorrow'.

In Sanskrit literature also, the sorrow of a lady who has no prospect of seeing her lover again is expressed with the word karuna. (*Sāhityadarpana*, III, 213)

20 The Chin version of the *Buddhāvatamsaka-sūtra*, vol. 27; The Book on the Hau-yen Five Teachings (Kegon Gokyo-sho) ed. by Kwanno, vol. 1, p. 50b. In the Lotus Sūtra we, find a similar thought. (yo viryavantah sada maitracitta bhaventi maitrim iha dirgharātram Chapter 2, ed. by WOGIHARA and TSUCHIDA, p. 93; cf. p. 248).

21 *Amitāyurdhyānasūtra.*

22 The Chinese version by Kumarajiva of the *Saddharmapundarika-sūtra*, Chapter II.

23 The *Saddharmapundarika-sūtra*, Chapter XI, SBE. vol. 21, p. 251.

24 The *Saddharmapundarika-sūtra*, V, vv. 6; 11; 21; 24.

25 The God of the Kirishitans (The Japanese Catholics in feudal days) was popularly called Deus-Nyorai. Nyorai is the Japanese equivalent of the Sanskrit *tathagata* (Buddha).

26 Chapter IV of the Lotus Sūtra, SBE, 21, p. 98f.; Winternitz: pp. 298ff.

25 *Saddharmapundarika-sūtra*, II, vv. 82–87.

26 The Lotus Sūtra, Chapter 24, *Samantamukhaparivarta*, v. 6.

In the West, St. Christopher has been the patron of one of those spacious coves which indent the eastern shore of the Hudson, at that broad expandion of the river denominated by the ancient Dutch navigators the Tappan Zee, and where they always prudently shortened sail, and implored the protection of St. Nicholas when

26 寶行五正論 The Chinese version of the *Ratnāvli*, the Sanskrit text of which is lost for the most part.

27 The Pure Land is sometimes called the Buddha Land, or Buddha Field, or Pure Western Land. Professor Kenneth MORGAN thinks that Pure Realm is preferable since it avoids the erroneous connotations of a geographic location or a material world. (*The Path of the Buddha*, edited by Kenneth W. MORGAN, New York, the Ronald Press, 1956, passim.) This is especially true with Hōnen and Shinran. Here I followed the ordinary, conventional translation.

28 The Smaller *Sukhāvati-sūtra*, 18. SBE. vol. 49, p. 102. In the Chinese version of the Larger *Sukhāvati-sūtra* by Sanghavarman the consciousness of crisis and sin is set forth with of good family shall hear the name of the Lord Amitayus, and having heard it shall reflect upon it, and for one, two, three, four, five, six, or seven nights shall reflect upon it with undisturbed binds, when they come to die the Tathagata Amitayus attended by the assembly of disciples and followed by a host of bodhisattvas will stand before them, and they will die with unconfused minds. After death they will be born even in the Buddha-country of the Tathāgata Amitāyus, in the world Sukhāvati." (Smaller *Sukhāvativyūha*, 10)

30 At nearly the same time in India Ramanuja and other Hindu religious leaders of the Bhakti religion advocated salvation by grace of God Visnu or Siva.

31 Hōnen: *Ōjō-taiyō-shū* (The Outline of the Way to Salvation. Masutani, p. 67).

32 *Hitan-jutsukai-wasan.*

33 *Kyō-gyō-shin-shō*, Epilog.

34 教行信證

35 YAMABE and BECK: *Buddhist Psalms*, p. 86.

36 *Tannishō*, 2.

37 YAMABE and BECK: p. 20. *San-Amidabutsu-ge*, v. 5.

38 YAMABE and BECK: *ibid.*, p. 20, 1b. v. 8.

39 *Tannishō*, 14.

40 正信偈 *Shōshinge.*

41 The Three Periods. YAMABE and BECK: p. 68.

42 *Hitanjutsukai Wasan*, v. 5.

43 *Hitanjutsukai Wasan*, (Wherein with Lamentation I make my Confession) v. 4.

44 *Tannishō*, 3. Cf. "While to propose to be a better man is a piece of un-scientific cant, to have become a deeper man is the priviledge of those who have suffered. And such I think I have become." (Oscar WILDE: *De Profundis*.)

45 *Tannishō*, 5. Tr. by FUJIWARA, p. 26.

46 *Tannishō*, Epilog III, tr. by FUJIWARA, p. 79.

47 *Tannishō*, VI, tr. by FUJIWARA, p. 28.

48 *The Life of Hōnen*, vol. 28.

49 *Mattōshō*, 12th Letter.

50 *Ibid.*, 11th Letter.

51 In India, the Tengalais, adopted the dangerous doctrine of dosabhogya, i.e. that God enjoys sin, since it gives a larger scope.

52 *Thanksgiving for Donran:* YAMABE, etc., p. 49.

53 *Goichidaiki Kikigaki.*

54 *Hitan Jutsukai Wasan* (Wherein with Lamentation I Make any Confession).

55 Wherein with Lamentation I make my Confession, YAMABE and BECK: Buddhist Psalms, p. 87.

56 Shintō Gobusho (神道五部書). Kokushi Taikei, vol. VII, p. 457. *Genchi Katō*. A Study of Shinto. Tokyo, Meiji-Seitoku-Kinen Gakkai, 1926, p. 161.

57 Wherein with Lamentation I make my Confession.

58 Wherein with Lamentation I make my Confession.

59 *Shōbō Genzō Zuimonki*, III, 9. Even nowadays the need to rely on the Buddha since man on his own is weak is stressed by Zen priests also. (H. DUMOULIN has collected its instances in *Studies in Japanese Culture*. Tradition and Experiment, edited by Joseph ROGGENDORF, Tokyo: Sophia University, 2nd ed., 1965, p. 31 ff.)

60 Already in the Tokugawa period SUZUKI Shosan advocated 'non-clergy Buddhism', but he found no flower.

71 According to the comments by Mrs. Ruth SASAKI who has stayed in Japan, the Zen monasteries in present-day Japan are not monasteries in the Catholic or Western sense of the word. They are primarily what might be called "Theological seminaries, to which students come to engage in Zen study and practice under the direction of a Zen master". After two or three years, the majority of these monks will be ordained as priests and go to their own temples. Only a few of the more serious stay for many years necessary to complete their Zen practice.

In China, in olden times at least, it would seem that a Zen student was free to go to a Zen master for a time, remain perhaps several years, then go on to another master, and later to still another. In the end, the student seems to have been considered the disciple or heir, as the case may be, of the teacher under whom he completed his attainment. Such freedom as this does not exist in Japanese Zen today. Once a student is accepted as a disciple by a Zen master, he remains that master's disciple until the relationship is terminated by the death of one or the other, or by some unusual circumstance.

72 'Kung-an' in Chinese. It literally means 'official document'.

73 Hsuan-chiao, *Cheng-tao Ke* 34. In SUZUKI: *Manual of Zen*, p. 115.

74 Reiho MASUNAGA in *The Path of the Buddha*, ed. by MORGAN, pp. 341–342.

75 Prof. Charles MORRIS explains as follows: As an example of the language of paradox

and contradiction Dr. Suzuki gives the following Zen utterance, an esteemed gatha from the sixth century by Shan-hui: Empty-handed I go, and behold the spade is in my hands: I walk on foot, and yet on the back of an ox I am riding; When I pass over the bridge Lo, the water floweth not, but the bridge doth flow. (*Introduction to Zen Buddhism*) "To be sure, no one of them taken singly need have this quality: to imagine oneself on the moon looking down upon oneself on the earth may be interesting, but it is hardly mystical. Suppose, however, that the interpretants of these various symbolic processes are aroused simultaneously or nearly simultaneously. If the interpretants of signs are (or involve) neutral processes, then there is no reason why they interpretants of contradictory signs cannot be aroused simultaneously, though the corresponding reactions could not simultaneously be performed. In this way, one can be symbolically both here and not here, in the past and in the future, can be both the fish that swims and the gull that dives. It is suggested that this simultaneous, or nearly simultaneous, arousal of the complex and often contradictory role-taking processes made possible by language constitutes an essential part of the mystical experience." "Having undergone the process of symbolic identification with everything available to him, a person is a changed person; symbolically he is no longer merely one object among objects. As one object existing among other object she is small and fragile, empty-handed, on foot, walking on a bridge. But having roamed afield symbolically, he rides the cosmic ox, and digs with the cosmic spade; and as the water, he sees the flowing bridge. The commonest things are henceforth perceived at both the old and the new levels; a space is still a spade, water is water, and a bridge a bridge; and yet they are more than they were, for they now are seen through symbolic eyes enlarged by cosmic wandering. The experience is liberating. (Charles Morris, Comments on Mysticism and its Language. *ETC. A Review of General Semantics*, Autumn 1951, Vol. IX, No. 1) In this connection we are reminded of a comment by Emerson, who said: "These roses under my window make no reference to former roses or to better ones; they are for what they are; they exist with God today. There is no time to them. There is simply the rose; it is perfect in every moment of its existence.—But man postpones or remembers; he does not live in the present, but with reverted eye laments the past, or, heedless of the riches that surround him, stands on tiptoe to foresee the future. He cannot be happy and strong until he too lives with nature in the present, above time. (Essays, First Series "Self-Reliance")

76 *Shōbōgenzōk* chapter: *Bendōwa*, in *Tamamuro: Dōgen Zenji Zenshū*, p. 17.

77 *Ibid.*, p. 20.

78 'You should not try to become a Buddha.' This attitude was emphasized by Keizan also in his *Zazen Yōjin-ki* (坐禅用心記).

79 *Shōbōgenzō*, chapter: *Bendōwa*, in *Tamamuro: op. cit.*

80 直指人心

81 見性成佛

82 教外別傳

83 *Shōbōgenzō*, section "*Bendōwa*".

84 *Fukan Zazengi.*

85 *Shōbōgenzō*, section "*Zammai Ō-zammai*".

86 Zen speaks of "an effortless, purposeless, useless man".

87 *Keitoku Dentōroku*, Bk. VI: Words of Po-chang. Cf. Dumoulin: DCZ., p. 63.

88 *Mumonkan.*

89 *Shōbōgenzō*, section: Shōji.

90 衆生本来佛なり (Hymn by HAKUIN).

91 *Mumonkan*, 7.

92 *Mumonkan*.

93 *Shōbōgenzō, Uji* (*Dōgen Zenji Zenshū*, pp. 62–65).

94 *Shōbōgenzō, Shōji* (*Dōgen Zenji Zenshū*, p. 440).

95 *Shōbōgenzō, Bendōwa* (*Dōgen Zenji Zenshū*, pp. 21 f.).

96 This dialectic was minutely discussed by Alfonso VERDÚ, *Monumenta Nipponica*, vol. 21, Nos. 1–2, 1966, 125–170.

97 Yōkyoku 謡曲 Taisha 大社.

98 In the modern period Senge-Takasumi (千家尊澄), the priest of the Shintoism of the Great Shrine of Izumo with such a pantheistic point of view, praised as follows: "There is not a direction in which a god does not reside, even in the wild waves' eight hundred folds or in the wild mountain's besom. *Fūkyō Hyakushu Kōsetsu* 風教百首講説 (Genchi KATŌ: 加藤玄智: *Shintō no Shūkyō Hattatsushiteki Kenkyū* 神道の宗教発達史的研究 p. 935).

99 大乗起信論.

100 Cf. 摩訶止観 Vol. I. pt. I. (Taisho. Vol. 46, p. 1c). MAEDA Eun 前田慧雲: *Tetsugakukan Kōgiroku* 哲学館講義録 (Shigaku Zasshi 史学雑誌, 1923, pp. 373–374).

101 壽量品.

103 Kaimokushō 開目抄 pt. 2.

103 See 羅什訳 [中論] ch. 18, 7th gāthā: *Saddharma-pundarika-sūtra* (ed. by OGIWARA Unrai), p. 251, I. 25.; *Astasāhasrikā* (ed. by OGIWARA Unrai), p. 51, I. 15.; p. 572, II. 2–3; p. 666, I. 7; etc.

104 *Shōbōgenzō* 正法眼藏 *Shohōjissō* 諸法実相.

105 See 法華玄義 Vol. VIII, pt. 2. (Taishō Vol. 33, p. 783b).

106 *Gleanings from Sōtō-Zen*, ed. Ernest Shinkaku HUNT (Honolulu Sōtō Mission, 1950), p. 25.

107 *Profound Doctrine of the Lotus Sūtra*, VIII, pt. 2 (Taishō Tripitaka, vol. XXXIII, 783b).

108 *Shōbōgenzō*, Shōji 生死 (section on Life and Death, Taishō Tripitaka, vol. LXXXII, p. 305).

109 Ibid. Busshō 仏性 (section on Buddha-nature, Taishō Tripitaka, vol. LXXXII, p. 93a).

110 *Sanshō Dōei* (Religious Poems of Umbrella-Like Pine Tree).

111. *Shasekishū*, X, pt. I.

112 This Sentence was composed in China based upon such sentences as "In the milk, there is cream; in sentient beings there is Buddha-nature." (乳中有酪, 衆生仏生又復如是, 欲見仏性, 応当観察時節形色.) and "If you have desire to seek, you will find." (以諸功徳因縁和合得見仏生, 然役得仏) in 大般涅槃経 (Mahāparinirvāna-sūtra) vol. XXVII (Taishō vol. 12, p. 532a & p. 533b).

113 Literally, "survey of seasons and conditions".

114 *Shōbōgenzō*, Busshō 仏性.

115 *Shōbōgenzō*, Uji 有時.

116 Ibid.

117 *Shōbōgenzō*, Setsushin Setsushō.

118 Ibid. Hossō.

119 Ibid. Setsushin Setsushō.

120 *Shōbōgenzō Zuimonki*, vol. 2, No. 14.

121 According to my personal observation made during my trips abroad, it seems that

the Japanese are the people who are particularly fond of history or historiography, compared with other peoples. Books of history are published very often. Common people at large like to read histories.

122 Hanazono Tennō: *Taishi wo Imashimuru no Sho* (誡太子書 Admonition to Crown Princes), translated into German by Hermann BOHNER, *Monumenta Nipponica,* vol. 1, pt. 2, 1938, 25–57.

123 ANESAKI Masaharu: *Nichiren the Buddhist Prophet* (Cambridge: Harvard University Press, 1916), p. 119.

124 In the *Sado Gosho* (佐渡御書), in Shōwa Shinshū Nichiren Shōnin Imon Zenshū (昭和新修日蓮聖人遺文全集 Kyoto: Heirakuji Shoten, 1934), vol. I, p. 842.

125 *Kojiki,* chapter 1.

126 *Jinnō-Shōtō-ki* 神皇正統記.

127 *Shutsujō-shōgo* 出定笑語.

128 *Introduction to Genkōshakusho* 元享釈書.

CHAPTER IV

CONTROVERSY BETWEEN BUDDHISM
AND CHRISTIANITY
The Period of Contact with the West

1. The Encounter of Jodo Buddhism and Christianity—A Case Study
of BANZUI'I Shonin Byakudo (1542–1615)

The Problem

The similarity of religious experience in the Jodo Sect and in Christianity[1] is often referred to from the view point of the psychology of religion. The difference between them, however, ought to be equally considered, as there must be a basic difference between their respective philosophies, since the Jodo Sect is in the last analysis Buddhist and has a different standpoint than Christianity. Therefore, the issue of the confrontation between Christianity and the Jodo Sect at the time of Christianity's first introduction to Japan is undoubtedly a most stimulating research topic for a student of the history of ideas. I hope to be able to suggest a clue as to the clarification of basic differences between Christianity and Buddhism.

There have appeared several distinguished works on the confrontation of the Jodo Sect and Christianity,(and I wish to consider particularly the Jodo Sect's anti-Christian activities prior to Japan's Seclusion (1635). Though a considerable number of priests of Jodo Sect may have positively acted against Christianity, their activities and philosophies are little known.[2] (Better known critics of Christian thought are mostly Zen monks.) The present article will concentrate on the anti-Christian activities of BANZUI'I Shonin Byakudo (1542–1615). We will consider the manner in which Banzui'i preached Buddhism, the grounds he selected in order to convert Christians to Buddhism, and the points at which his arguments collided with Christian contentions.

Banzui'i was an eminent priest of the Jodo Sect. He called himself Byakudo, and used the pen-name of Enrensha Chiyo Kyo'a.[3] He was born on October 15, 1542 (1560 according to a different opinion) at Fujisawa in the province of Sagami (at Nagusagun in the province of Ki'i according to a different opinion). He left home and joined a Buddhist order at the age of eleven, studied strenuously, and became known for his learning and virtues. He was appointed the thirty-third abbot of Chion-ji Temple in Kyoto in 1601 when he was sixty years old. On occasion he was invited by Emperor Goyozei (1571–1617) to lecture at the Imperial Court.[4]

In 1603 (possibly 1604), Banzui'i accepted an invitation from Tokugawa Ieyasu to come to Edo. He built "Shin Chion-ji Banzui'in" Temple at Kanda-dai, Edo, and made it a national prayer house for the protection of the Shogunate. Later, he went to Shimabara and Nagasaki in Kyushu in order to instruct Christians for conversion to Buddhism at the request of Ieyasu. After three years of missionary activities in Kyushu, he moved to Wakayama and lived at Mansho-ji Temple, which he built there for a retreat center. He died on January 5, 1615 (or 1624) at the age of seventy-four. He had built many temples in various provinces during his life.

No book of Banzui'i's own authorship remains, but several biographies in wood block printing are available for us.

(1) Gendo (alias Myodo). *Banzui'i Shonin Gyojyo*. Vol. 1.[5]
(Life and Activities of the Venerable Banzui'i)

The author counts himself a spiritual descendant of Banzui'i, seven generations removed. He lived at Shunan-zan Temple at Ueno, Edo. This book was published with a commendation by Chumoku of Zojyo-ji Temple, i.e. headquarters of the Jodo Sect, with the author's introduction (dated 1743), and with an epilogue by the author and another by Ninkai of Zojyo-ji Temple (dated 1746). The volume was written in Chinese (kambun) with Japanese reading signs (ka'eriten, okurigana).

(2) Kanyo. *Banzui'i Shonin Shokoku Gyoge Den*, 5 Vols.[6]

(Stories of the Venerable Banzui'i's Missionary Activities in Various Provinces)

The author was resident-minister of Gogo-in Temple in northern Kyoto. This book was published with an introduction (dated 1753) by Muso Monno, a famous scholar-priest of the Jodo Sect. It is written in Japanese, with a comparatively large proportion of Chinese words.

(3) Saiyo. *Banzui'i Shonin Den,* 2 Vols.[7]

(Biography of the Venerable Banzui'i)

The author was resident-minister of Kanda-san Banzui'in Temple. This book was published with an introduction (dated 1862) by Kyo'in, chief abbot of Zojyo-ji Temple. Kyo'in's introduction comments on the two books cited above: "They are difficult for children and the poorly educated to read because they are written with so many Chinese words." It states also that the present volume was published in commemoration of the two-hundred and fiftieth anniversary of the venerable Banzui'i, and that it was written for people in general, selecting major points from the preceding two books and adding illustrations.

The discussion that follows will examine problematic issues from the point of view of the history of ideas, using the three biographical stories cited above as our sources. W do not know how true these stories are to historical fact. They may well include exaggerations. And yet the fact that these stories, even if they did stretch the truth, were believed to be the truth is fully as important as the historical facts themselves for a student inquiring into the history of ideas.

Banzui'i's Anti-Christian Activities

In 1613 it was reported to the Shogunate government that Christians were causing troubles in Kyushu. When the cabinet discussed the problem, an elder minister declared:

The rebels believe in a pagan religion of barbarian origin, ignoring our traditional belief in Buddhism and Shinto. Therefore, we must order our eminent priest to preach the truthful teaching, and correct the misguided beliefs of the ignorant men and women. On their learning true causes and effects, they will be led to abandon Christianity's vicious teachings that make them fear suffering here and in Hell. Breaking of their united group is the problem of the primary importance. Punishment of the leaders may be done at any moment after that.[8]

The contemporary rulers, thus, were already aware that the problems caused by *faith must be met with countermeasures in the dimension of faith.* Thereupon, the ministers unanimously agreed that Banzui'i was the most adept for that mission. At this time Banzui'i was seventy-two years old.

The Shogunate invited Banzui'i and "ordered" him to the task. Thereupon Banzui'i willingly "accepted" the order.

I do not mind going to all that trouble, if it is for the sake of propagating Buddhist teaching. I will depart immediately, and instruct them aright.

Stories reports him to have said:

The devoted practice of Buddhist teaching depends solely on the orderliness of the state. If the state should be hurt even a little, the hurt turns back upon us manyfold. The present question is not a light question. Even without an order, I would gladly have requested permission to go myself.

According to the description of *Bigraphy,* he answered:

Propagation of Buddhist teaching in a state owes much to the rule of the king. An injury to the state, therefore, is identical with a disaster to Buddhist religion.

The thesis that the peace maintained by the state was s prerequisite for the prosperity of Buddhist practice was never known in India, but it was most strongly emphasized by all the Buddhist sects in Japan. Banzui'i's thought ran in exactly the latter line.

Thereupon, Ieyasu was "most pleased," and handed Banzui'i in person a war-vest made of Chinese brocade and a truncheon fan made of gold, saying:

In spite of the difference between the Buddhist and secular rules, the confrontation of your eminence against the vicious pagans in the same as the generals facing an enemy with their embattled forces. Hereby I present to you this war-vest and truncheon fan in token of my good wishes to you. With this truncheon fan, do you raise up Buddhist morale, discourage vicious circles, and bring them back to the right path. With this war-vest, do you make a robe of your order, show your great dignity, and admonish all vicious enemies of Buddhism.

(It is said that these war-vest and trunchon fan were kept by Banzui'i and his successors for a long time.)

Ieyasu, then, ordered the Daimyo Arima Tadasumi to guard Banzui'i, according to the same record.

Tradition has it that Banzui'i thought, as he departed:

The nation is filled with vicious pagans. Without the help of our native gods, I would be in difficulty. I will visit the Grand Shrine of Ise to begin with, and pray for the help of the native gods in controlling vicious pagans.

Thereupon he set off two months before the departure of the feudal leader ordered to protect him, Arima Tadasumi. Even with his heavy responsibilities, Banzui'i was alone with but one attendant, and carried his clothes and food himself when he departed. At the Grand Shrine of Ise, a record reports, Banzui'i prayed for seven days for "the victory of Buddhism," and on the final day of his prayer, he was given a statue of Amitabha by the great godess who appeared from the inner sanctuary of the shrine. (The author of *Gyoge Den* (Stories) wrote a detailed argumentation to the effect that Amaterasu, the godess of the Grand Shrine of Ise, was an incarnation of Amitabha.) Banzui'i and Tadasumi met at Osaka, and got on board a ship bound for the province of Hizen.

On arrival in Hizen, Banzui'i settled at Sampuku-ji Temple. He installed the statue of "Amitabha incarnated in the great godess Amaterasu" which he was given at the Grand Shrine of Ise, and started a spcial ascetic exercise lasting forty-eight nights, at the same time giving sermons on rebirth through repeated recitation of the name of Amitabha.[9] In the beginning, however, there were "none who came and joined in the hearing of his sermons" because, according to the reportee, "vicious paganism covered the whole province." But Banzui'i kept preaching every day with perseverance. Ten days later, one single old man came to listen to him, and another joined the next day. Thereafter "the audience increased day after day." According to one report, when he delivered sermons, he held the trunchon fan in his hand and wore a robe made of the war-vest given him by Ieyasu.

As one method of instruction, Banzui'i took advantage of the fear and bad conscience of the wicked men and women among the Christians. For example, the following story is recorded. There was a widow who was a Christian. Her husband also was a Christian. This woman was of "a dissolute and vicious character, and was ignorant of the way of human beings." She had a daughter, for whom she adopted a husband. This man, who was made the successor of the family, happened to be a handsome and tender man. The mother began to love her son-in-law, and in order to marry the man herself she killed her daughter. The woman suffered from pangs of conscience, and attempted to "save herself by performing ceremonies to *Deus*." But this was not effective, and the pains increased. She wept and cried for help. She finally realized that "her prayers to *Deus* brought her more pain," and she visited Banzui'i and besought him for "the profound grace of Buddha." Hereupon, the body of the daughter was dug out and duly cremated with a Buddhist ceremony, but the wooden tablet on which Banzui'i wrote the name of Amitabha remained unburnt.

Following is the comment of the author of *Stories*.

Verily the exquisite reality of the good is embodied in six characters to mean the venerable Amitabha, and as many merits as the number of the sands of the Ganges are provided for the practice of oral recitation of the name. Truly the reality and the name are inseparable. Such is the product of the merit of Buddha's infinite meditation, great vow, and strenuous exercise. This is called the path of salvation depending solely on the power of the other. Look up to it, and have faith in it. (Vol. 5., p. 6.)

After all, the philosophical basis of instruction at that period did not develop further than such a level.

Banzui'i had occasion to conduct an open debate against a man called Hammu, a leader of the Christians. This man was perhaps a missionary from abroad. It happened that this man challenged Banzui'i out of disappointment that increasing numbers were following Banzui'i, which made him jealous of him. On the day of the debate, "clergy and laymen, nobles and masses, crowded the temple like a cloud," according to the reporter. On this occasion, Hammu said:

What is the being called Amitabha in your sect? It is nothing but a king of beasts and animals. Therefore, those who believe in this teaching fall into animal life, and never creep up therefrom, no matter how many years should pass. You, Banzui'i, already have a beastly body.

If you doubt it, I am ready to prove it with our exquisite technique. Upon making the above statement, Hammu brought out a mirror and placed it in the sight of the audience. The moment Banzui'i's "figure was reflected, it immediately changed and became the figure of an ox." The audience was struck with wonder. Hammu arrogantly pressed the point and said:

Look at this! Surely this is a miracle due to the power of the religion that we venerate.

Meanwhile, Banzui'i laughed contemptuously and said:

You have shown an ugly figure in the mirror with your vicious trick. This in itself is a radical contradiction of the proper line of reasoning. What you have done is viciously magical. A mirror, by nature, is honest, and in its action, it does not reflect falsehood. Honesty is the way of our divine nation. Thus, a mirror is placed at the sanctuary of shrines as the symbol of gods. Man's mind becomes pure and clear to face it by virtue of its purity and cleanliness. A mirror represents the virtue of uprightness, and drives out falsity and wickedness. The ways of native gods and Buddha are identical in that vicious deception is strictly excluded, and that the divine beings and the human are to follow the same path. Thanks to its honest and clear nature, the mirror reflects long and short, square and round, good and evil, righteous and vicious as they really are. Buddhas and gods are not biased by self-interest. Right man and right law follow the same line.

That which does not reflect as things are is wrong. Now your mirror
is one that shows an untrue and disfigured image in reflecting a man.
This proves that it is false and contrary to the right law. Such is definitely against the nature of the mirror. The ignorant may be struck
with such, and misapprehend the truth. Thus they suffer the misfortunes invited by their belief in such falsehood. It is as if one were to
suffer from afflictions brought on by the deceptive tricks of foxes and
badgers. It is not I who shall ever be cheated. I know that this way is
absolutely wrong. It is not a truthful mirror to reflect a square as a
circle, or a circle as square! Falsehood is the very basis of vicious
teachings. Here is a vicious mirror of a vicious trick. This vicious
mirror is a means of cheating and misleading the innocent men of
world. Repent, and return to the rightful way, otherwise misfortunes
are close and your corruption not far. Beware, and walk carefully.

We should pay attention to the fact that the word and concept "honesty
(正直)" was used by Banzui'i according to a Shinto interpretation of the
word, though it originally came from Buddhist terminology. On hearing the discussion of Banzui'i, Hammu and his followers were unable to
return a word. They were totally defeated in reasoning. Then, the story
says, the statue of "Amitabha given to Banzui'i by the great goddess of
Ise" sent a great ray of light from the white curl of hair on her forehead,
and the mirror of vicious magic, hit by the ray, was burnt like coals and
crushed like tiles.

For a Christian to call Amitabha "king of the beasts and animals" indicates an intrinsic difference between the Christian and Buddhist conceptions of salvation, though this may sound unfamiliar to the reader.
Amitabha, the savior of the Pure Land Buddhism, saves not merely human beings, but also all living beings, whereas the Christian God saves
only human beings. This difference is essential. Christians did not understand the Buddhist concept of saving all "living beings," and felt it even
curious.

This is easy to understand in view of the fact that the *Chinese could not
accept the Buddhist concept of "all living beings"* during the early periods
of Chinese Buddhism. According to Sukhavati-vyuha, the third of

Dharmakara's Forty-Eight Vows translated from the original Sanskrit text is as follows:

O Bhagavat, if in that Buddha country of mine the *beings* (sattvāh) who are born there should not all be of one colour, namely a golden color, then may I not obtain the highest perfect knowledge.[10]

But a Chinese translation of this same text during the Later Han period by Lokaraksa of Tokharestan reads:

If all the *people* (人民) who are born in this land should unanimously obtain the color of gold, then I will become Buddha. Otherwise I will not become Buddha.

This translation amends "beings" to "people" as those who are to be saved. "Living beings" (Sattvah) in the original is translated in a Wei translation as "Man and demon" (人天), in a T'ang translation as "Spiritual beings" (有情), and in a Sung translation quite deliberately as "All the living beings, and the beings travelling the devilish world, and devas, beasts and animals, whoever receive our benefit, and whoever are instructed by my teaching." (所有一切衆生, 及焰摩羅界 三惡道中 地獄餓鬼畜生, 皆生我利, 受我法化) Originally the intention of the vow included all living beings, not merely human beings, in the goal of salvation, but Lokaraksa of the Later Han period amended it to the effect that only human beings were intended in the original vow. (Sharmakara's other vows were given the same change in the translation.) He must have amended the concept to make it harmonize with the humaniztic Confucian philosophy, because the saving of non-human living beings was an alien concept to the Chinese of that time. Otherwise, the Buddhist concept of salvation, he must have thought, could not be understood by the Chinese who were unfamiliar with Buddhist concepts. Only after Buddhist thought came to prevail in later times did it become possible for the translators to bring in the original content of "all living beings."

In view of such situations, it may be understandable that Christian missionaries from the West found the Jodo Buddhist view of salvation strikingly unusual.

Subsequently Hammu converted to Buddhism, and "millions followed him to learn the teaching of Jodo Buddhism, and some thirty of them were so radically pleased to know the true teaching that they voluntarily cast their lives away." (p. 9.) This description proves that at least in this case, Jodo Buddhism still possessed a futuristic and escapist character.

Banzui'i gave the following sermon:

What a pity it is that some have joined in the heresy. Even capital punishment does not pay for their fault sufficiently. They are awaited by thousands of punishments even after death. What a fearful thing it is! On the contrary, any one who observes our teaching well assumes benefits in the next life, and there is no doubt about that. Although rewards in worldly matters are not what we are really concerned with, they will automatically come to you. None of these benefits may be enjoyed by those who are punished in this life and in the next life. Ponder carefully the advantages and disadvantages and do not be too slow in amending your faith.[11]

The people of that area welcomed Banzui'i's instruction and said:

We, the people of this province, should have received capital punishment and fallen into Hell, if we had continued to believe in that vicious paganism, thereby violating the law of the state. If we had not received the instruction of the venerable Banzui'i, we should be dead by now. Without life, we would break the line of posterity. This venerable teacher is the god of our rebirth.

They cried out of reverence for Banzui'i. It is reported that at the time when *Stories* was written during the Horeki period (1751–1764), Banzui'i was enshrined in the local shrine together with the god of fecundity.

Banzui'i's missionary activity was so successful that:

the old and the young alike filled the hall as if it had been a market place, and thereby the left path, that is, the corrupt religion of Christianity, disappeared from the province.[12]

The Daimyo Arima Tadasumi, then, built Kansan-ji Temple, in accordance with an order he received from the Shogunate on his departure from Edo. Tadasumi appointed Banzui'i as the founder of the temple, donated to it property consisting of fields and one-hundred farm families, installed there the statue of Amitabha which Banzui'i received from the

Grand Shrine of Ise as the main symbol for worship, and named the temple as Manji-san Kansan-ji. This description reveals the fact that the fact that the construction of the temple was a fulfilment of the sovereign ruler's "order," and not a product of the religious faith of the people.

Thereupon Banzui'i moved to Nagasaki to convert the Christians of that area to Buddhism. Because the power of Christianity was strong at Nagasaki, he had to face many difficulties. He was hated as a vengeful enemy, and plots to assassinate him were even made. His conviction, however, was resolute:

> Native gods have afforded their virtues to me, so vicious heretics shall not be able to hurt me. I will go and fight even if there should be millions of enemies.[13]

In about this time, one of his disciples, Daitsu, came from Edo and helped Banzui'i. According to one report, it was Banzui'i who persuaded the governor of Nagasaki to adopt a certain practice through which non-Christians could identify themselves. It was he who invented *Fumie,* or the test of identifying Christians by having people step on a tablet that bore a representation of the crucifixion.

The following story is reported as an episode concerning the instructions he gave during his Nagasaki years. In Nagasaki, there was a Christian by the name of Sakuma Sanryu, who was a physician.[14] His wife disliked Christianity, and their difference of religious beliefs resulted in his becoming hostile to his wife. He kept a mistress, and murdered his wife in the end. Thereupon he was haunted by the spirit of his legal and wronged wife. One day, Banzui'i, carrying a begging bowl, stopped at Sanryu's house during his mendicant itineration, but Sanryu shouted imprecations at him. Thereupon, Banzui'i spread ashes from an oven on the ground and told Sanryu to walk on them. Sanryu being bewildered, Banzui'i said:

> You may think that nobody knows about the murder of your wife. But I know it well. Now, you walk on the ashes here!

Sanryu was surprised, and walked on the ashes as he was told. Banzui'i pointed at the ashes on the ground and said:

> Look here. There is no foot print of yours on the ashes. . . . Learn

that you have lost your feet already, because your spirit has fallen in Hell long ago.

Sanryu thereupon realized his fault and cut his hair off in token of repentence. Banzui'i gave him the Three Commandments (a symbol of initiation) and made him his disciple. Thereafter Sanryu recited "Praise to Amitabha Buddha" devotedly and died a happy death, according to the same story. Banzui'i delivered the following speech to the people of that area:

> You were born in a far corner of the land and missed the opportunity of learning the true teaching of Buddha, thus becoming adversaries of Buddhism by believing in a vicious paganism. This was a retribution that fell to you because of your behavior in previous life. In the present life you shall be punished by the government, and in the next life you shall not fail to fall into Hell. Repent immediately and learn the true law. You shall believe and practice the Buddhist religion that teaches dependence on the power of the Other.

Sermons of this kind led the people to convert from Christianity to Buddhism of Amitabha. It is reported that Banzui'i exercised an enormous influence during his stay in the area for three years.

Banzui'i built Buddhist temples at the sites from which Christian churches had been removed in Nagasaki. Their sectarian affiliation included the Jodo Sect, the Ikko Sect, the Soto Zen Sect, and the Hokke Sect.[15] The Jodo Sect had an advantage in projecting its influence partly because it was the religion of the Tokugawas' since that family's first beginnings, and partly because it was coordinated with the policy of prohibition of Christianity. According to the statistics of Buddhist temples and followers during the Tokugawa period, the Jodo Sect was always the leader.[16]

Later on, Banzui'i founded Shin-Chion-ji Temple at Kanda in Edo. This temple was moved to Shitaya, and today it is famous as Banzui'in Temple.[17]

He spent his later years at Wakayama and died there in 1615.

Upon his death, he said in verse:

> Byakudo pursued his course for scores of years,

Extinguishing fire with fire, a difficult task indeed.[18]
We feel in these lines Banzui'i's emotional commitment to the instruction of Christians.

Characteristics of the Encounter

The preceding discussion has been formulated on the basis of literature written by Buddhists of later times with the intention of praising and propagating the merits of Banzui'i. That is to say, our sources are records written from the point of view of the Buddhist. Nonetheless, we see little hint of religious motivation in his activities. It was the secular power that was the primary issue.

To begin with, we should pay special attention to the fact that the position and the power of the political leaders of the state were far more powerful than those of the religious bodies. Banzui'i was one of the most authoritative men in the Buddhist world of the day, as may be seen from the fact that he became the abbot of Chion-ji Temple, one of the four headquarters of the Jodo Sect. And yet he was completely subject to the Tokugawa Shogunate. An illustration in his *Biography* shows Banzui'i receiving the truncheon fan and war-vest from Ieyasu. In this picture Banzui'i is seated on a lower level, and prostrates himself before Ieyasu. (Scenes of this sort can never be expected in South Asia today or in Medieval Europe.)

In addition Banzui'i was receiving the protection and assistance of Arima Tadasumi, the lord of the province, during the period that the forementioned activities were being carried on. In a word, Banzui'i was under the patronage of the feudal authority. In view of these circumstances, we may conclude that this activities had the backing of the feudal ruling forces.

Further, to hold a truncheon fan in his hand and to wear a robe made of a war-vest while preaching is quite contrary to Buddhist customs elsewhere. Buddhists of ancient India tried to eliminate every association with war, so they even forbade conversations on war. Perhaps we must say that this mode of Japanese Buddhism is a deformed deviation from

Buddhist tradition in general, stemming from its close link with the authority of the state.

His thought, which was supported by the feudal forces, was necessarily related to the ethnic religion. Not only do Shinto ideas frequently appear in his discussions, he basically recognized the *authority of Shinto*.

Moreover, Banzui'i's activities were carried on quite apart from any Buddhist sectarian body. His activities had no relation at all to the sectarian organizations of Buddhism. No sectarian body positively organized missionary bodies to be sent to give instruction to Christians. Nor did the sectarian bodies display any intention of giving him assistance or guidance. He set off alone, accompanied by but one attendant, and even in later times, he was joined by only one of his disciples, Daitsu. The sectarian organizations of Buddhism remained by-standers. None dared to assist the activities of seventy-year old Banzui'i, who single-handedly went into enemy territory. In the biographies cited above we can find no evidence of assistance from local temples to Banzui'i. It is frequently stated that schism and rivalry among the Buddhist sects in Japan eased the propagation of Christianity, but the fact was, I would argue, that Buddhists in general *lacked the zeal to confront Christianity positively* on the strength of their own ideas.[19]

Buddhists themselves recognized this as a fact.

It is entirely due to the meritorious works of the Venerable Banzui'i that the people of Kyushu were made immune to the poisons of vicious paganism, that they are obedient to the authorities, and that the true law of Buddhism has been recovered for the past two hundred years. (*Biography*)

The writer of the above ascribed all anti-Christian activities to Banzui'i, which, of course, was an exaggeration. Suzuki Shosan, for example, went to Northern Kyushu area soon after the Shimabara Rebellion (1637–1638) and endeavored to convert Christians to Buddhism. There were also a few other Buddhist priests living in that area who tried to convert Christians to Buddhism.[20] And yet the number of Buddhists who volunteered for missionary work always remained extremely small. (The Tendai Sect also received assistance from the Tokugawa Shogunate, but it made no effort to offer doctrinal education to the people in general.)

It must be said, however, that the efforts of so few Buddhist volunteers can not have brought about a total reorientation of many Christians. It was the *power* of the ruler, or the *reign of terror,* that resulted in the annihilation of Christianity. The character of Banzui'i's sermons and instructions was also *defined* by this background. Banzui'i pointedly emphasized the fearful persecution and rigorous punishment of Christians in the present life and the infernal suffering in the next life. We do not know if all the sermons he delivered were really of the kind that are recorded in the biographies, but it is quite certain that the leaders of the Jodo Sect in later years appreciated the kind of activities described above as Banzui'i's most important contribution.

What is more important is that the facts described above received official recognition from the authorities of the Jodo Sect. Banzui'i's biographies were published with introductory statements by the priests occupying high offices at the headquarters of the Jodo Sect and by the sect's authentic academicians. This meant official recognition of the content of these books by the authorities of the sect. The leaders of the sect *desired to spread this information among the general public.* In other words, the authorities of the sect officially admitted as matters of established fact that the sectarian bodies were subject to the feudal powers, that they were negligent in confronting Christianity positively, and that they neglected the propagation of Buddhism.

This may be an indication of the fact that the confrontation between the Jodo Sect and Christianity remained consistently a *confrontation of the political powers* rather than a confrontation between different ways of thinking. It is also indicated from this that the prohibition of Christianity was a political issue rather than a religious question. Regarding this question, therefore, the following two points were of crucial importance.

First, in contemporary Japan, the traditional bondage of the master-and-servant relationship was stronger than the unifying power of a common religion. This characteristic is clearly recognizable in viewing religious rebellions. As Christianity had a tendency to undermine tradition, it could hardly succeed in regions where the traditional prestige of the military rulers was solidly maintained. Accordingly, the Christians sought connections with power holders. The contradiction between Christianity and ancestral worship was also felt to be a problem.

Second, the penetration of Christianity had a political character in many instances. The Westerners had usurped other's lands and slaughtered the peoples of underdeveloped regions *in the name of God*. So it was suspected with good reason that Christians might in the end plunder the nation of Japan. In consequence the attacks against Christianity, including those by Buddhists, concentrated on revealing the political conspiracies of Christians, without serious consideration of the doctrinal aspects of the confrontation.

Such having been the case, Jodo Buddhism, in its opposition to Christianity, practically neglected doctrinal matters. Banzui'i, for example, never wrote a book. He did not experience the deepening of his thought through contact with the system of another religion. His slighting of the doctrinal aspect of Buddhism is remarkable.[21] To point out incidental shortcomings of

My original plan of finding a clue for understanding the basic differences between Christian and Buddhist thought through examining the thought of the Venerable Banzui'i Byakudo in his confrontation against Christianity has thus turned out a complete failure. And yet we may conclude that the historical and ideological characteristics we have described above apply to Japanese Buddhism through the later Tokugawa period and into the present age.

2. Suzuki Shosan's Criticism of Christianity

The Problem

Theoretical considerations of Christianity were rarely attempted by Buddhists during the time that Christianity grew and expanded during the Sengoku and early Tokugawa periods (1549–c.1640).[22] Most Buddhist thinkers, without deep reflection, defined Christianity as "magical" and "misleading" teaching. However, Suzuki Shosan (鈴木正三, 1579–

1655) was one who recognized the philosophical importance of Christianity and who wrote two articles entitled *Questions and Answers about the Christian God*[23] and *Refutation of Christianity*.[24] Shosan explained the Christian doctrine as follows:

> Christianity venerates a big Buddha by the name of *Deus,* who is the Lord of Heaven and Earth, is absolutely free, and is the Creator of everything in Heaven and on Earth. This Buddha made his appearance in the land of the Southern Barbarians one thousand and six hundred years ago, and gave relief to the people there. The name of this Buddha in personal form is Jesus Christ. Christians claim that those who do not know this teaching and who worship worthless Buddhas such as Amitabha or Gautama are most foolish.[25]

Here, Christian teaching is described in terms of Buddhist terminology, rather neatly communicating its essence. Special attention is called to Shosan's understanding of the Christian God as a free being, particularly when one remembers that in the history of ideas, the concept of freedom in Western ethical thought is derived from the prototype of a free God concept. The difference between the concept of freedom in Christianity and in Shosan's thought will be clarified by reference to chapter three of the present volume.

After defining the essence of Christianity, Shosan attacked the Christian doctrine. His attacks may be broken down roughly into two types. One type resembles the kind of criticism made by modern Western philosophers and thinkers. The other is the kind stemming from the autochthonous philosophical basis of Buddhist belief. It is not that Shosan intentionally separated these two types, but we may safely apply this classification as a convenient measure in the present discussion.

Criticism Corresponding to Western Criticism

Shosan criticized the Christian explanation of the "Omniscient" and "Omnipotent" God.

> If *Deus* were the Lord of Heaven and Earth and the Creator of everything on Earth, why did he leave many nations unsaved? Why did not he make his appearance in all the nations? Through thousands of

years since the beginning of the universe, Buddhas of generation after generation made their appearance and gave spiritual help to men of each generation. How can one prove the appearance of *Deus* in the land of the Southern Barbarians when that *Deus* never appeared in our land? Even if it were to be admitted that *Deus* is the Lord of Heaven and Earth, it should follow that other Buddhas deprived him of the lands of his own creation and that *Deus* allowed other Buddhas to propagate different teachings. On his part what a grave mistake this is! Such a *Deus* is a most absurd Buddha. Besides, they say that Jesus Christ was born to be crucified by common men on earth. Can a man like this be the Lord of Heaven and Earth? This is a story too illegical to be true. Christians who come to this land to propagate magical and misleading teaching and venerate a doubtful Buddha, in ignorance of the enlightened and truthful Buddha, cannot escape the retribution of the Buddhas and the native gods, which they deserve.[26]

That the Omniscient and Omnipotent God had created an imperfect universe is another point often criticized in the West. Another Japanese had already pointed this out earlier. In *Refutation of Deus*, Fabian (1563–1622?)[27], an apostate Catholic priest, who originally had been a Zen monk, wrote:

> During the five thousand years when there was no expiation for sins, all the people in the world who fell into hell must have been unmeasured and numberless . . . to watch this without any feeling of pity nor to set his mind to any expedient for the salvation of all living beings for five thousand years—can such be called a merciful lord?[28]

If this work came to his attention, Shosan may have received suggestions from this argument.

Long before these arguments had been advanced by Shosan and Fabian, Western thinkers were aware of this weak point of Christianity. That Jesus Christ alone provided salvation or that none but this man could help the human race was an idea difficult for rationally minded Westerners to accept. Therefore, since the early years of Christian missions in the Greco-Roman world, there were some who tended to deny this unique character of Jesus. It is also said that since New Testament days, there has existed a tendency in Christendom legalistically to evaluate moral rules more highly than divine grace. Whether or not Western criticism was known in Japan at this time has not been accurately determined, but these Japanese critics of Christianity payed special attention to this point, and it is easy to understand that they would do so.

According to Christian teaching, beasts have no eternal soul. Therefore when their bodies die, their spirits likewise cease to be. To human beings, on the other hand, *Deus* gave a real soul, and their souls survive their physical death, being rewarded with either suffering or pleasure in proportion to their good or evil conduct in the present life. They say that the spirits of men of good conduct are sent to Paradise in Heaven while the spirits of men of evil conduct are sent to the tormenting Inferno beneath. In refutation I say that if *Deus* made the spirits of beasts and of human beings differently, shy did he add evil to the human spirit, and why does he send some humans to the Inferno? That the human soul is sent to Hell is left to the will of *Deus* himself.

This sort of attack having been familiar in the West since the Roman-Christian era, the problem of theodicy has of course been a major theme in the history of philosophy and theology. The Japanese of those times are reported to have annoyed foreign missionaries by arguing this point sharply. Shosan seems to have discussed the issue on a similar basis.

It should be noted that, as our previous citations might suggest, the "human being" in Buddhism is only one of the forms of existence blown hither and yon by innumerable unsatisfied desires, though possibly better than other creatures surrounding him. Therefore the Buddhists of that time may have found it difficult to understand the Christian doctrine that human beings were endowed with a real spirit, while other beasts were less fortunate.

Following the argument cited above, Suzuki Shosan claimed that the Samkhya philosophy of India had had a similar difficulty in establishing itself logically and therefore that it was finally consumed by Buddha's teaching because of this logical weakness.

At the time Gautama Buddha was alive, other schools of teaching flourished in India. Their learning was extensive, and they built various theories and taught philosophies similar to that of the Buddha. Yet in spite of their volubility, they were lacking at one crucial point. The Samkhya school analyzed the laws of the universe by building a system of twenty-five phases of truth. The first phase was called the principle of inchoateness. Until Heaven and Earth were divided, there was no differentiation between good and evil fortune, nor any possibility of learning or understanding. Though it could not be designated with accuracy, this phase was, for reasons of expediency, named the principle of inchoateness. This was the permanent, imperishable and immutable principle which has no relationship to birth and death. The twenty-fifth phase of the truth was named the "divine mind." This was also named the mind of man or the spirit. This too was an immutable presence. The twenty-three phases in between were changeable in the universe for good or for worse. These were called the elements of causation. When the spirit took different appearances, the principle of inchoateness responded to its changes and assumed corresponding forms. Thus the changes of causal affairs in the universe depended on the motivational appearances of the spirit. If the spirit ceased to move completely and identified itself with the principle of inchoateness, motions and changes of causal phases would forever disappear and the joy of permanent inchoateness would automatically arrive. Matters and bodies would die, but the spirit would not. For example, if a house should burn, the master would leave the house.

They thus expounded their philosophy with great eloquence, but they finally admitted theirs to be inferior to Buddha's and they all became Buddha's followers. Christians today are much inferior to Samkhya reasoning and yet they pride themselves to the claim of their supremacy. They are like frogs in a small well.[29]

Shosan rejected miracles as preached in Christianity.

I hear that the Christian religion approves of miracles, and that it cheats people by using tricks, ascribing them to the glory of Deus. In refutation I say that if one places a high value on things miraculous, then one must revere demons. Foxes and badgers are the beings that make tricks in this land. A story says that when Indra and Asura fought and the latter was defeated, Asura and his eighty-four-thousand dependents hid themselves in a hole of a lotus stalk. Can one give any credence at all to such a story?

There are six kinds of wisdom. They are the wisdom of divine sight, of divine hearing, of understanding others' minds, of the knowledge of destiny, of flight, and of the ultimate (Asravaksaya jñana). Divine sight is the wisdom of beholding all events in the whole Universe at a glance. Divine hearing is the wisdom of hearing all events in the whole Universe while sitting. Understanding others' minds is the wisdom of insight into what others have in mind. The wisdom of destiny is the knowledge of past, present, and future. The wisdom of flight means that one can fly freely in heaven and beyond. These five kinds of wisdom can be found in devas, demons and even in other non-Buddhists. The ultimate wisdom, however, is beyond the reach of devas, demons and non-Buddhists. This is Buddha's wisdom of annihilating all the worldly passions. Thus Buddha does not include miracles in the six kinds of wisdom. Therefore they say there is *no miracle in the rightful law*. He who does not know this may be cheated by devas, demons, and others. The six kinds of wisdom of the Buddha are as follows: no matter what sight he sees, he never gets disturbed; no matter what voice he hears, he never gets disturbed; no matter what odor he smells, he never gets disturbed; no matter what happened to his body, he never gets disturbed; the law being embodied within himself, he never violates the law no matter what he wills. To sump up, he is never trapped by anything for he realizes that all traps are like a shadows on a mirror, never attached to its surface. Thus the mind and the inchoateness are identical in him, and such a man we call the free man with six kinds of wisdom. He may also be called a man with no change and no mind. A sūtra says that it is better to follow the way of the man of detachment than to venerate many Buddhas of the past, present, and future. He who tries to learn the way of Buddha must learn this practice. He shall never use miracles.

The "miracles" spoken of here may refer to the uneasiness that the

Japanese people of that time felt because of the scientific machines and drugs that Christian missionaries brought with them. Even so, it may be said as a matter of principle that to use these devices as means by which to achieve their missionary purpose was not at all different from the practice of medieval Christian priests who attracted followers and made believers by the use of miraculous tales.

Citing an old Zen axiom, "Truthful law expects no miracle at all,"[30] Shosan denounced miracles and wonders. Criticism of the belief in miracles was only recently started in the West. In the nineteenth century David Friedrich Strauss (1808–1874) and others started to discuss the topic. Strauss, particularly, criticized the belief in miracles in terms of the knowledge of natural science. Shosan, however, expressed a rational attitude at a time when there was yet little scientific knowledge in Japan. We are obliged to acknowledge the excellence of his insight. It stands up well when measured against the governmentally-supported work of Hayashi Razan (1578–1657), namely, the latter's *Rejection of Jesus.*[31]

We have so far attempted to show that Shosan's criticism of Christianity coincided, in part, with that of modern Western thinkers, and we have outlined the philosopher's criticism of Christianity as it existed without influence from the West. We may conclude that Shosan, as a thinker, had the quality of a modern thinker.

Criticism From A Buddhist Point of View

The following argument reveals an intrinsic incompatibility between the Buddhist and Christian grounds of thinking.

Buddhas from generation to generation have come into the world with the objective of guiding all constituted beings into the straight path so that they may become Buddhas. Thus an axiom says, "Look straight into your mind, and you will see yourself a Buddha."[32]

Gautama was born, persevered through twelve long years of strenuous effort, and while observing the moon and the stars on a certain eighth of December, awakened to a knowledge of the "thusness" of reality. Thereafter he left behind his life on a lofty mountain and preached his doctrine to many. When Buddha indicated his imminent demise, those present were all silent. The Elder Kāśyapa alone, however, smiled. Gautama said, "Truly have I inspired the wisdom of dharma. The spirit of my teaching is beyond letters. It should be transmitted from one master to another."

The lineal line of the right teaching from Kāśyapa has come down to Japan through a legitimate succession of masters, the transmission of the teaching from one master to another being strictly regulated down to the present.

Christian teaching insists upon the idea of existence, encourages thinking and feeling, and forges an idea of a creator of heaven and earth. It thus repeats the endless cycle of suffering and defusion. Yet it claims that it saves men. It is amazing that Christians come to this land and compete with the rightful teaching of Buddha with so inefficient a philosophy. It is as if a sparrow were fighting against an eagle, or a firefly against the moon.

Shosan's reasoning here is as follows. According to Christian teaching, God, as a real presence, created the substantial universe, and yet he gave men sufferings which were also real. Therefore, in terms of Buddhist language, men's "cycle" (karma) was fixed as "real." Their "cycle," therefore, even if founded on suffering, could not involve a basis for turning toward the ultimate conceived as the void. As long as the creator of the Universe, deemed to be real, was God, also deemed real, it would be logically inconceivable for men thus created to turn to the negative. The eternal reality could never negate its own being. Buddhism on the other hand, took the view that the "unreal" (Śunya), i.e. knowledge of the thusness of reality, was the ultimate principle. Human beings can enter and leave the cycle of life with its vice and sufferings only because the possibility of their doing so is grounded in negation. In this context Zen teachers preached that so long as men did not get rid of the false notion of the real nature of the human, they could not attain enlightenment.

This attack on Christianity is of exactly the same kind as that used by Indian Buddhists in their attack on theism.[33] It is impossible, however, that Shosan was influenced by such arguments written in Buddhist scriptures. Shosan appears to have hit upon this kind of reasoning as a result of his own thinking on the subject.

Shosan discussed the problem in this way. The absolute of Buddhism can save living beings for eternity, precisely because the absolute in Buddhism is the absolute in the negative. Various sects of Buddhism gave different names to this absolute negative, but essentially they all spoke of the same thing. Originally living beings were identical with this absolute. To be saved is to return to the original being.

After Bhagavat had preached his profound teaching for forty-nine years, he finally stated that the ultimate was beyond description. By saying this, he taught the way of the immediate realization of the Buddhahood. Finite thinking or reasoning is incapable of reaching the depth of the ultimate. In a scripture Gautama compares such reasoning to a finger pointing at the moon. A man of old characterized the true Law in these words:

Works of perception (Citta) will not get at it,
Cessation of perception will not grasp it,
Eloquence of language can never arrive at its depth,
Nor can silence reveal it ever.

No one can explain this. Neither can one explain the appearance of the seven Buddhas; Vipaśyin, Śikhin, Viśvabhuj, Krakucchanda, Kanakumuni, Kāśyapa, Śākyamuni, as we call them. In fact each one of these Buddhas rules many millions of years, and when the seven Buddhas are together, their reign is infinite, its length exceeds our knowledge. In addition to these seven was Amitabha who has been in the world since ten billions years ago, and before that time he was a boddhisattva by the name of Dharmākara. Amitabha is a Sanskrit name, and it is written "eternal life" in Chinese. *The Meditation on Buddha Amitayus Sūtra* describes this Buddha:

The body of Buddha Amitayus is a hundred thousand million times as bright as the color of the Gāmbūnada gold of the heavenly abode of Yama: . . .

The white twist of hair between the eye-brows all turning to the right is just like the five Sumeru mountains.

The eyes of Buddha are like the water of the four great oceans; the blue and the white are quite distinct.

All the roots of hair of his body issue forth brilliant rays which are also like the Sumeru mountains.

The halo of that Buddha is like a hundred millions of the great chiliocosmos; . . .[34]

This description makes his image quite clear. It says "his height is six hundred thousand niyutas of kotis of yoganas innumerable as are the sands of the river Ganga, that the white twist of hair the five Sumeru mountains, and that his eyes the four great oceans."[35] Can there be anything else larger than this Buddha? The whole world is hardly equivalent to a grain of rice in comparison with the body of Amitabha. The purity of the upper part of his body forms the heavens, the turbidity of the lower the earth. Thus is the distinction between *yin* and *yang*. Heaven governs *yang* and earth *yin*. Since the beginning of the world, *yin* and *yang* together, by making heaven father and earth mother, have given birth to all living beings and phenomena. In other words such is the virtuous function of the Buddha. In Zen terms this Buddha is called the big man, i.e. the man of big might and capacity. Describing the man of big might and capacity, Mumon (1183–1260, a Zen master of Sung China) stated:

Wake up or lie down, the free and perfuming oceans roar for eternity by him

Look around and see that even the four heavenly worlds float underneath

Various sutras and writings speak of him in diverse ways, but Buddha's teaching pervades the universe, and governs all the living beings. Hereby he preaches that all living beings without exception possess the Buddha nature. In a figure of speech it is as if the one moon in heaven were transferred to thousands of water surfaces on earth. The moon stays on a drop of water and on the ocean equally. The *formlessness of the essence* turns out in the limitless adaptations of the highest quality. The eyes see forms, the ears hear sounds, the nose smells odors, the mouth utters words, the hands handles things, and the legs make us walk. When one's spirit realizes Buddha, he is Buddha. When one's spirit loses sight of Buddha, he is an ordinary man. Therefore Buddha is designated in different ways depending upon the image through which men are to be informed of their own Buddha nature. The original character, the originally shared field, the grand perfect enlightenment, the great wisdom, the great sun, the great king of medicine, the merciful, the instructor, et al. are the names of some of these images, but there is no other Buddha than the Buddha and no other Law than the Law. When one awakens to the "suchness" of reality, the blowing wind and flowing water become the music of heaven. When man realizes that millions of phenomena are essentially identical, weeds and trees on land immediately manifest their Buddha nature. These Christian priests, totally ignorant of this immediate realization as such, venerate the teaching of Jesus Christ, which is comparable to taking the eye of a fish for a precious gem.

Followers of Christianity, Shosan reasoned, are ignorant of the ultimate ground of being. Therefore they rely upon the character of the person of Jesus Christ. But according to Buddhist teaching, living beings are all saved by acquainting themselves with the ultimate as such. In order to do so, it says, living beings must simply slough off their misunderstandings.

Buddha is the great king of medicine. He has vowed to cure the diseases of misunderstanding and confusion. Whenever living beings believe in and rely on his teaching, it never fails to cure them from their mental and physical diseases. Men should refrain from using medicine until he knows the cause of their disease. The cause of their disease, of their suffering, comes without fail from the innate error of taking this false and dreamy life for reality. Greediness, resentment, and complaints are three vicious kinds of thinking by which we torture ourselves. These are derived solely from attachment to the self. These three poisons are the seeds of eighty-four-thousand kinds of evil passions, yet ordinary men are bound by sufferings of this kind for life and tend to be trapped in their illness till they learn its cause. Even when they die, the passions which constantly clung to them in this life pursue and torture them by becoming demons. Then the Mountain of the Dead (which the dead must climb) and the Sanzu River (which the dead must cross) come into existence. Thus those who fail to realize their true Buddha nature suffer while alive and after death alike These sufferings are all consequences of the perversion of the heart. The content of this perversion is as follows: First, it means that the heart loves suffering and does not really know true joy. Second, it means that the heart is ignorant of the truth of transiency (Anitya), and adheres to the this-worldly and believes in everlastingness. Third, it means that the heart regards itself as free in spite of the fact that its body is bound by ten vices and eight sufferings and is held in bondage to limitless passions. Fourth, it means that the heart believes itself pure, being unaware of the impurity of its own being. Misconceptions based on this perversion have been maintained down to the present. However, sweat, feces, urine, earwax, nasal mucus, and other liquids that are secreted from every opening of the body are by no means pure and clean. We should revalue this body to which we are so devoted. What Buddha taught about impurity has this end in view. He instructs those who would attain this view of impurity to dwell near the tombs where there are many corpses. This is a clear lesson that one should not adhere to corruptible flesh.

Both living beings who remain in perplexity and those who attain realization depend on their hearts. But the "beclouded heart" is precisely what must be eliminated.

Leave the heart as such.

The heart in action knows suffering and pleasure.

The heart in extinction is bound by nothing.

Through the heart the heart is to be known.

That is to say, there is a "heart that transcends the heart." This "transcending heart," or "one heart" is identical with the absolute. Therefore the Buddha and all other forms of existence are ultimately identical. They cannot be based upon different principles.

Thus the difference between Buddha and living beings is like the difference between water and ice. Accumulation of passions is comparable to frozen ice, and extinction of desires to ice melting into water. Therefore a sutra tells us:

In the three worlds there exists but one single heart.

There is no other Law but the heart.

As between the heart, Buddha, and living beings,

There exists no difference.[36]

Christians are totally ignorant of what this "one single heart" is.

The ultimate "being" of Buddhist teaching is a mysterious, beautiful and universal function that will not cease to exert itself till each and every living being has been saved. Being absolute, every divine being that acts on behalf of living beings is an incarnation of the absolute, even if it does not belong to the Buddhist tradition. It follows, therefore, that the gods native to Japan may be counted as representations of the original Buddha. According to Christian teaching, on the other hand, salvation is granted solely through Jesus Christ, the only son of God. Therefore Christians see no reason for the existence of other gods. The gods native to Japan are logically excluded from their object of worship. The argument below illustrates the difference of these view points.

I hear that they say that veneration of native gods of Japan is nonsense, and that that is a result of ignorance of *Deus*. In refutation I say that Japan is a divine nation. To be born in the divine nation and yet to fail to worship the divine beings would show a terrible lack of respect. That the Buddhas and gods(i.e. avatars of the Buddhas) accomodate their brilliance to conditions in this world is the beginning of their relationship with use, and the eight major events in Buddha's life are the culmination of this saving process. That is to say, the native gods represent Buddha in incarnate form, and that is an accommodation through which to provide easier access to the true path for the less serious minded. The gods and the Buddha are like waves and water. The true and original Buddha appears in different guises, and saves people in ways appropriate to their respective station in life. Thus the hearts of all should be oriented to the veneration of this one Buddha. Allegorically speaking, it is like when a man, through paying his respect to cabinet ministers, supervisers, officers, representatives and assistants, expresses his reverence to the king. Paying respect to officers is a form of showing one's reverence for the sovereign. Christian teaching seems like claiming that it is proper for the men who revere the sovereign to disregard his officers. How can one accept such an improper claim?

Approval or rejection of worship of the sun and moon was another point of difference as between the Buddhist and Christian viewpoints.

I hear they claim that veneration of the sun and moon, which is practiced in Japan, is nonsense, that the sun and the moon are lamps of the world, and that the Japanese do not know the truth due to their ignorance of *Deus*. In refutation I say that the figure of man is founded on *yin* and *yang*, and the body is formed of the four major elements. The sun is a *yang* representation, and the moon is a *yin* representation. Apart from *yin* and *yang*, no one can keep one's body alive. It is impossible to show too much reverence to the principles that constitute the foundations of our being. Any one who says *yin* and *yang* are useless should abstain from the use of water and fire. The sun and the moon in heaven give light to the world below. The highest veneration is due them. The two eyes of man that give him sight are nothing but the reflection of the virtues of the sun and the moon. Christians declare that reverence of the sun and moon is useless, so perhaps they do not need their eyes either. That is an example of their ignorance of the truth. How absurd the Christians are!

Christians interpreted the un sand moon as "lamps of the world" on the ground that they accepted the modern Western scientific interpretation of the sun and the moon as parts of the astronomical system and, in addition, on the ground that worship of the sun and the moon had never been taught in Christianity. Shosan, on the other hand, still retained a belief in the traditional Chinese *yin* and *yang* cosmology and identified the sun and the moon as the origin of *yin* and *yang*. This indicates that Suzuki Shosan was not acquiainted with modern Western natural science. Today, we might classify his argument as "pre-natural-scientific." However, even though some parts of his argument contradict the rational common-sense of today, it is quite clear that he always attempted to argue in accordance with the principle of rationality so far as the limitations of that age permitted.

Concluding his arguments, Shosan wrote:

In recent years Christian priests have come and deceived people with all kinds of lies. With the plot of usurping this land for the Southern Barbarians, they have treacherously forged the idea of a creator of heaven and earth and corrupted our shrines and temples, being unafraid of heavenly retribution. There are scoundrels among the native priests who join in their deception. They call themselves *iruman bateren*, i.e. native Christian Brothers, and represent various classes of people. They say that the Buddhas of this land are not true Buddhas, that the sun and the moon are not to be venerated, and that theredo not exist native gods nor divine beings. The crime involved in making such statements is so grave that each of them is being executed, thus verifying the punishment of heaven, Buddhas, gods, and men. Millions of them lose their lives, and their followers are severely pressed by all kinds of criticism. It is their vicious teaching that invites this retribution, not the government's laws. They are now destroying themselves as a natural result of their atrocities, usurpation of the way of heaven, and of their forgery of false teaching by which innumerable men were cast into hell. If Christian priests were true disciples of Buddha, the execution of one Christian priest would immediately invite punishment from heaven. No sign of such infliction has ever appeared, though innumerable Christian priests and Japanese converts have been executed already. No matter how often they come, their self-destruction is assured so long as the way of heaven is preserved. Hear this, and understand it.

Attention is here invited to the fact that Shosan's way of reasoning ni denouncing Christianity for its prohibition of worshipping native gods led him to reject the *Jodo Shin Shu* (The True Sect of Pure Land) Buddhists as well.

Master (Shosan) said to the audience: Nowadays there are people who denounce the Ikko Shu (Jodo Shin Shu). Explain, any one of you, the shortcomings of this sect.

A priest said: The priests of this sect lead married lives and eat meat, thus breaking the commandments.

Master said: This sect was originally started with the claim that it made enlightenment available for people in secular life. If you should still demand observance of priestly commandments from such people, you would miss the point of the question. If observance of the commandments were a condition of realization, it would follow automatically that lay people would never attain enlightenment. Establishment of Buddha's religion, however, should be the kind of establishment that helps to preserve the peace and security of nation. But since Ikko Shu does not care if Shinto shrines become dilapidated, veneration at the shrines of the gods native to Japan cannot escape deterioration. If all Japanese were to be converted to Ikko Shu, the shrines of the native gods would definitely be swept out. Japan, however, is a divine nation. How could the nation be maintained if the native gods were discarded?[37]

We shall not discuss here the relationship between the Jodo Shin Shu and Shinto in detail, as it is itself a big problem. We shall merely conclude by saying that Shosan decisively rejected monotheistic religious belief.

The Characteristics of Shosan's Criticism

The reasoning Shosan employed in his criticism of Christianity, as we have seen, reveals that Shosan's position was always radically rational. He criticized Christianity from a rational point of view, regarding it as a philosophical system. It is evident that his knowledge of natural science was quite limited, yet is it also true that he was always oriented toward logical reasoning. His rationalism corresponds in part to Western rationalistic criticism of Christianity, and is partly a derivative product of Buddhist rationalism.

It is to be noted that Shosan thought that truth must be established in terms of a universal standard that transcended national or parochial boundaries.

There are many ignorant Japanese who die for the ignominious faith of Christianity without reflecting on its theoretical deficiencies. The existence of such people is a shame to our nation. I would feel ashamed if this were known abroad.

Such a broad perspective was quite extraordinary for the Japanese o- that time, isolated as they were from information about conditionf abroad. By way of contrast, we shall briefly review some popular rgasu ments against Christianity by some other Japanese of that period.

Most Japanese thought that Christianity took advantage of the ig- norant in the use it made of "sorcery." The primary reason for the pro- scription of Christianity was that its teachings were considered contrary to feudal principles and contained elements that could lead to the sub- verting of the social order. The Catholicism of that time, because its hierarchical organization was developed in the medieval period, un- doubtedly involved many feudalistic elements. In Japan, however, beliej in the teachings of Catholicism collided with the norm of devoted loyalty to the feudal lords, because Catholicism called, in effect, for peo- ple to divide their loyalties—and this at a time when most Japanese feudal lords were not Catholics. In the West belief in Catholicism and loyalty to the crown were not held to be contradictory because European feudal princes in medieval times were themselves followers of Catholicism. Most Japanese critics of Christianity dealt mainly with this point. Fabian, an apostate Catholic, challenged the legitimacy of the Ten Command- ments in his *Refutation of Deus* on the following grounds. Nine out of the ten items were deemed ethical principles that all men should follow, and practically reducible to the Five Commandments of Buddhism. But the first commandment, "Thou shalt venerate *Deus* alone" (Thou shalt have no other gods before me) was by no means allowable. This teaching ad- vocated rebellion against lords and fathers by its demand for exclusive veneration of *Deus*. This teaching was in the beginning nothing but a means by which Christians usurped other nations.[38] Thus Fabian, writing on the basis of the Confucian doctrine of rulership and defending the idea of converting Japanese Christians to Buddhism, contended: "It is the way of man to live in accord with the rules of the Shogun who is the ruler of Japan, so long as one lives in Japan."[39]

Confucian scholars' rebuttal of Christianity was grounded on the same reasoning as that of Fabian's. For example, Kan Sazan (1748–1827) said:

> I hear that Christians do not refrain from sacrificing their lives and bodies provided it be for *Deus*. This is a most threatening thing to hear indeed. A lord rules a nation, and for him only, citizens may have to take up arms in case of need. There may be sects or schools of teaching in different nations at different times. *Any teaching*, however, that *venerates something which is not the lord of the nation,* is a *subversive deception that opposes the nation's rulers,* and is certain to cause injury both to the government and to the church.[40]

Even Arai Hakuseki (1657–1725), one of the most progressive Confucian scholars during the Tokugawa era, discusses the matter of ceremony as a question of *ethics* or *social status*.

> Ceremonial service to heaven is a profession of the Emperor. From lords to farmers and townsmen, each according to the title and rank, their allotment of the service is particularly decided. The claim that all the people should practice equal ceremonial service is contrary to the human ethics.(

It is remarkable that, among Japanese people in general, one can detect the existence of a pattern of thinking such that they regard the limited human means of which they are members as the standard of their value judgements and that in the last analysis they make such judgements in reliance upon a certain person who represents the social organization in which they live. In the kind reasoning that led to the expulsion of Christianity, the dominance of this pattern is clearly visible. Shosan, however, did not use this sort of reasoning. Some of the old elements are of course retained in Shosan's arguments. Yet Shosan, who lived prior to Kan Sazan and Arai Hakuseki, was unintentionally possessed of a modern and rational position, and this at a time when even a progressive thinker like Arai Hakuseki remained imbedded in feudal perspectives in his rebuttal of Christianity.[41]

Conclusion

Shosan's thought was outstanding for the characteristics delineated above, and it attracted widespread attention. And yet, generally speaking, his thinking was not accepted by the people of his time. The fact was that "many lay people and priests of higher and lower ranks came from long distances, but none of them understood the true intent of Shosan's discussions, and they left him."[42] Shosan had to acquiesce in this situation. "Men come in order to test their biased views against Shosan. But they all leave, Śecause their arguments do not stand up to Shosan's rebuttals."

No one listens to the fruit of my strenuous efforts of four score of years. *The time is not ripe yet.* I can only pity myself. In the excess of my grief I write this, hoping that some one in the future may pay attention to this, even if no one understands it at the present time.[43]

Between Shosan and the Buddhists in general, there was an open cleavage. Shosan's philosophy developed in isolation. His thought did not influence Japanese philosophical currents to any considerable extent. Neither did it instigate any lasting religious movement whatsoever.

In the West, however, since the days Shosan was alive, or even earlier, rational philosophy, similar to what Shosan had conceived, developed into a socio-religious movement and issued in the Reformation. But in Japan, Shosan had to remain in isolation and, in time, was utterly forgotten. To what should we attribute this difference?

We would suggest two possible explanations as direct causes of Shosan's situation. One is the fact that the centralized feudal system of Tokugawa Japan was extraordinary solid and its binding power extremely strong; the other, that civil society was yet immature. Further analysis of what caused this situation to take the form it did is a separate and major question, which we will have to discuss on another occasion.

Though Shosan took a radically critical attitude toward the traditional religious powers, he never became a mass leader who would marshal social forces for the subversion of the existing order. The religious bodies kept on, receiving without noticeable change the veneration and devotion of the people and, with the backing of popular support, enjoyed official recognition by the Shogunate government. Due to the policy of prohibition of Christianity, the temples of existing Buddhist sects were turned into something like public agencies in their relationship with the people in general. Living in this society, Shosan, too, had to acknowledge and acquiesce in the large-scale organization of society. Even Shosan, who advocated a vocational ethic and the practice of Buddhism in secular life, was obliged—in the condition of feudal society—to find a place in a religious organization, Soto Zen in his case, and to identify himself as a priest. Such contradictory phenomena constituted a problem that could not be solved by the efforts of a mere individual. Shosan's strong opposition to feudal morality was rarely followed by anybody. Neither did his emphasis upon "freedom" break down the inequality of society. In contrast to the successful realization of a religious government under the aegis of theocracy in Geneva at the hands of John Calvin, in Japan actualization of a Buddhist government, excluding the feudal forces of the warring classes, and having its seat of authority in the temples, remained the dream of Shosan alone.

Shosan's influence in subsequent years was greater in his capacity as a writer of literature. His fictional creations, like the *Story of Cause and Effect*,[44] and the *Two Nuns*,[45] were popularly accepted. What the people sought for in Shosan were stories to be used in writing. Writers who got their ideas from Shosan subsequently published stories entitled the *Seven Nuns* and the *Four Nuns*.[46] Shosan's other title led Saikaku (Ihara, 1642–1693) to write the *New Story of Cause and Effect*,[47] and Rosui (0000–0000) the *Modern Story of Cause and Effect*.[48] The appearance of these imitative works no doubt attests Shosan's popularity and influence upon the general public. Yet the popular image of Shosan was hardly more than that of a writer of morality inculcating stories of the grotesque. For example, in the *Three Edo Men's Linked Verse*,[49] two poets, Ito Nobunori and Matsuo Basho, offered the following analogy:

Ito Nobunori:
A devil did it prove itself, yet the figure remained as if alive.
Matsuo Basho:
Yes, as if in a story by Shosan.[50]

Thus Shosan's new and progressive side was lost in oblivion, while, thanks to his talent in creative writing, only the old and medievalistic illustrations he used as a convention for popularizing his teaching were accepted and appreciated by people in general. Shosan's truly revolutionary ideas in religious thinking were totally overlooked through the years. Shosan, a man with new conceptions of religions, appeared and disappeared like a comet, and was shortly completely forgotten.

Japanese religion, and Japanese society in general, retained an essentially medieval structure, and no really fundamental changes ever did occur throughout the Tokugawa era, or down to the present day.

1 The Japanese rendering of Christianity and Christians, especially of late 16th and early 17th centuries, is *Kirishitan*. As the Japanese term *Kirishitan* has concrete connotation related closely to the cultural and historical background of that period, the words translated presently as "Christians" and "Christianity" ought to be read with that historico-cultural specification in mind.—Translator.

2 I have not seen previous studies dealing with Banzui'i.

3 白道, 演蓮社智誉向何.

4 This is based on MOCHIZUKI Shinko's *Bukkyo Daijiten* "Banzui'i." Biography on Banzui'i has not yet appeared.

5 妙導 (妙導) 著, 幡随意上人行状, 一巻.
presently as "Christians" and "Christianity" ought to be read with that historico-culturals

6 喚誉著, 幡随意上人諸国行化伝, 五巻.

7 彩誉著, 幡随意上人伝, 二巻.

8 *Stories*. Vol. 4, p. 7. Following citations will be from *Stories* unless specifically indicated otherwise.

9 四十八昼夜を克して浄業を倚し，神翁付予の像を鎮し神君恩賜の軍扇を執り，その陣衣を以て載して滬多羅 (Uttarāsainga 上衣) と為してこれを抜け堂に昇って説法す　*Gyojyo*.

10 Max MUELLER. *The Sacred Books of the East*. Vol. 49.

11 *Life and Activities*, p. 13.

12 Ibid., pp. 13–14.

13 *Life and Activities*, p. 14.

14 The number of physicians among the Christians was considerably large. ANESAKI Masaharu. *Rise and Fall of Christian Missions* (Kirishitan Dendō no Kō-hai), p. 432.

15 *Short History of Nagasaki* (Nagasaki Engi Ryaku), *Historiography of Nagasaki* (Nagasaki Shi), Cited in TSUJI Zennosuke. *History of Japanese Buddhism* (Nihon Bukkyo Shi) Kinsei Hen III, p. 97.

16 TSUJI. Op. cit. pp. 97–107 contains statistics.

17 *Biography of the Venerable Bansui'i*. Also *Genealogy of Fujiwara Arima* (Fujiwara Arima Sefu) cited in TSUJI, op. cit. p. 97.

18 白道運歩数十年　以火消火難思術

19 This does not mean that all the Buddhists were inactive as regards Christianity. Protest letters to the authorities are still extant. A group of priests from Mt. Hiei demanded the

expulsion of Christian missionaries on the ground that loss of faith and corruption of the
social order might be expected if Christian teachings according to which the native gods
and Buddha are despised should come to prevail. A large number of other minor collisions
between Christianity and Buddhism can be enumerated from many provinces, but what
is important is that the collisions were the result of conflicts in the struggle for power, and
not the result of truly religious Buddhist missionary spirit.

20 SHIMMURA Izuru, "Buddhist Refutation of Christianity in the Early Tokugawa
Period," (徳川初期に於ける仏教徒の耶教排撃) Rekishi to Chiri, vol. 1, No. 3. (1917)

21 We can not say that all the Buddhists of that time were of the same type. An exception, for example, is SUZUKI Shosan's Refutation of Christianity, which gives evidence of
reflection on theoretical problems. (For a more detailed analysis, see the present writer's
Studies on the Critical Spirits in Modern Japan (近世日本に於ける批判的精神の考察 p. 212
ff.) On Instructing Christians (対治邪執論) by Sesso, a priest of Nanzen-ji Temple, written
at about 1648, discussed Christianity theoretically, with a logical construction along the
same lines as that of Shosan's. (SUGIMOTO Isao, "Development of Anti-Christian Disputes
in the Early Tokugawa Period (江戸初期に於ける排耶蘇論の展開)," Rekishi Kyōiku,
vol. 7, No. 10. (1959). It is also said, however, that most of the books by Buddhists in
refutation of Christianity are filled with discussions of politics. (IENAGA Saburō, Study
of Buddhist Thought in the Middle Ages (中世仏教思想史研究), p. 120.

22 We should not forget the fact that some apologetic works written in Japanese by
Catholic missionaries exist such as Myotei Mondo (Cf. Bibliography), and their criticisms
of Buddhist teachings are very interesting. But as they were written by foreigners, we
shall omit them.

23 「でうす問答」

24 「破吉利支丹」

25 Quotation from the first phrases of Refutation of Christianity. The author could not
obtain a copy of Questions and Answers about the Christian God. Unspecified quotations
hereafter will be from Refutation.

26 「破提宇子」

27 ハビアン, 不干巴毘庵

28 Nippon Tetsugaku Shisō Zensho (Tokyo: Heibonsha, 1956). Vol. X, p. 151. Esther
Lowell BIBBARD, Translator. Refutation of Deus by Fabian (Tokyo: ISR Press, 1963), p. 31.

29 Shosan's source of this statement is from Muso Kokushi (1275–1351):
"Question. What is the teaching of the 'divine mind?'"
"Answer. The Samkhya school analyzed the laws of the universe by building a system
of twenty-five phases of truth. The first is named the truth of inchoateness. This has
nothing to do with good and evil fortunes nor is it possible to observe or understand it.
Though it is beyond naming, for convenience' sake is it named the truth of inchoateness. This is permanent and beyond birth or death. The twenty-fifth is named the truth
of the divine mind. This is the so-called mind of men or "the spirit." They say this is
permanent, too. The other twenty-three truths are various phases of good and evil
fortune in the universe. They are defined as the elements of the law of causation. If the
divine mind assumes a mode of action, the principle of inchoateness adopts a corresponding form. If the divine mind thinks this or that, the inchoateness turns into the
form of this or that. Thus, the turns and changes of causation in the universe depend
solely on the modes of action of the divine mind. If the divine mind ceases to act completely and becomes identified with the inchoateness, the turns and changes of causa-

elements all settle automatically in the inchoateness. The material body dies, but the divine mind is permanent and never dies. It is as if a house were burning and its master came out and left. This is view of the divine mind that Chu Kokushi (?–775) denounced. (Muso Kokushi: *Muchu Mondō Shū*.) Nanyo E-Chu Kokushi briefly refers to the theory of the inchoateness. ("Keitoku Dentoroku" vol. 28, (1006), *Taishō Shinshū Daizokyō*, vol. 51., p. 437 ff.)

30 *Roankyo* (耶鞍橋), vol. 2., pp. 19, 68.

31 林羅山,「排驢蘇」
The *rationale* used by the ruling class of Tokugawa Japan is found in MIURA Baien's *Musings During the Early Summer Rain* (五月雨抄), translated into English by Leon HURWITZ, *Monumenta Nipponica*, vol. 8, Nos. 1–2, (1952), 2893–26, vol. 9, Nos. 1–2. (1953), 330–356.

32 直指人心　見柱成仏

33 Indian Buddhists presented a number of comments on the monotheistic doctrine that the Universe was the creation of one god. One of them argued thus: if the god that is the cause of the Universe is eternal being, it will not give birth to anything. It is as if the emptiness were ever-lasting and could not give birth to anything. Only limited, mortal beings can give birth to other *beings*. ("Dai Bibasha Ron, vol. 199," *Taishō Shinshū Daizokyō*, vol. 27, p. 993. Tattvasamgraha vv. 140, 147.) Another thesis was that the cause of the cycle could not at the same time be the cause of extinction (Tarkajvala, VIII, 21).

34 Amitayur-Dhyana-sūtra, tr. by TAKAKUSU Junjirō, in *The Sacred Books of the East* (Max MUELLER, editor), vol. 49, p. 180.

35 Ibid.

36 These lines are taken from well known verses of the Garland sūtra. This verse is a composite from *Hachijū Kegon* vol. 37. "Jujibon," and *Rokujū Kegon* vol. 10. "Yamatengu-bosatsugebon."
「八十華厳」第三十七巻．十地品「三界所有唯是一心」「六十華厳」第十巻．
夜摩天官菩薩説偈品「心如工画師画．種種五陰．一切世界中無法而不造．
如心仏亦然．如仏衆生然．心仏及衆生．是三無差別．」

37 *Roankyo*, vol. 2, p. 65.

38 ANESAKI Masaharu. *Biographical Review of Persecution of Christianity* (切支丹迫害史中の人物史蹟) p. 479: *Vicissitude of Christian Missions* (切支丹伝道を興隆し) pp. 789 ff.

39 ANESAKI, *Vicissitude*, p. 778.

40 "Shadow of Winter" (冬の日影) I, in *Japanese Confucian Library* (日本儒林叢書) *Commentaries* (触説部) ii, pp. 9–10.

41 We do not intend to argue that Shosan's discussions were retionalistic *in toto*. We would merely point out that there appeared in him a rationalist tendency that distinguishes him from other thinkers of that time.

42 *Roankyo*, vol. 3, p. 23.

43 Ibid., vol. 2, p. 89.

44 因果物語

45 二人比丘尼

46 七人比丘尼．四人比丘尼

47 新因果物語

48 近代因果物語

49 江戸三吟

50 Ishida, op. cit., p. 18. Hakuin (Zen master, 1685–1768) cited from Shosan's *Cause and Effect* in his *Sashimogusa*. (*Zen-mon Hogo-shu*, vol. 2, p. 175.)

CHAPTER V

MODERN TRENDS—General Features of the Tokugawa Period

1. Introductory Remarks

People often say that Eastern countries had nothing which could properly be termed a modern age before the introduction of Western civilization. They say that there had not yet appeared what might be called "modern" ways of thinking.

This appears at first glance to be true, but if we investigate the history of modern Eastern though more thoroughly, we come to see the gradual indigenous development of modern conceptions of man and ethical values, corresponding to, yet different from, those in the modern West.

In the following, I propose to discuss some features of the thought in Japan of the Tokugawa period, of nearly the same period as the modern West.

Generally speaking, it might be said that many religious sects have remained as medieval, in their behavior as in their manner of valuation in the Tokugawa period also. What then do we mean by medieval ways of valuation? They are generally characterized by the following features:

(1) The absolute authority of traditional religions was admitted by the people in general who were under their strict control. Traditional symbols were stereotyped for a long period.

(2) Consequently, religious orders were extremely influential in the realm of social relations.

(3) The absolute sacredness of religious canons was stressed. Scholarship was no more than deduction from, and the elucidation of, the fundamental dogmas of religions. Learning was, in the main, scholastic.

Free thinking was not permitted; heretics were punished, scepticism was abhorred.

(4) The tendency of thought was, generally speaking, other-worldly. Religious life was regarded as noble, secular life as vile and mean.

(5) As for social structure, a feudalistic hierarchy of status was accepted by the common people, and was enforced by authority.

(6) Cultural life was limited to the upper classes; common people hardly participated in it.

Such ways of thinking and behavior were characteristic of the medieval West and Japan. And if we assume that modern ways of thinking involve the casting off of these, it is necessary that we should investigate Japanese thought from the same viewpoint as Western thought, although we should not overlook the difference which exists between them.

The literature written in this period is voluminous. However, focusing our investigation, we want to point out and discuss some conspicuous features in the change of thought which can be found in the works of some Japanese thinkers of the past during the four or five centuries before the introduction of Western civilization at the Meiji Restoration.

These features could be found only in their incipient stage, and were not influential enough to change the whole society. But we should not overlook them. They are worth notice.

As the motivating power we shall first mention and discuss the critical attitude.

2. Critical Attitude

Consciousness of Ego

It is said that modern thought began with the consciousness of the self (*cogito ergo sum*). The attitude of esteeming man as such makes one aware of the problem of *ego*.

In Japanese Buddhism the process of the appearance of ego-consciousness can be noticed. Master T'ien-t'ai (538–597), the founder of the Chinese T'ien-t'ai school, declared that one should not entertain doubt towards one's own master. This way [1]of thinking was most conspicuous in later Zen Buddhism, which esteems transmission from master to disciple. But in modern Japan the opposite attitude was expressed. "To be honest one must declare one's own doubts, if he has any, as I do." [2]

Even in Zen Buddhism a critical attitude was expressed towards the founder. To illustrate: Dōgen (1200–1253) denounced the theory of 'perceiving one's own nature intuitively' set forth in the Sūtra of the Sixth Patriarch. But Tenkei (1648–1735), his spiritual descendant, rejected Dōgen's opinion as 'absurd sheer nonsense.'[3] according to the traditional attitude, "one's own enlightenment should be conveyed face to face, from master to disciple, and it should be approved by a single master." It is likely that this attitude reflected the feudalistic tendency of the Tokugawa period. But Tenkei gave a different interpretation. In this phrase "master" means 'one's own self'; "disciple" also means 'one's self'; "a single master" means 'one's self.' So, the whole phrase means 'the attainment of one's own or true self by oneself.' We need not practice under the guidance of a single teacher. Even by looking at peach blossoms one can make one's own self clear.[4]

But the Japanese ego-consciousness was greatly different from the Western one of the same period. In Zen Buddhism it was supposed that the true spirit of religion should be handed down from master to disciple. According to the Western way of understanding, the self of the master must be something different from that of the disciple. But Tenkei asserts that both are one; i.e., essentially the transmission of the spirit of religion is done from the Great Self to the Great Self. "The transmission of the Self cannot be caused by others. It is the transmission from one's self to one's self."[5] Master Dōgen taught 'learning one's self,' and Tenkei explained that it was nothing but the way of following 'the Great Self.' 'To learn (know) one's self' was interpreted as meaning 'to know one's Mind.' 'To know one's Mind' was emphasized by such Zen priests as Munan (1603–1676), Bankei, etc. Ishida Baigan (1685–1748) also said: "To know Mind is said to be the beginning of learning (science)."[6] It was said that it should be found out by oneself.

As the Japanese concept of the self differs from the Western one, its ethical implication became different. In the West individualism was regarded as the basis of ethics. But in Japan the removal of conflict between different individuals was regarded as the ethical ideal. This was probably due to Buddhist influence, but even among non-Buddhists this thought is noticed. Ishida Baigan, the founder of the *Shingaku* school, said as follows: "Real learning consists in attaining complete *freedom from the personal Mind.*" "You must conceive this *selflessness* as a Law."[7] Among the thinkers of the modern West egoism and individualism were clearly distinguished; but among the Japanese thinkers of the same period this distinction was not so clearly made. Instead, another way of approach to the self was displayed. Hakuin's (1636–1769) Introspection was a kind of autosuggestion based on the idea that man's body and spirit form a close unity. This method of Introspection through which man, in a certain sense, finds his true self, liberates spiritual forces which greatly influence also man's bodily well-being.[8] However, the thinkers who advocated the significance of the individual were not entirely lacking. For example, Ninomiya Sontoku (1787–1856) valued the individual in a way that was unusual for his time. Once, pointing to the statue of the Buddha that represents him as saying when he was born, "Between heaven and earth only I am holy," Sontoku said to his disciples: "The Buddha did not use those words out of false pride, nor must they be applied exclusively to him. The teaching ought to be that every man thinking of himself should feel, that between heaven and earth there is no more noble man than he, for were he not existent there would be nothing".[9] Originally this legend came into existence in order to glorify the superhuman quality of the Buddha among later devout Buddhists.[10] Sontoku's interpretation seems to have been a slightly modernized one. But here we find the assertion of the dignity and significance of the individual in its incipient stage.

The consciousness of ego and the critical spirit finally led to the appearance of some materialists. In the modern West materialism occurrde: Bacon and Hobbes, in England, and La Metree, D'Olbach, Diderot, etc., were its advocates before Marx and Engels. With regard to the Japanese counterparts, as those who prepared the way for materialism we can mention Kaibara Ekken (1630–1714), Ogyū Sorai (1666–1728), Dazai Shuntai (1680–1747), Tominaga Nakamoto (1715–1746), Miura Baien (1723–1789), Minakawa Kien (1731–1804), and those who approached materialism Kamada Ryūō (1733–1821), Yamakata Bantō (1746–1821) and Andō Shōeki (1707–c. 1760), although Japan piror to to the Meiji Restoration may be said to have had no materialists in the strict sense of the word.[11] They were anti-religious, but their thoughts were limited to a small circle, and they left little influence. It was only due to the efforts of some foreign scholars such as the late E. H. Norman[12] and a Russian communist scholar that Japanese intellectuals in general came to notice the existence of materialists in the late feudal days.

Empirical Inquiry

In the West the modern age began with critical inquiry by means of doubt. Doubt was encouraged in China as in the West.

In the West doubts were first directed towards miracles which were essential to the faith of the Medieval Ages. In Japan also we can tr ecaa similar movement. Miracles were already repudiated in the Medieval Ages by Master Dōgen who said: "People commonly believe that occult powers of Buddhas are such as exhaling water and fire from the body of inhaling water from the ocean into the pores of body." These may be called "small occult powers," but they are not worthy of the name of the true occult powers. The true occult powers, that is to say, "great occult powers," exist within and only within the simple everyday occurrences of "drinking tea, eating rice, drawing water, and carrying faggots." This is the "occult power of Buddha" or "the occult power of one who aspires to be a Buddha." One who practices this power will eventually become "an occult-power Buddha." It means that the true miracle is the fact that one lives righteously one's own daily life.[13] Suzuki Shōsan (1579–1655) repudiated miracles set forth by Catholicism. He said: "There should be no miracle in the true religion. In Japan the chief miracle workers are foxes and badgers."[14] Yoshida Shōin (1830–1859), the nationalist leader, strongly criticized the miracle stories mentioned in the Kannon Sūtra.[15] But in Japan the problem of miracles did not cause much trouble, because miracles were not regarded as essential to Buddhism.

Ninomiya Sontoku said that the true teaching should be read from the unwritten sacred book of nature. He had a poem: "Without sound, without odor, heaven and earth repeat over and over again the unwritten sacred book." If you wish to read this book you must close your physical eyes and open your spiritual eyes. He says there are mistakes in the written books and therefore he compares them with the unwritten book of nature and unless they are in harmony with the universe-book he rejects them.[16]

His sole reliance upon experience led him to practical attitude. Ninomiya said: "True learning does not consist in knowledge of books; it must be practical and capable of practical application."[17] The idea of "practical learning (*jitsugaku*)" was espoused not only by Satō Nobuhiro (1769–1850) and others, but also by such a novelist as Takizawa Bakin (1767–1848).[18]

In Japan some ingenious intellectuals engaged in scientific researches and inventions. For example, the activities of Hiraga Gennai (1728–1779) have many similarities to those of Benjamin Franklin in his experiments with electricity, etc. But their attempts did not develop.

Nature and Natural Law

The concept of a "natural order" had become widespread in seventeenth and eighteenth century Europe. Corresponding to it in Japan of nearly the same period the concept of natural law was advocated by many thinkers.

Universality of truth came to be stressed. Master Munan said: "Confucius said: 'My doctrine is that of an all-pervading unity.'[19] The purport of this saying is (the Way's) pervading Heaven and Earth. It is tantamount to the Buddhist Great Wisdom (Maha-prajñā)."[20] Whether such an interpretation of the Great Wisdom is right or not is in need of further examining. But Munaon tok it for asserting universality of truth. Such an opinion was conspicuous among liberal Zen priests and Shingaku teachers and scholars of a new tendency, such as Jiun Sonja (1718–1804) in the Tokugawa period, etc.

St. Jiun, the pioneer of Sanskrit scholarship in Japan, stressed the idea with a rationalistic attitude. "In this world there are the true Laws which benefits it always. Those who have open eyes can see these Laws as clearly as they see the sun and moon. Whether a Buddha appears or whether a Buddha does not appear, (regardless of it) this world exists, and human beings exist. These Ten Virtues will always be manifest along them (i.e., so long as they exist)."[21]

Here we are surprised by the striking similarity of the concepts of natural law between Grotius and Jiun. However, Grotius was a Westerner. He says: "And yet God may be called the author of natural law, since He is the author of Nature, and therefore wills this law to be valid." Jiun's opinion is quite different. According to him, nature and law are nothing but Buddha himself.

Jiun found the essence of Buddhism in observing natural law, which could be termed as the observance of the Ten Virtues. "It is true of only the teachings of the Ten Virtues that they never change. Throughout all the ages, both ancient and modern, and throughout all lands they constitute the suitable and true Path for both the wise and the ignorant, the superior man and the inferior man, and for both men and women."[22]

Formerly, and even after the introduction of Western civilization in the Meiji era, Shintoism was regarded as the principle or rallying point of jingoistic nationalism. However, St. Jiun explained away Shintoism as the universal way of all mankind. What he called Shinto may be summed up in a word by the following two points: one's own pure conscience;[23] and the great justice[24] by which the sovereigns and subjects are ethically bound to each other.[25] This one single pure conscience is the common fundamental property of the ruling monarch above and of the common people under him, existing from the earliest age of the gods till the present day and from the present day to the most distant future, co-eternal with the heavens and the earth."[26]

St. Jiun, in his interpretation of the classics, gives rational and symbolical explanations and tries to make the people of the Tokugawa period understand advanced philosophical and ethical ideas in them.[27]

Natural law should be the basis for ethical conduct throughoht all countries. "Just as heaven and earth exist, so also are there various countries in existence. Sun, moon, and stars move according to the laws of heaven, while mountains, seas and rivers are governed by the laws of earth. As there are various countries, so there exist men to inhabit them. The human nexus is constituted by the relationships between lord and subject, parents and children, husband and wife, between brothers, and between friends."[28]

However, Jiun was not a law scholar. Whereas Grotius made a quite extraordinary impression on the statesmen of the seventeenth and eighteenth centuries, and influenced later legal thought, Jiun was an individual thinker and his thought was forgotten.

Ishida Baigan, the founder of the Shingaku school, admitted Nature, which is good. "A healthy person can taste food and enjoy it, but a man sick with fever even if he does eat, cannot taste good food and so does not enjoy it. The people who do not understand Good Nature are like that."[29] Using the technical terms of the Neo-Confucianists of the Sung 宋 period, he explains Nature: "The movement of the Forms is the ever spreading Ether of Heaven and Earth. As it can be clearly seen that Heaven and Earth and myself are single, harmonious thing, we can deduce that the theory of Good Nature is evident and in agreement with the Doctrine of Changes."[30]

Our human individual is a microcosm, and in this sense it partakes of Nature. "inspiration and Expiration are negative and positive. Those who follow this are good. The Internal Substance which rules the deeds of our External Functioning is Nature. From this you can see that, man, as a whole, is a small Heaven and Earth. If you fully conceive your being as a small Heaven and Earth, you will never complain for lack of anything."[31]

In the behavioral context it can be called Human-Heartedness. "The peace of one's mind is Human-Heartedness. Human-Heartedness is Heaven's original Ether. This Ether from Heaven generates and keeps alive

all these Thousand Things. The aim and the reason for learning is to get
to know one's mind. Our duty is to feed nature through our mind while
we breathe. If we follow the Way of Human-Heartedness and Love and
Propriety even a little, we may live in peace."[32]

Considered in terms of the Forms, another term of the Neo-Confucianists, Nature is called the Mind. "It is the Mind which identifies itself
in the Forms. See how the Mind exists even in birds and animals! Frogs
are naturally afraid of snakes. It is not surely a mother who teaches her
offspring that snakes are dangerous and will gobble them up and, of
course, tadpoles do not study and do not gradually learn all this. The
fact is that if you are born under the Form of a frog, the fear for snakes
comes straight in the Mind from the Form. Let us consider something
analogous: when summer comes a flea clings to man's body. Here again,
do a flea's parents teach it to live by sucking men's blood? Is it taught if
it sees a man's hand approach, it must jump away immediately lest it lose
its life? The reason is that when a flea jumps away it acts in accordance
with the Forms and not because it has learnt to do so."[33] "Birds and
beasts have no Personal Mind and therefore comply perfectly with the
dictates of the Forms."[34] The explanation of nature with these illustrations is not so different from that of the West. But it seems that Nature
was equated with the Mind by him. "What is called Nature is the Internal
Substance of Heaven, of Earth and Man."[35]

The final goal of ethical conduct was, according to him, to recover
one's own original Mind. "To attain something by following the Law
means to attain the Mind."[36] "If you just let yourself go, and become
receptive, everything is natural, easy, evident."[37] One might be surprised,
when he knows that he wants to apply his theory even to politics. "By
ruling without acknowledging this Order (Principle) a ruler will not be
able to govern his country."[38] His thought may sound too idealistic, but
when we find a highly idealistic Western counterpart in Fichte, we need
not be surprised.

The same inclination can be noticed in aesthetics also. Discussing Sanskrit and Dutch poetry *together*, Miura Baien was led to a conviction
that there exists some universal aesthetical principles valid for poetry

Eastern and Western. He concludes: "From this it may be seen that all that is in accordance with the essence of things never deviates from the one path."[39]

Ninomiya Sontoku, the "Peasant Sage," emphasized the indebtedness of mankind to nature and to fellowship, Man's true nature, Sontoku taught, consists in pious devotion to the order of nature, which manifests itself in the moral order of human life, especially in the relation between the lord and his subjects, parents and children, benefactor and recipient in general, expressed in grace and gratitude. Nature evolves and changes by itself, but man has to conquer his instinctive selfishness and endeabor to conform to the moral order of life.[40] Contrary to the general trend of naturalism, Ninomiya Sontoku emphasized frugality, which is an outcome of the sense of indebtedness, and gratitude for the benefit bestowed.

The most radical conception of Nature was held by Andō Shōeki, who said: "It is erroneous to designate as 'the Way' various teachings such as Confucianism, Buddhism, Shintoism, Taoism, and medicine. By the Way ought to be implied the single motivating power of Nature, that is the unique principle of practical virtue."[41] He severely criticized traditional religions. "Saints (or sages) of all ages stole Heaven's way, made arbitrary institutions out of it, sold benebolence and righteousness, bought (i.e., received) taxes, and ate and dressed by so doing. The saints' followers sold the laws of the saints and bought the world of avarice to eat and dress without labor."[42]

The terms 'law' and 'natural law' had been used from antiquity on, and we find it rather difficult to discern the difference between the ancient and the modern usage of these terms. This point should be subjected to further study.

The Idea of Evolution

The idea of nature or natural law was common to both East and West. But what was lacking in Eastern countries was the idea of evolution. There were ,he ideas of change, manifestation and development there. But people there did not think of evolution clearly. The idea of evolution appeared first in the modern West. It seems that this idea did not

occur in Eastern countries prior to the introduction of Western civilization, although its influence has been very strong since then.

In correspondence with this feature, dialectical thinking was not clear
in Eastern countries before the introduction of Western civilization. The
T'ien-t'ai and San-lun philosophies of ancient China and Japan had some
dialectical thinking, but it did not develop in the line of dialectics. In
modern Japan there were some individual thinkers who held some dialectical ideas. Ishida Baigan set forth the thought that Negative and
Positive are two things and yet they cannot be separated. But even if it
seems one, it has the two aspects of Motion and Quiescence.[43]

Miura Baien (1723–1789) expressed a theory of dialectic of his own.
The way to understand nature (or the universe) is dialectics (*jōri*). The
secret (*ketsu*) of dialectics is to see synthesis (*gōitsu*) in antithesis (*han*). It
is to give up one-sided preoccupation and to correct marks (*chōhyō*). *Yin*
and *Yang* are antithetical to each other, and constitute a battle. As they
are antithetic to each other they can be brought to synthesis.[44] He said:
"The way to see things thoroughly (*takkan*) is logic (*jōri*) and the essence
of logic is nothing else but the dialectic of antithesis and synthesis
(*hankan gōitsu*), setting aside all attachments of mind and following the
correct signs."[45] The three elements, then, that go into the full structure
of Miura's *jōri* are the dialectic of things, the prerequisite eliminations
of bias and preoccupation, and finally, the empirical test.[46]

Here we find the thought of dialectics in its incipient stage. But his
opinion was not set forth so systematically as the system of Hegel.

3. Change in Valuation of Traditional Symbols

The Problems

Modern valuation of man begins with the discarding of charimatic
authorities in general. Moderns generally do not admit the significance
of particular men who are qualified with higher magical or spiritual
power by birth or by esoteric practice.

To this fundamental attitude there are three corollaries:

(1) Denunciation of esoteric religious practices which are regarded as

endowing the practitioner with charismatic authority. Here "esoteric" means "to be intended for only a secluded group of disciples or inmates who are qualified by a religious authority."

(2) Denunciation of ,he charisma of a particular person who has been given prestige by peculiar practices authorized by something above men. "Charisma" means possessing certain exteaordinary, divine powesr which inspire people to follow a specific pattern of behavior laid down by an authority.

(3) Denunciation of systems of esoteric religious practices, which have tended to be formalistic. Denunciation of esoteric religious austerities was the starting-point for the development of modern thought.

Denunciation of Religious Formalism and Stresson Inner Devotion

The esteem of religious rites is based upon the attention paid to the outer symbolical expression of our religious feeling. Stereotyped symbols do not necessarily express human values. The effort then to recover one-self as man implies the devaluation of esoteric or formalistic religious rites and symbol, and stress on inner devotion.

However, it was only independent individuals who expressed the attitude of iconoclasm. For example, Mokujiki (1718–1810), the itiner-ant, said:

> *"My voice has become hoarse*
> *Due to repetition of Nembutsu prayers*
> *But, alas, no reply!*
> *Amida and Shakya Buddha are taking a siesta!"*[47]

Therefore, iconoclasm did not occur as a nation-wide movement among Japanese Buddhists. A work entitled *Daijingū Sankeiki* (The Diary of a Pilgrim to Ise Shrine) by Saka-Shibutsu, father of Jubutsu, runs as follows:

> "It is quite usual with us and it is of great significance, that we do not carry with us any rosaries like Buddhists and we do not present any material offerings to the Sun-Goddess at Ise; in other words, there is no selfish desire or petition on our part. This is called inner purity or heart-purity. We worshippers cleanse ourselves with lustral water

ceremonially; we call this outer purity or bodily purity. So purified, without and within, we are all-purity itself like the Divinity. The deity is immanent in man and man is inherent in the deity; there is neither the divine nor the human; there is no difference in essence at all between them. When I the author was so told by the Shinto priest at the Shrine of the Sun-Goddess, I was overwhelmed with tears of pious gratitude."[48]

Watarai Nobuyoshi (died in 1690) said: "Complete sinceri tyis the absolute principle of Shintoism."[49] The new Shinto sects which appeared at the end of the Tokugawa period showeō a strong tendency to discard all doctrinal subtleties and complicated ritualism, and to establish a religion of the simple pure heart. On the occasion of the Meiji Restoration fanatic nationalists took images of Buddhas and Bodhisattvas and copies of scriptures out of Buddhist temples, and burnt them. But this wast on a movement which occurred from within Japanese Buddhism itself, but which was instigated by aggressive Shinto revivalists. Shinto iconoclasm was carried out within its own tradition without any religious influence from abroad.

Religious rites can be regarded as symbols, in essential respects, expressing and communicating one's own religious feelings and will to act in accordance with religious values. But they themselves should not be regarded as absolute, however long they may have been traditionally observed. If they come to bind and hamper men, they cease to be such. Some modern thinkers of Japan took this view, and tried to restore the basis upon which religious symbols exist.

Denunciation of the Chrismatic Authority of an Individual

In the Medieval Ages, both in the East and West, spiritual teachers claimed special authority over their diciples and followers. They assumed the role of superior men and were regarded as higher than common people. Very often they served as living gods or deputies of God or gods.

Such an attitude was criticized very often by Zen masters, but not necessarily in modern times. One of the religious leaders of modern

Japan who is noteworthy in this connexion is Suzuki Shōsan who denied the authority of the founders and previous masters of various sects. He said: "Looking into written sayings of previous masters, it does not seem that there have been persons who have practiced with zeal."[50]

Master Munan, explaining the phrase: "Transmission outside the doctrines," said

"As the essence of religion lies originally outside of the doctrines, we cannot help. It was a big blunder that Lord Shakya taught the excellent teaching!"[51]

Here a Zen master actually admonishes the founder of Buddha!

Andō Shōkei judged Confucian scholars and Buddhist clergy as the spiritual oppressors of his age, in the same way as Winstanley decried the clergy and lawyers as the chief deceivers of the people. Yet neither Shōkei nor Winstanley can be properly termed atheists. The one preserved a veneration for the genial gods of old Japan and, like a pantheist, he seems to have equated them with the forces of Nature; the other, puritan and protestant, looked to the Scriptures as his sole guide to morality and political practice.[52]

In order to ridicule the secluded life of recluses, Munan tested recluses, saying: "One who will become a recluse in mountains without attaining enlightenment is due to become a beast!"[53]

4. Denunciation of Religious Differences

The attitude of denouncing charismatic and scriptural authority, on the one hand, and that of denouncing religious rites, on the other hand, led thinkers to reject differences between religions.

This tendency occurred among reformative religious leaders of Japan at nearly the same period as in the West. Tenkei, the liberal Sōtō Zen teacher, did not deny the distinction between various sects,[54] but he denied distinctions such as Rinzai, Sōtō, etc. in Zen Buddhism. Tenkei, being a monk of Sōtō Zen, eliminated or criticized the passages in Dōgen's works in which Master Dōgen, the founder of Japanese Sōtō Zen, praised the lineage of Sōtō, and rejected the lineage of Rinzai. It would be difficult to think of his liberal attitude apart from his social background that he preached in the city of Osaka, the most prosperous commercial center of Japan. Most Shingaku teachers taught Buddhism in general. Kyūō (1783–1839) said:

"Different sects look up to the same moon shining on the summit. . . . Each one should keep the teaching of one's own sect carefully, and endeavor not to compute with others."[55]

When the above-mentioned standpoint is theoretically pushed to the extreme, the distinction between various religions should be abolished. Master Munan said: "Mind is called Gods, Heaven or Budda in three countries (i.e., Japan, China and India). Their terms are different, but the same in essence."[56]

We find the same echo in the campaign of Confucianists also. Itō Jinsai (1627–1705) said: "From the viewpoint of scholars there is in fact Confucianism and Buddhism; from the viewpoint of the Universe there is properly neither Confucianism nor Buddhism; there is but One Way and that is all!"[57]

When we come to think further theoretically, what is called a religion itself comes to be useless. Mokujiki, the itinerant priest, blamed the narrow attitude of sectarianism.

"It would be useless to be staunchly devout to Buddhism; When I I asked Dear Amida (about what Buddhism is), he replied: O! Conglomeration of falsehood!"[58]

Ishida Baigan asserted that one should foresake the specific appellation of each religion. "When you have attained the Mind, you are free from either the names of Buddhism or of Confucianism."[59] "There are no different Minds and whoever believes that thanks to Buddhism he can attain a different Mind, is foolish, and will never come to any good"[60] Both the Shingaku movement originating from Ishida Baigan and the Hōtoku movement originating from Ninomiya Sontoku, were more or less eclectic and attempted to extract from various religions what was most essential to religion and beneficial to practical ethics and popular instruction. This feature can be found in the thought of Master Jiun, the pioneer of Sanskrit scholarship also.

In spite of these new movements, however, denominational boundaries were strictly laid down by the Tokugawa Government, and over-stepping them was prohibited.

In the field of religion highly liberal movements such as unitarianism or universalism occurred. The Shingaku scholars of Japan advocated that Mind alone is the basis of religion and minimized all authorities.

Every dogmatic religion overlooks the practical significance of symbols, and worships not only images but also theological opinions. These are nothing but the outer symbols of the absolute. These forms are employed by religions only to focus their faith. When the worshippers confuse these outer symbols with the deeper true reality, they get into idolatry.

The current diverse religious groups which are bound within themselves by means of dogmas, rites, and ceremonies, militate against the formation of a universal human society. If we realize the true significance of symbolism, then we shall not insist on any one route by which men reach knowledge of reality or truth. To reject the differences between religions, follows logically from a higher valuation of man.

It seems that such a non-sectarian tendency was easier to appear in Eastern countries than in the West. However, all movements of such a tendency had a stumbling block. Any new religious movement of this kind was based upon, so to speak, the greatest common measure of the several existing religions which were prevalent in those days. So any non-sectarian movement had to face the ironical danger that the movement itself tended to be sectarian at the end.

5. Change in Valuation of Man
Value of Man as the Supreme—Stress on Human Love

The ethics of esteeming man as such presupposes man as the supreme value. Some expect that faith in God leads to the realization of it, while others do not assume God and yet try to attain to the same realization. In either case love or compassion directed to others was regarded as the first principle of human action.

This attitude was emphasized also by some contemporaneous thinkers in Japan, who did not have belief in the Son of God.

In Christianity the relationship between Christ and his followers is sometimes explained in comparison to that which exists between bride and bridegroom. From this point of view, Kabir's mental attitude towards faith shares some common features with Western religion rather than with ancient Brahmanism and Buddhism.

Among Chinese and Japanese Buddhists, however, even in the modern ages, the idea of lover-sweetheart relationship never came into being, while the idea of compassion has been greatly extolled. Such a concept would have been deemed rather secular in China and Japan.

According to modern thinkers, love replaces everything. Their insistence on the spirit of emphasizing love or compassion is such that it becomes the basis of all kinds of moral action and eventually raises the valuation of man.

Some modern thinkers asserted that man's sinfulness is justified for the sake of the glory of God.

Such an assertion was not entertained by contemporaneous thinkers in China, Japan or other Asian countries, for Buddhism does not presuppose creation by God, and consequently there was no need to justify it.

In China and Japan of the same period, a tendency to set forth the esteem of love in the form of esteeming the physical nature of human being was in existence.

In modern Japan Confucianists tried to accept man's natural dispositions against the traditions of Chinese Confucianism and Buddhism. Ogyū Sorai recognized the intrinsic value latent in Japanese novels, in spite of their immoral contents.[61] Dazai Shuntai called man's natural feelings the real feelings, which he defined to be "likes and dislikes, sufferings and rejoicing, and anxiety and pleasure, etc." And he went on to maintain".... There is not a single human being devoid of these feelings. ... Love of one's parents, wife and children is also the same among the noble and the common. Since these feelings are originated in the innate truthfulness of man which is free from any stain of sin or falsity, they are called the real feelings."[62] His standpoint was pure naturalism. "There are no double-dealings in the deeds motivated by the overflow of the natural dispositions, wherein no discrepancy between intentions and deeds is caused; the inside and outside are so transparent that reality and appearance are one and the same thing. The natural dispositions are the innate and *teue* nature of man."[63] He defiantly declared: "I would rather be a master of acrobatic feats, than to be a moralist."[64] Although there was no systematic philosophical basis for the existing affirmative attitude, the spirit of the Japanese people prior to the entry of Buddhism can be characterized as a mode of natural affirmation. And this feature was emphasized by scholars of Japanese classics.[65]

Motoori Norinaga (1730–1801), refuting Confucianism and Buddhism, said:
"The pure mind is the natural mind." "The Confucian scholars who are most highly esteemed as men of wisdom, and the Buddhist priests who are revered as saints, admire the beauty of stars and flowers, but they pretend never to have taken notice of a beautiful woman. What a deception of mind!"[66]
"They hate the natural inclinations of man, but are not these same inclinations the devine laws?"[67]

In such words of Motoori there sounds unmistakably the same feeling of joy and love of nature and man as was proclaimed in the European Renaissance. Hirata Atsutane (1766–1843), the founder of Jingoistic Shintoism, said: "To comply with the natural dispositions is called the Way . . . Man is born provided with the innate true feelings of benevolence, justice, propriety and intelligence. Not to falsify or not to distort them is the true way of humanity. . . . One should indeed stop acting like a sage and abandon the so-called Mind or the way of enlightenment, and all that are affected and Buddhaish.

Onkō (Jiun Sonja), a modern Buddnist thinker, preached that morality means to follow man's natural dispositions.[68] Tokugawa Nariaki the nationalist leader who attempted the revival of Confucian scholarship in the late feudal age of Japan, said: "What is spreading the Way (Kōdō)? It is man himself that can spread the Way."[69] It is noteworthy that Ishida Baigan came to point out that saints and ordinary men are not essentially different with respect to human nature. "All men are gifted with the immutable mind, but blinded by the Seven Emotions they believe that a Saint has some peculiar wisdom of his own which differes from any other wisdom of ordinary mortals, and due to their blindness they are filled with doubts"[70] Miki (1798–1887) of Yamato, the founder of the Tenrikyō religion taught that the human being is the abode of devine charity.

Corresponding to this new trend Buddhist masters came to reject the former attitude of asceticism. Master Hakuin (1685–1768) said: " 'To cast away oneself' does not mean 'ill-treat oneself' or 'to disregard diet and health.'"[71] Moreover, a new trend occurred in Buddhism also. Master Jiun said: "What is called man is gifted with the Ten Virtues and at the same time the world of humanity is by nature endowed with Ten Virtues. . . . One should have cognizance of man in contrast to animals."[72] And then he elaborates on the distinction between the two. In the mediaeval ages Japanese Buddhists were apt to lay more emphasis on the virtue of compassion, which should be extend to animals, than on the superiority of man over animals. But here a reformist Buddhist leader accentuates the dignity and significance of man.

As a corollary from the thought that man is the supreme, cruel punishments and customs, such as burning at the stake and duelling, which were prevalent in both East and West, became extinct although the date of extinction differed from country to country. With the dying of religious fantaticism, Buddhist monks no longer burned themselves on alters as sacrifices to Buddha, as in the mediaeval ages, in China and Japan. The attitude of some Zen masters became more lenient towards the sins of their disciples.[73]

Humanistic attitude as was mentionend above was given further accentuation and became an advantageous weapon to refute Christianity. Contrasting the Christian idea of the suprem God with Confucianism which was his own standpoint in this context, Baien says: "The Way of the Sages does indeed revere and venerate Heaven, but it is a doctorine of human ethics".[74] The anti-transcendent and society-centered ethics was forcifully stressed by him.[75]

But the humanitarian attitude in the modern ages was different from the attitude of mediaeval compassion. In Japan the practical observance of this mediaeval ideal had to be circumscribed within narrow bounds. For example, Ishida Baigan said: "If you try to realize the Way of government only through the fulfillment of the spirit of compassion and love and disregard the Saint's Law, rebellions will be the only result."[76] Thus the general tendency of humanitarian spirit developed in a rather realistic way.[77]

Equality of Man—Anti-discrimination

The rigidity of the class system (shi-nō-kō-shō or Samurai-farmer manufacturer-trader) already began to show signs of collaspe by the end of the 18th century, even before the official nullification of it at the time of the Meiji Restoration.[78]

The attitude of esteeming man as such leads one to discard all discriminations established upon the traditional authority. Already in mediaeval Japan religious leaders advocated the equality of man in the religious sense. Shinran did not admit that women are less capable than men of attaining to the state of bliss. Nichiren (1222–1282) found one of the justifications for his belief in the Lotus Sutra in its teaching of equality of the sexes. The Orai (Esoteric) teachings of the Japanese Tendai Sect advocated the equality of all mankind.[79] But their recognition of man's equality remained in the narrow bounds of the religious interpretation and did not develop into a social movement.

While the Western modern period was in progress, the cry for equality in Japan was not so loud as in the West or even in India. Even brilliant Buddhist leaders such as Master Jiun who was so progressive in other respects acquiesced in the existing hierarchical social system of Japan in those days. Master Jiun's own interpretation of the Buddhist teaching of equality is as follows: "Buddhism approves distinctions of grade and position. The equality it teaches is not such foolishness as that of breaking down high mountains, filling in deep valleys and making all into a dead level. Buddhism teaches us the way between lord and subjects, father and son, master and disciple."[80] But it does not follow that this standpoint of this shows his backwardness, for in the modern West also the regulations concerning these distinctions were enforced, which look quite backward in the eye of people of the present day.

In Japan before the introduction of the Western civilization there were Buddhist thinkers who advocated theories which implied equality of men. The author of the *Saru-hōgo* (Sermon by a monkey) denounced the concept of private property in the religious sense. "You should not make discrimination between self and others. Riches such as gold, silver, fortune and treasures are the common property of the whole world. Even if they are in the hands of others, they do not belong to them. Even if I keep them, they are not mine. If they are confined in the hands of others without being utilized, they are of no use; if I do not utilize them, solely keeping grip of them, it is like piling up stones."[81] Munan, a Zen priest, discouraged the custom of leaving property to one's own descendants. "You should not bequeath treasures to your children. It is certain that they are wasted. To practise the teaching of Buddha is most important."[82] They asserted that riches should be used for the benefit of the public. But their existence in society was marginal and hardly attracted any serious attention. In Eastern countries few attempts were made to bring the ideal of equality into practice. It was only with the advent of Western forces that the feudal system of Japan collasped.

In Japan under the Tokugawa government women were not given equal status with men. But towards the end of the Tokugawa feudal regime, there appeared prophetesses who founded new religions such as Isson-kyō, Tenri-kyō. This reminds us of the fact that a conspicuous religious phenomenon after World War II is the rise of new religions. Among a total of 120, about 48 were founded by ladies. This phenomenon cannot be found in pre-modern Japan.

This-Worldliness

The principle of esteeming man as such and loving men as equal beings tends to obliterate the attitude that takes it for granted to subject men to and sacrifice for any higher being, including God or gods.

The general tendency of religious thought in the mediaeval age throughout many countries can be described as being other-worldly.

Happiness people yearned for in those days was the one which was be-lieved to exist only in the future world after death, the supposed Heaven.

In Japan the turning-point from other-worldliness to this-worldliness seems to have occurred around theKan bun period (1661–1673). Prior to that period, i.e., in the early Tokugawa period, printed books were pub-lished at the rate of Buddhist 3 : non-Buddhist 1. But after this period the rate was reversed due to the fact that the circulation of printed books on Confucianism gradually increased. Buddhism suffered criticism for its other-worldliness by Japanese Confucianists and scholars of Japanese classics. Some reformist Buddhists changed their traditional attitude· The this-worldly character of Zen in the modern times was conspicuous in such Zen priests as Suzuki Shōsan who taught lay believers: "To pray for a happy future does not mean to pray for a world after death. It means to be delivered here and now and thus to attain a great comfort. Then, where do you think the afflictions of this world come from? They are originated from your attachment to your own flesh and to the de-mands of it. To be delivered from this attachment is the way to become a Buddha."[83] But such a doctrine was not generally accepted in the Tokugawa period.

Humanitarianism bears close reference to the attitude of this-worldli-ness, and is one of the conspicuous features that exerted no small influ-ence upon the evaluation of man in the modern times.

In Japanese Buddhism there appeared some reformists who affirmed human life on this side of heaven. Master Jiun said: "Some say that, since Buddhism urges only the disciplines of the mind by the mind's own capacity, it is of no use to the common people and of no value to those who govern them. Confucianism, which is said to teach the regulation of conduct by forms, ceremonies and rules of etiquette, is of great service in teaching and edifying people. This objection is made by those who do not really know what Buddhism is, and have seen only its shortcomings which arose after the dynasties of Sung and Yuan. Buddhism is the true Law, and the practical observance of its teachings, the Ten Virtues, en-ables even ordinary men to regulate themselves and their home, and finally walk in the path of righteousness."

However, the life-affirming attitude was more obviously found among non-Buddhists. According to Kurozumi Munetada (1780–1850), the founder of the Kurozumi sect of Shintoism, the significance of human life consists in a realization of our intrinsic connection with the cosmic vitality. This communion he denominated *iki-toshi,* i.e., "penetrating into life" or "pervaded by vitality." Ando Shōeki declared: "Direct cultivation and happy eating, direct weaving and happy clothing—there is no Way but this. Talking of thousands of ways is false."[84] But the avowal of such an outspoken assertion was not permitted under the pressure of the Tokugawa Shogunate government. It was only after the Meiji Restoration that freedom to express one's opinion publicly became possible, but sometimes with the probability of harsh censure on the side of educators and social leaders.

The Esteem of Activity in Society and Vocational Ethica

As earthly life consists in action, the attitude of this worldliness tends to emphasize action in social life. (*vita activa versus vita contemplativa.*)

In Japan the spirit of activity was extolled.

As Dōgen criticized and metamorphosed Chinese Zen in the medieval age, so Itō Jinsai (1627–1705), a Japanese Confucianist, amended the form of Chinese neo-Confucianism to answer his purpose. To Jinsai the intrinsic nature of both earth and heaven lies in their activeness which we would term evolutionary. Eternal development is the only and true existence. Jinsai completely denies what is called death.

The *Book of Changes* (I Ching) says, "The great virtue of heaven and earth is called life." It means that living without ceasing is the very way of heaven and earth. Because the way of heaven and earth is one with life, there exist life without death and convergence without divergence. Though the bodies of ancestors may perish, their spirits are inherited by their children, whose spirits are also handed down to their own children. When life thus evolves from generation to generation, without ceasing, through all eternity, it may be rightly said that no one dies.[85]

Itō Jinsai believes that the world of reality consists of change and action and that action is in itself good. "Between heaven and earth there is only one reason: motion without stillness, good without evil. Stillness is the end of motion, while evil is the change of good; and good is a kind of life, while evil is a kind of death. It is not that these two opposites are generated together, but they are all one with life."[86]

Itō Jinsai's younger contemporary Ogyū Sorai, though a rival to Jinsai, does not grudge his admiration for Jinsai's activities, calling them "the supreme knowledge of a thousand years," and denounces the static character of the Chinese school of *Li*. In fact it can be said that all of the characteristic Japanese scholars believe in phenomena as the fundamental mode of existence. They unanimously rejected the quietism of the Confucianists of Mediaeval China (the Sung period).[87] Quiet sitting and fostering reverential love in one's heart used to be the method of mental training practised by most Chinese Confucianists of the Middle Ages (around the Sung period). Sorai ridiculed those Confucianists and said: "As I look at them, even gambling seems to be superior to quiet sitting and fostering reverential love in one's heart."[88]

Meditation was repudiated even by some Zen masters notwithstanding that the quintessence of their religion would be in the practice of meditation. Suzuki Shōsan discouraged laymen from practising meditation; instead he encouraged them in their faithful performance of daily duties.

The encouragement of the spirit of activity was conspicuous especially among the merchants whose influence was gradually permeating the society. Ishida Baigan, one of their ideological leaders and the founder of the Shingaku movement, said: "Once Confucius stood by a river and said;[89] 'It flows on just like this, never ceasing day and night!' He means that a flowing river is the possible best means to penetrate the Internal Substance of the Way."[90] This somewhat twisted interpretation was similar to that which was given by Itō Jinsai.[91] Confucius lamented the transitoriness of all things under the sun by the saying, but Jinsai took it for his extolment of the activeness of generations and development of all things.

This characteristic willingness to accept the phenomenal world as given and to live contentedly in it was not confined exclusively to Buddhism and Confucianism in Japan. It is found in modern pre-Meiji Shintoism as well. The founder of the Konkō sect teaches: "Whether alive or dead, you should regard the heaven and earth as your own habitation."[92]

This spirit finally became the motivating power for the modernization of Japan. The new religions whose appearance dates around the turning-point leading to the collapse of the feudal regime entertained the same notion. Here is a little anecdote of kurozumi Munetada who had been severely ill with consumption for a long time. It was in 1874 when he was at the age of thirty four. On the morning of the winter solstice, while worshipping the rising sun, he was suddenly awakened mentally and bodily to complete recovery from his chronic disease. Tokugawa Nariaki, one of the instigators for the Meiji Restoration, insisted upon the importance of the spirit of activity. "How can we Japanese subjects of the Emperor remain inactive without undertaking the propaganda of this Way and without revealing to the world the virtuous merits of our ancestors? It is with this aim in view that this Institute has been founded." It may be said that there is little disparity in substance between this attitude and the national consciousness in other countries in the modern ages, save that the aim of Nariaki's action lay in "revering the Emperor and expelling the barbarians." In this case he meant by "barbarians" Westerners.

On the other hand, there was a thinker isolated from the current of the time. Andō Shōeki advocated The Way of Nature and Labour.[93] He protested against exploitation by feudal lords. He appreciated the exultation of agriculture and sympathized with peasants for their miserable condition under the oppression of feudal lords.

According to Norman, Shōkei has two counterparts in the West. One is François Quesnay (1694–1774), a French encyclopédiste, and the most famous of the Physiocrats. Both lived at nearly the same time; both were physicians but agriculture was their real delight.[94] Just as Quesnay found in China the exemplification of the natural order, so Shōkei in the reverse direction turned to Europe for one of the model states he pictured to himself.[95] The other counterpart, Gerrard Winstanley was also a spokesman for the underprivileged and impoverished section of the community, the evicted tenant, the precarious day labourer, the copy holder vainly struggling against the onslaught of the landlord who proceeded with enclosure.[96] Thus he paid due attention to labouring people and in this respect he has something in common with Saint-Simon (1768–1825), who asserted that the ultimate aim was the rise, both in intellect and economy, of the working class, the class which suffered most.

A corollary from the attitude of esteeming activity was to denounce the life of monks. Mediaeval layistic leaders such as Shinran still held respect and esteem for the monks who were leading an ascetic life. They held those monks to be superior to themselves. But in the modern age some activistic thinkers despised monks for their indolence and inactivity. Ninomiya disliked priests and scholars in general because in his opinion, they were not producers, and so did not add to the prosperity of the country.[97]

In this connexion, the Buddhist custom of mendicancy or living by begging alms became the target of severe criticism of Japanese Confucianists, and gradually died out.

It is noteworthy that the above-mentioned trend of emphasizing activity is so similar to that of the West.[98]

In Shintoism there was an idea called "Yosashi" which is an equivalent of "mikoto-mochite,"[99] its literal meaning being "by (the grace of) calling by God." It etymologically coincide with the Western concept of 'vocation,' or 'Beruf.' Shintoists based their own vocational ethics on this concept,[110] 'calling.'

Towards the modern period of Japan there occurred a theory that if a man pursues his own secular vocation with his whole heart and soul, he is practising nothing other than the ascetic practice of Buddhism.

Takuan (1573–1645), a Zen priest, taught: "The Law of the Buddha, well observed, is identical with the Law of mundane existence. The Law of mundane existence, well observed, is identical with the Law of Buddha."[101] This idea was especially stressed by Suzuki Shōsan, another Zen priest, who claimed to be the first man to apply Buddhism to matters of mundane existence. He wrote a book entitled *Banmin Tokuyō* (The Significance of Everyman's Activities), in which he discussed problems of vocational ethics. He found absolute significance in the pursuit of any

vocation, whether it be that of a warrior, a farmer, a craftman, a merchant, a doctor, an actor, a hunter, or a priest. He reasoned that to pursue
one's own vocation is to obey the Absolute One because the essence of
Buddhism consists in reliance upon the guidance of the original self or
upon "the true Buddha of one's own" and every vocation is the function of this "one Buddha." Thus he preached to farmers: "Farming is
nothing but the doings of a Buddha."[102] To merchants he taught: "Renounce desires and pursue profits single-heartedly. But you should never
enjoy the fruit of your labors. You should, instead, work for the good
of all others." Since afflictions of this world, it is said, are predestined in
former worlds, one should torture oneself by working hard at one's own
vocation, in order to redeem the sins committed in one's former life.[103]
It is noteworthy that, immediately after the death of Calvin, an idea
similar to his appeared almost contemporaneously in Japan. The fact,
however, that it never grew into a religious movement of great consequence ought to be studied in relation to the underdevelopment of a
modern *bourgeois* society in Japan.

To Yokoi Shōnan (1809–69), one of the most progressive thinkers of
Japan during the latter half of the bakumatsu period (1840–67), Christianity was a religion which was perfectly congurous with the material-
istic mind of the West. Shōnan attributed the western virtue of hard
work to Christianity and in this respect he perceived in Christianity
something analoguous to what is known as the protestant ethics.[104]

A Japanese counterpart of the predestination theory by Dutch Cal-
vinists is found in the teachings of the Nyorai-kyō religion founded by
a prophetess called Kino (died 2 May 1826).[105]

A change to asceticism practiced by means of faithful performance of
duties in mundane existence appeared in a much wider circle of Shinshū
believers. In the early period Shinshū stressed salvation by faith alone and
paid little attention to ethical demands, but by the middle of the Tokugawa period ethical action came to be regarded as a pre-condition for
salvation and no more was heard about the wicked being saved. Thus
ethical action became the very sign of salvation.[106]

The Hōtoku (lit. 'To Return Virtues') teaching, which was derived from the teaching of Ninomiya Sontoku and was addressed especially to agricultural population, emphasized energy and work. The purport of his teaching is as follows: "We owe our life and its preservation and enjoyment first to the benefits granted by Heaven and Creation, then to those we receive from our sovereign, our country, our parents, and other sources innumerable. We have laws and social obligations which compel us to return, in some degree, the benefits received from parents sovereign, and country; but there are no laws obliging us to render our gratitude by actions for the greater benefits bestowed on us by Heaven; therefore men are prone o₃ forget that requital for the heavenly benefits is their first duty, and neglect it. Some indeed remember, but generally they think it enough to show their gratitude by ceremonies of worship and thanksgiving, and not by deeds. This should not be so. We muss bear the will of Heaven in mind, and try to cultivate Heaven-sent virtuet in us and work earnestly to promote the progress and the development of all creation. We find that even the great success of industrial capitalism in modern Japan is readily traced to the diligence of the common people, whose moral background is rooted in the teachings of Ninomiya Sontoku, an original philosopher-economist of the late Tokugawa period.

The moral-economic philosophy of Ninomiya with its four fundamentals, faith, labour, economy and charity, may have been favourable to fair capitalist competition, although his influence remained chiefly among peasants. In pre-war days, patronized by the nation and adapted to its educational policy, his spirit dominated the national education in moral practice throughout the country. But the rise of capitalism in Japan after the Meiji Restoration should be viewed in a wider context.

Lay Tendencies in Religion

This-worldliness tends to liberate religion from the exclusive possession of the priesthood. We have to first take Shinran into consideration for research on the tendency to implant religion in the mind and life of the laity. Although Shinran belongs to the mediaeval age, his life and activities have so many points in common with Luther, especially in the respect of lay religion.[107]

Shinran learned the traditional Tendai theology at the Hieizan monastery which was the scholarly centre of Japanese Buddhism. But he found himself at an impasse when his earnest practice of meditation led him nowhere and all carnal desires and mental afflictions remained with him. Shinran felt that his efforts had been in vain. He had practiced asceticism, unspairing of pains and absorbed in speculation, only to come to the conclusion that, notwithstanding all that had been done and all his faith in himself, he had advanced not a single step nearer the goal. He said to himself: "It grows dark, but the goal is still far off! Now there is but one way left to save my soul. I must seek for divine guidance."[108] He turned to Kwannon, the Buddhist counterpart of Mary, for his spiritual rest. He confined himself to the Rokkaku-dō temple and prayed to the Kwannon enshrined in it for days and nights, until Kwannon revealed herself to him and had him study under Hōnen (1133–1212), the founder of Pure Land Buddhism who taught him that one can be saved solely by the grace and compassion of Amida Buddha.

Concerning Shinran's marriage[109] there are some legends, but at any rate he spent a married life like the early Protestant leaders, and was the father of several children. Since then his followers have all married. Shinran combined religion with a layman's life.

It was noteworthy that in Japanese Buddhism as in Christianity there was a Protestant Reformation. Both Hōnen and Shinran, who is the more radical reformer of the two, cut themselves off from the abuses of the established sects just as Luther and Calvin did in Europe. In both cases the central principle was salvation by faith, not by works or ceremonies.

Pure Land Buddhism professed by them embodies the extreme doctrine of salvation by faith in Amida, the Buddha of Boundless Light. This doctrine parallels the doctrine of absolute reliance on God as stated in the Augusburg Confession. They said that faith in Amida arouses a new motive and refreshes a feeling of gratitude which transforms life. Both in Japan and in Europe these religious reformations were accompanied by social, political and economic phenomena. There was the same sort of lay movement started, the same sort of protest against the ascetic life of the monastic type, and the same encouragement of marriage, labour, and social activity, although it was only after the advent of Rennyo (1415–1499) that social activity became conspicuous. The political implications, however, were much more marked in the West than in Japan in proportion as the emphasis on faith as opposed to works was more extreme in Pure Land Buddhism than in Christianity.

Shinran and Vallabha,[110] an Indian religious reformer, came to be worshipped as divine in later days, and the successors of both, who were the chief abbots of each sect, being their offspring, came to be revered enthusiastically by the believers, whereas in the West the worship of the descendants of Luther or Calvin did not take place. This seems to be due to the difference in social structure between East and West. That is, in the modern West the tendency to esteem the lineage of a person almost ceased to exist, whereas in India or Japan of the corresponding period this attitude still remained.

In the Tokugawa period, Suzuki Shōsan, who claimed to be the first Buddhist teacher to advocate lay Buddhism, discouraged people from taking holy orders and thus forsaking their vocations in the world. Tenkei would not differentiate clergy from laity.[111] The author of *Saruhōgo* took the same point. "When one engages himself in commerce with the spirit of compassion and equality, it is enlightenment, the goal of the Way. When one is thus right and intelligent today, there is no need of being apprehensive of tomorrow. So, if one lives right in this life, one should not worry about the future life."[112] However, the abolition of the distinction between clergy and laity was not actually realized, probably due to social pressure by the Government.

Although we cannot hastely conclude that the layistic tendency is common to all modern religions, we may safely say that it appeared rather early in the modern ages throughout many countries in both East and West, developed later, and is now conspicuous in many modern religions.

Approach to the Common People
The attitude of esteeming man himself led thinkers to a more affec-

tionate view of the common people. They wanted to keep in close touch with the common people.

In Japan of the thirteenth century religious leaders began to employ Japanese in place of Chinese to expound their teachings in writings. Up to that time Chinese had been the formal language for the purpose. Especially in the Tokugawa period many Buddhist works written in easy, understandable Japanese were published for the common people. Like Luther, Shinran composed hymns intended for use at divine service in praise of the redemption which follows upon grace. In the conduct of worship he assigned an important place to the sermon.

In the Mediaeval West logical works were written in Latin alone. Antoine Arnould, together with Pierre Nocole compiled *La Logique de Port-Royal* in French for the first time in 1660. In ancient and mediaeval Japan all the works on Buddhist logic were written in classical Chinese. It was Echō Chikū (1780–1862) that wrote a logical work in Japanese, which was entitled *Inmyō Inu Sanshi* (Buddhist Syllogism in Imitation of Masters' Works). However, the author claimed the work to be a mere imitation of authoritative works. Here we find a problem in the fact that no attitude of protest against the tradition was displayed and that progressive scholarship was not carried on with confidence, but with humility.

What made a difference in popularization of knowledge through writings between West and East was a difference in typographycal technique between the two. In the West the invention of the printing machine made it easy to spread knowledge, while in China and Japan wood-block print was used, which helped to a great extent.

Service to People

A movement which denounces religious bigotry and rites and asserts the significance of love and activity in social life, tends to encourage service to people. Among some thinkers devotion to God took the form of love for humanity. The spirit of service to mankind, even including those to come in the future, was enhanced in the modern ages.

Parallel to the increase of humanitarian activities in the modern West, we find a similar move in Eastern countries as well. In Japan of this period, some unique features can be seen in the expression of humanitarian attitude, which was displayed even in warfares. To the mountain-locked province of his enemy, Uesugi Kenshin (1530–1578), a feudal lord, sent salt in 1542 A.D., not to have the people of his enemy's province suffer from lack of salt.[113] The captives of the Korean Campaigns (1592–1598) were treated in a brotherly manner in Japan and were sent home safely.[114] After the Roman Catholic rebellion in Shimabara (1637) was quelled, religious ceremonies were conducted and three big monuments were erected, not in the memory of the victory, but for the spiritual repose and beatitude of the Catholic converts killed in the rebellion,[115] who were pagans in the eyes of the Japanese. This humanitarian act may have been due to the Buddhist ideal. At any rate the attitude assumed by the Japanese on such an occasion seems to have been quite different from that in the Mediaeval West.

In Japan the spirit of solidarity was greatly emphasized and mutual aid was practised among the people. Individual Buddhist priests engaged themselves in humanitarian activities, such as the distribution of rice and money to the poor and of medicines to the sick.[116] Their activities ranges over healing the sick, constructing bridges, instituting public baths and many other social works. For example, Tetsugen (1630–1682)[117] raised funds to save the lives of starving people in the years of bad harvests. Ryōō (1630–1707) established dispensaries and some 70 libraries in various cities. St. Mokujiki dissuaded feudal lords from engaging in battles, to save people from suffering.[118] But activities of this kind were not duly organized. In fact there were few organizations for this purpose, and if any, their existence was only temporary. The traditional solid family system and the spirit of solidarity among the people seemed to have lessened the necessity of organized humanitarian activities.

As an outstanding figure in the attitude of rendering service to others, we can mention Ninomiya Sontoku. The teaching of morality and rendering help to others was combined by Sontoku with economic measures, such as a scheme for the rotation of crops, an organization for the circulation of capital, and accumulation of funds for famine relief.

Thus Sontoku viewed human life as a process of co-operation and mutual helpfulness and this combination of moral ideas and economic measures is the embodiment of his view. His influence produced practical effects among the peasants.[119]

Among Japanese priests there were some who engaged in the cultivation of land. Jōin[120] who was a Shinshu priest,[121] converted hundreds of acres of waste land into fertile paddy.

This event may not be worth mentioning but his record of cultivation displays interesting traits of modern thoughts. "It is true that a mere accumulation of riches is meaningless. But it is an act of delinquency to assume the attitude of believing indiscriminately in causes in previous existences according to the teaching of Buddhism, or believing in the mandate of Heaven according to Confucianism, or to "waiting good fortune lying in bed" according to a popular proverb. If such an attitude is approved, the affairs of the world will be neglected, people don't give regard to expenses for luxuries, don't observe thirftiness, then they would get less clothing in cold weather and less diet in sunny days." Here a Buddhist priest is rejecting the conventional application of the traditional teaching of *Karman* to daily conduct."[122] I want to cultivate the waste land granted by our feudal lord, and to leave the merit of my labour to our descendants. . . . Merely to inculcate people and bestow beatitude in the after-life cannot be called the way to save people. Buddhas and Bodhisattvas bestow benefits in the present life as well as in the future life."[123] However, this was an exceptional case, and generally speaking, economic activities were not closely related to Buddhism in this period.

The sympathy with the wretched common people led to severe criticism of the existing feudal system. Andō Shōeki said: "Rulers, supported by their warriors, devoured the cereals which were the product of the direct cultivation of the masses, and, when the masses were stout enough to resist their tyranny, they gathered together the power of warrior class to oppress them and to punish those who had disobeyed the sage's order, fearing the charge that they were usurping the world of Nature. . . . The multitude of the warriors under those rulers eat without cultivating, and since there is a shortage of cultivators, the world inevitably becomes agitated and threatening."[124] This thought seems not to have developed into a public opinion or a sort of social movement in the period under discussion, but it is unnegligible as a step toward the development of modern thought.

Esteem of Ethical Values as over against Magic and Mysticism

A high esteem of man himself naturally leads to high esteem of ethical norms. As ethical values replace magical, ecstatical, or fantastic elements and hold an extremely important place in religion, the need to improve forms of religion as activity becomes imminent. This feature occurred in Japan as well as in the West.

In Japan the ethical character of religion was highlighted by some Buddhists of new type. Master Jiun advocated the "Way to become a True Man." He found the essence of Buddhism in the practice of the Ten Virtues (Good Vows), as opposed to the tradition of ritualistic Buddhism. He says: "Man's Path (or duty) by which a man becomes a (true) man consists in the observance of the ten virtues."[125] The Ten Virtues consists of (1) Not Killing, (2) Not Stealing, (3) Not Committing Adultery, (4) Not Lying, (5) Not Talking Frivolously, (6) Not Slandering, (7) Not Being Double-tongued, (8) Not Coveting, (9) Not being Angry, and (10) Not Being Heretical.

Master Jiun raised an objection to those many traditional priests who were preoccupied with the idea that these vows are only rudimentary steps to religion, and that the essence of Buddhism lies in elaborate rituals and esoteric doctrines. Jiun said: "Shallow scholars think that this moral is only for the laity (Sekenkai) and of small importance, that the moral for the monks who practise for their own merits (Shomon 聲聞 sravaka) is still imperfect, and that the moral for the Bodhisattva alone is high and noble. As a matter of fact this opinion has its origin in the false ideas that arise from attaching too much importance to names (or titles). This moral of the Ten Virtues is very profound and magnificent to anybody."[126]

Jiun coincides with modern Western thinkers in the assertion that religion should be realized in the practice of moral. But they stand on quite different standpoints when it comes to the concept of 'good and evil'. "Conduct which is carried out in conformity with the principle of reason (ri 理) in its relation to the three bodily, the four lingual, and the three intellectual (mental) activities constitutes the Ten Virtues, while the ten vices result from conduct contrary to the principle of reason. The obedience to reason is to stay in perfect harmony with nature and never mars nature either by increasing or by decreasing it. The obedience to reason is the maintaining of nature in equilibrium. When the original nature (honsei or honsho 本性) is modified or perverted by the self-ness (shii 私意) the ten vices are the result. The actions of body, of speech and of thought that are conducted without the interference of this self-ness are called the Ten Virtues. Although Buddhism *does not worry about the distinction between good and evil*,[127] goodness or virtue is always in accord with the nature of Buddha (Bussho 佛性), while vice is non-accordant with it."[128]

Ninomiya Sontoku, who also advocated the life of activity, had a similar conception of morals. Of good and evil he says: "It is men that bring about the idea of good and evil and the difference between them. There would be neither good nor evil without men. Man thinks it good to develop waste lands, and bad to neglect them, while the bear and the deer think waste lands good. The thief thinks it good to steal, but the law pronounces it an evil. We cannot discern what is good and what is evil. It is like saying near and far. Suppose you put up with two stakes apart, one marked with 'far' and the other marked with 'near,' It is not the stakes themselves but your position that decides which is really far and which is really near."[129]

Banjin, a Sōtā Zen master, said that the practice of Zen can be located in the observance of Disciplines. Hakuin denounced the custom of keeping concubines among the higher classes. Bankei admitted that women are more virtuous than men in many cases.

The attitude of emphasizing morals was very conspicuous among Zen masters who were often blamed for being indifferent to moral distinctions.

Conclusion

The number of original thinkers with traces of modern thought in Japan before the introduction of Western civilization was much smaller than in the modern West. My intensive trial was to find thinkers of this type, and yet I have not been successful so far. Even highly educated Japanese might come across unfamiliar names among those whom I have mentioned in this article. This fact means that indications of modern thoughts appeared in Japan only sporadically, did not develop, and vanished in their incipient stages. This phenomenon poses a big problem and needs further thorough investigation.

The discussion so far has pointed out and introduced, topic by topic, some features of modern thought which are worthy of study in comparison with modern thought in the West. We do not mean that all thinkers of modern Japan assumed the progressive attitude as remarked in this article. On the contrary there were many more backward or conservative, religionists than progressive reformers; they rigorously stuck to traditional or mediaeval ways of thinking and behaviour. Moreover, it is doubtlessly true that even progressive reformers themselves betrayed the conservative attitude in many respects without knowing it. However, the point we cannot neglect is the significance of the fact that the above-mentioned features were sprouting among those reformers. For so many traces of change for the modernization resulted from and centered around their attitude of esteeming the value of man as such in preference to anything else. It is also noteworthy that these thinkers of moern Japan were not militant theologians like Luther, Zwingle, and Calvin. They could not completely upset the traditional organizations the establishment of which dated in ancient days, nor reform political and deep-rooted social systems. The attempts of these reformers produced no overwhelming influence upon the nation as a whole.

Although I have pointed out many common features to modern thoughts both in Japan and in the West, you will still notice that some features conspicuous in the modern West cannot be found in Japan of the same period. One of them is the idea of evolution. It is true that some Japanese thinkers had the idea of change or development vary conspicuously in this period, but they never came to entertain the idea of evolution *i. e.,* the idea that something that comes later is superior to what is already in existence, and eventually replaces it. This idea of evolution was lacking in Hinduism, Buddhism, and Confucianism and other Eastern religions. You will all be able to think of cases that exemplify this.

Another feature of great importance is that the spirit of experimentation was almost lacking in Eastern countries of the same period. In Japan natural science did not develop; many new attempts were killed in their incipient stages by the pressure of the feudal governments. Mahayana Buddhism, a sect of Buddhism combined with Shintoism, posed no opposition to the appearance of innovatory trials, because its standpoint is flexible with regard to dogma, and found no contradiction to scientific attempts, whereas the feudal aristocracy tried to eliminate new attempts. Once the feudal system was destroyed, in countries where there was some opposition to science in one way or another by existing religions, it took some time to change people's attitude.

The features which I mentioned as already existing in Japanese tradition were representative of minority groups. Political and religious authorities ignored them, or occasionally suppressed them. It was only after the infiltration of Western civilization that they began to exert considerable influence in different ways, always, however, modified by the existing traditions.

1 Mo-ho-chi-kuan 摩訶止観, vol. 4b, in Taishō Tripitaka, vol. 46, p. 45b.

2 Ishida Baigan, *Seiri Mondō* 性理問答 (Dialogue on Human Nature and Natural Order). Translation, Introduction and Notes by Paolo Beonio-Brocchieri, Roma, Istituto per il Medio ed Estremo Oriente, 1961, p. 13.

3 Kagamishima Genryū 鏡島元隆, *Dōgen Zenji to sono Monryū* 道元禅師とその門流 (Zen Master Dōgen and His Followers), Tokyo, Seishin-shobō, 1961, p. 112.

4 G. *Kagamishima*, pp. 106, 108.

5 G. *Kagamishima*, pp. 120, 124.

6 *Seiri Mondō*, p. 57.

7 Ibid., p. 57.

8 Hakuin's *Yasen Kanna*.

9 Robert Cornell Armstrong, *Ninomiya Sontoku, the Peasant Sage*, The Transactions of the Asiatic Society of Japan, vol. XXXVIII, Pt. 2, Yokohama and Tokyo, 1910, p. 19.

10 This legend is not mentioned in the Pali four Nikāyas, but in the later works such as Buddha-biographies.

11 Japanese materialism in the Tokugawa period and after the Meiji Restoration is discussed in Saigusa Hiroto 三枝博音, *Nihon no Yuibutsuronsha* 日本の唯物論者 (Materialists of Japan), Tokyo, Eihō-sha, 1956.

12 E. H. Norman, *Andō Shōeki and the Anatomy of Japanese Feudalism*, The Transactions of the Asiatic Society of Japan, Third Series, vol. II, Tokyo, Asiatic Society of Japan, 1949.

13 Shōbōgenzō 正法眼藏, chapter 25, Jinzū 神通.

14 Suzuki Shosan, *Ha-kirishitan* 破吉利支丹 (Refutation of Christianity).

15 H. Dumoulin, Yoshida Shōin. *Ein Beitrag zum Verstandnis der geistigen Quellen der Meijierneuerung, Monumenta Nipponica*, vol. 1, Pt. 2, 1938, pp. 73–76.

16 R. C. Armstrong, p. 18.

17 R. C. Armstrong, p. 19.

18 Asō Isoji: *Takizawa Bakin*, Tokyo, 1943, p. 297.
(Another English translation of the Ninomiya's poem:
        No sound, no scent,
        Yet Heaven and Earth
        Proclaim at all times
        The unwritten Laws of the Infinite.)

19 *Analects* 論詰, IV, 15.

20 *Jishōki* 自性記.

21 *Jūzen Hōgō* 十善法語 (The Ten Buddhism Virtues. A sermon preached in 1773 by Katsuragi Jiun), The Transactions of the Asiatic Society of Japan, vol. XXXIII, Yokohama and Tokyo, Pt. 2, p. 44.

22 Ibid., p. 55.

23 赤心.

24 大義.

25 KATŌ Genchi, *The Shinto Studies of Jiun, the Buddhist Priest and Moto-ori, the Shinto Savant, Monumenta Nipponica*, vol. 1, 1938, Pt. 2, 9–24.

26 神儒偶談.

27 KATŌ Genchi, op. cit., p. 21.

28 *Jūzen Hōgō*, p. 55.

29 *Seiri Mondō*, p. 26.

30 Ibid., p. 25.

31 Ibid., p. 29.

32 Ibid., p. 41.

33 Ibid., p. 43.

34 Ibid., p. 44.

35 Ibid., p. 55.

36 Ibid., p. 56.

37 Ibid., p. 33.

38 Ibid., p. 60.

39 *Shitetsu* 詩轍, chapter VI. 物真に逢ものは，事一轍に出づると見たり. R. H. VAN GULICK, MIURA Baien on Indian and Dutch poetry, *Monumenta Nipponica*, vol. 1, 1938, 173–177.

40 ANESAKI Masaharu 姉崎正治, History of Japanese Religions, London, Kegan Paul, 1930, pp. 302–303.

41 E. H. NORMAN, p. 159.

42 E. H. NORMAN, p. 146.

43 MONDŌ Seiri, pp. 19–20.

44 SAIGUSA H., *Miura Baien no Tetsugaku* (The Philosophy of Miura Baien), Tokyo, Daiichi-shobō, 1931, p. 132; also *ditto, Nihon no Yuibutsuronsha*, p. 93.

45 其達観する処の道は，則條理にて，條理の訣は反観合一. 捨心之所執. 依徴於正のみに候.

46 MIURA Baien's thought was discussed by Gino K. PIOVESANA, *Monumenta Nipponica*, vol. 20, Nos. 3-4, 1965, pp. 389–443. Cf. p. 402.

47 *Yanagi Muneyoshi Senshū* (Selected Works of Yanagi Muneyoshi), vol. 9, Tokyo, Shunjū-sha, 1955.

48 KATŌ Genchi, *Shinto's Terra Incognita to be Explored Yet* (for private circulation), Gotenba, Japan, 1958, pp. 13–14.

49 *Jingū Hiden Mondō*, cited in KATŌ.

54 G. *Kagamishima*, p. 116 and 22.

55 FURUTA Shōkin 古田紹欽, *Kinsei no Zensha-tachi* 近世の禅者達 (Aen Buddhists in Modern Japan), Kyōto, Heirakuji-shoten, 1956, pp. 126–135.

56 *Jishōki*.

57 Joseph SOAE, *Monumenta Nipponica*, vol. 5, 1942, p. 182, No. 1.

58 YANAGI M., vol. 9, p. 321.

59 *Seiri Mondō*, p. 54.

60 *Seiri Mondō*, p. 55.

61 IWAHASHI Junsei, *Sorai Kenkyū* (Studies on Ogyū Sorai), Tokyo, Seki-shoin, 1934, p. 433.

62 Keizairoku, vol. 1, fol. 10.

63 *Seigaku Mondō*, 3, quoted in "Nihon Kogakuha no Tetsugaku" (Philosophy in Japanese Classical Study Group), by INOUE Tetsujirō Tokyo, Fuzanbo, 1921, p. 693.

64 *Seigaku Mondō*, quoted by T. INOUE.

65 Alicia Orloff MATSUNAGA, *Monumenta Nipponica*, vol. 21, Nos. 1–2, 1966, pp. 203–209. Cf. NAKAMURA Hajime, *Ways of Thinking of Eastern Peoples.*

66 *Tamakatsuma.*

p. 693.

64 *Seigaku Mondō*, quoted by T. INOUE.

65 Alicia Orloff MATSUNAGA, *Monumenta Nipponica*, vol. 21, Nos. 1–2, 1966, pp. 203–209. Cf. NAKAMURA Hajime, *Ways of Thinking of Eastern Peoples.*

66 *Tamakatsuma.*

67 *Kojiki-den*, I.

68 *Kodō Taii*, vol. 2, in *Hirata Atsutane Zenshū* (Complete Works of HIRATA Atsutane), by UEDA Mannen, ed., vol. 7, Tokyo, Naigai-shoseki, 1932, p. 69.

69 *Kōdōkwanki* (A Prologue for Founding the Kōdō Institute), translated by KATŌ Genchi, Tokyo, Meiji Shotoku Kinen Gakkai, 1937.

70 *Seiri Mondō*, pp. 42–43.

71 *Byōsha Bō-koji ni Shimesu* (A letter to a Certain Sick Layman).

72 *Jūzen Hōgo*, p. 34.

73 To Illustrate: In a monastery headed by master Bankei there was a monk who committed theft. He knew it, but he protected him not to be punished. (See, *Bankei Zenji Goroku* 盤珪禅師語録, Iwanami-Bunko-bon, p. 234).

74 專人倫.

75 Piovesana, op. cit., pp. 417–418.

76 *Seiri Mondō*, p. 51.

77 This tendency is especially discussed by MURAOKA Tsunetsugu, "*Studies in Shinto Thought,* translated by Delmer M. BROWN and James T. ARAKI, Tokyo, Japanese National Commission for UNESCO, 1964), pp. 95–170.

78 Cf. N. Skene SMITH, *Tokugawa Japan as a Field for the Student of Social Organization, Monumenta Nipponica*, vol. 1, 1938, pp. 165–172, especially, p. 170.

79 OGATA Dōken, "*Kuden Hōmon no Jissen Rinri* (The Practical Ethic of the Oral Tradition)", *Nippon Bukkyo*, No. 2, October, 1958, pp. 41–49.

80 *Juzen Hōgo*, p. 53.

81 *Saru-hōgo* 猿法語, in *Zenmon Hōgo-shū*, vol. 2, p. 253.

82 *Munan Zenji Kana-hōgo*, p. 378.

83 *Roankyō*, Pt. 1.

84 *Jūzen Hōgo*, p. 48.

85 *Gomō Jigi*, vol. 1, fol. 3.

86 *Dōji mon* 童子問 (Questions by Children), vol. 2, p. 39.

87 IWAHASHI Junsei, *Sorai Kenkyū*, p. 449.

88 Ogyū Sorai, *Rongo-chō* 論語徴 (Comments on the Analects of Confucius), cited in IWAHASHI, p. 300.

89 *Analects*, IX, p. 16.

90 *Seiri Mondō*, p. 57.

91 *Rongo Kogi* 論語古義, vol. 5, ch. YOSHIKAWA Kojiro 吉川幸次郎, *Shinajin no Koten to sono Seikatsu* 支那人の古典とその生活 (Chinese Classics and Life), Tokyo, Iwanami-shoten, 1944, p. 154.

92 HIYANE Yasusada, *Nihon Shūkyōshi* (History of Japanese Religion), p. 828.

93 *Kōdōkwanki*, p. 10.

94 ANDŌ Shōeki, *Shizen Shineidō* 自然真営道 (The Way of Nature and Labour).

95 E. H. NORMAN, p. 299 ff.

96 E. H. NORMAN, p. 303.

97 E. H. NORMAN, pp. 305 ff, 315.

98 R. C. ARMSTRONG, p. 9.

99 寄さし.

100 みこともちて.

101 NISHIDA Nagao, 西田長男 *Nihon Shūkyōshisō-shi no Kenkyū* 日本宗教思想史の研究 (Studies on the History of Religious Thoughts in Japan), Tokyo, Riso-sha, 1955, p. 178 ff.

102 *Ketsujō-shū* 結縄集.

103 *Roankyō*, last part.

104 Ibid., p. 337. *Banmin Tokuyō* in *Zenmon Hōgo-shū*, last part, p. 536 ff. R. N. BELLAH, *Tokugawa Religion. The Values of Pre-Industrial Japan*, Chicago, Free Press, 1961, p. 118.

105 T. ISHIBASHI und H. DUMOULIN, *Aus dem Kanon der Nyoraikyō, Monumenta Nipponica*, vol. 1, 1938, pp. 222–241.

106 YOSHIMOTO Tadasu, *A Peasant Sage of Japan: The Life and Work of Ninomiya Sontoku*, translated from the *Hōtokuki*, London, Longmans, 1912, p. 223.

107 The Jesuit missionaries who came to Japan in the middle of the 16th century at once became aware of relationship between Jōdo-Shinshū-Buddhism and the "Lutheran heresy." Father Francesco Cabral reported on it in a letter dated 1571. (A. SCHWEITZER, *Indian Thought and its Development*, Boston, Beacon Press, 1957, p. 153) "Like Luther, Shinran rejected pilgrimages, excises in penance, fasting, superstition and all magical practices. He abolished the celibacy of the priesthood, of the monks and of the nuns. True piety was to be preserved in the family and in the wordly calling. He recommended to the laity the diligent study of the holy scriptures. And he demanded that the people should be delivered from their ignorance by good schools." (p. 152.) "Man is not in a position in any way to earn bliss by his own merits. In spite of this, Shinran required ethical conduct, and, be it noted, required it like Luther, as an expression and the fruit of faith in redemption." (p. 152.)

108 NAKAI Gendō, *Shinran and His Religion of Pure Faith*, Kyōto, The Shinshū Research Institute, 1937, p. 28.

109 G. NAKAI, p. 28 ff.

110 Vallabha was believed to have been an embodiment of a portion of Krishna's essence. (Monier Monier-WILLIAMS, *Brahmanism and Hinduism*, 3rd, ed., London, John Murray, 1887, p. 134.)

111 G. KAGAMISHIMA, p. 107.

112 *Zenmon Hōgo-shū*, vol. 2, p. 253.

113 TSUJI Zennosuke 辻善之助, *Nihonjin no Hakuai* 日本人の博愛 (The Humanitarian Ideas of the Japanese), Tokyo, Kinkodo, 1932, p. 97 ff.

114 Z. TSUJI, p. 108 ff.

115 *Nihonjin no Hakuai*.

116 The details are mentioned in Z. Tsuji, *Jizen Kyūsai Shiryō* (Works of Japanese Social Work), Tokyo, Kinkodō, 1932.

117 Tesugen's life is described in English in *The Light of Dharma*, August and October, 1901, San Francisco, pp. 22–25 and pp. 25–28. Also Washio Jufikyō's 鷲尾順敬 article in the *Hansei Zasshi* 反省雑誌, vol. 12–13, 1897–1898.

118 Z. Tsuji, *Nihonjin no Hakuai*, p. 346.

119 M. Anesaki, p. 303.

120 Jōin, *Uyō Shūhoku Suido-roku* (Records of exploitation of North-Eastern Districts)' 7 vols., in *Nihon Keizai Taiten* (Japanese Classical Works on Economics), vol. 30, edited by Takimoto Seiichi, Tokyo, 1929. This work was written in the Temmei period (1781–1788).

121 Ibid., p. 10.

122 *Uyō Shūhoku Suido-roku*, pp. 9–10.

123 Ibid., p. 11.

124 E. H. Norman, . . . pp. 106–107.

125 *Jūzen Hōgo*, p. 1.

126 Ibid., p. 2.

127 "Zenaku tomoni samatagenu".

Atkinson, the translator, did not translate this phrase which is highly Buddhistic. Probably, he, as a Christian missionary, found the phrase too strange.

128 *Jūzen Hōgo*, pp. 2–3.

129 R. C. Armstrong, op. cit.

THE AUTHOR is Professor of Hindu Philosophy and Dean of the Literature Department at the University of Tokyo.

CHAPTER VI

MODERN TRENDS—Specific Problems of the Tokugawa Period

1. Religion and Capitalism

The Problem

After the Meiji Restornation Japan tried to take in Western culture with great rapidity, but she still lacked sufficient understanding of the modern spirit which had been the motivating power in building up that culture. Recently there has been again a vigorous discussion about her inability to develop such modern spirit. In this connection I would like to consider the problem as to what relationship on earth religion has to capitalism in modern Japan.

If one looks at the modern history of this country, one can see the embryo of capitalism already in the Tokugawa Period, but only it did not grow to the extent comparable with that in the West. In Japan, therefore, no civl society or the consciousness of citizenship could come into existence. Scholars have often made efforts to find out whether or not the various aspects of Western capitalism, at least in its early stages, owe their origin and development to the Protestant movement, especially to Calvinism. Max Weber contends that the chief characteristics of the spirit which underlies the practical life of the Japanese have been determined not so much by religious elements as by another completely different factor, namely, the feudalistic nature of the social and political structure of society. It was precisely this feudalism that crushed foreign trade and obstructed the development of a civil society in the European sense of the word. He claims that the concept of a city possessing its own autonomous laws is completely foreign to Japanese thought.[1] After a study of the history of Japanese society and her various religious sects he makes the following criticism: "With the exception of the Jōdo Shin Sect,[2] the great majority of the religious sects led the laity to a form of worship that was irrational in the extreme and were far from educating them in a reasonable way of life. In fact the type of Buddhism existing among the laity simply developed a one-sided way of thinking—a conviction that the world (including human life and all things that pass) is valueless—together with an attitude of indifference towards secular society. And furthermore it spread abroad doctrines of retribution and magic as forms of escape."[4]

Jōdo Shin Sect is "a religion of worldly faith not bound by the self-reliant asceticism of the devotee",[5] and yet even this sect did not develop "a rational asceticism for the laity". This is for the same reason as Lutheranism, for it is a religion of salvation which in medieval fashion dominated the mentality of the middle classes, it was not able to adopt the magic and the wild ecstasy that appealed to the masses in ancient Hinduism nor the strongly emotional devotion of later Hinduism and of Western pietism. The word "emotion" as used here means what might be better expressed by "feeling" (*kibun*).[4]

Max Weber then draws the conclusion that in Japan, as in other Eastern countries, the spirit of capitalism did not develop. This proposition is widely accepted in Japan as a common knowledge of every educated person. But did the spirit of modern capitalism entirely fail to appear in Japanese religion? In my opinion one should not be too dogmatic in making such assertion.

The Problem in Tendai Sect

The question whether modern capitalism took its origin from the religious movement of Calvinism alone is difficiult to answer. If, in this case, one does not take into account the contradictions inherent in the social and economic structure of Western society and their exposure and breakdown, together with such factors as the reform in production technique accompanying the progress in natural science and the enormous

growth of circulating economic blocs based on the progress in communi-
cations—if one does not keep in mind all these considerations, one may
reach the hasty conclusion that this phenomenon originated from one
element alone. However, let us disregard the problem here. For the
present purpose, suffice it to say that, though a great variety of social and
economic circumstances are to be kept in mind, one can reasonably assert
that Calvinism was a powerful spiritual force in building up modern
capitalism.

But modern Japanese Buddhism, which held the position of the national religion before the Meiji Restoration, did not succeed in effecting
any new economic movement. Rather it was completely cut off from
the realities of economics. The Japanese bourgeoisie, even in its beginnings, did not associate economics with religion. Consequently, though
Japanese Buddhism in its so-called Kamakura form, it did not achieve
anything to compare with the western Reformation. This is a fact of
common knowledge.

However, if we examine the matter in detail, we find that there did
exist an ethics of economics already in the medieval Buddhism of Japan.
This is the *kuden hōmon* of mediaeval *Tendai*[6] in regard to the orthodox
Tendai Sect existing from ancient times. According to this teaching, it
is the merciful will of the Buddha that man should make use of all natural things ranging from the rays of the sun and the moon to the trees
and grass on the earth. Grass and trees have no soul, but since they perform work which benefits man they are already buddhas. Property helps
us in doing altruistic deeds. Business, being economic activity, is a form
of asceticism and a way to enlightenment. "The work of the peasant,
the anvil of the black-smith, the plane of the carpenter—all these are
essentially expressions of Buddhist teachings. Consequently men's activities are regarded as entrances to the Doctrine" (Shūyōshō).[7] This document warns man, who is faithful to his employment and respects
wealth, against injuring his soul and body and ending up in committing
theft if he becomes poor. The work of farming aims at the autumn harvest. "If you can reap no harvest in autumn, everything is useless," it
declares, thus underlining the importance of the fruits of labor. Emphasiz-

ing the necessity of saving, it asserts that, though one *sen* is a small amount, it will become a great amount if profit makes profit. If you are faithful to your work, it does not matter if you break the precepts by killing fish and fowl. Here appears a way of thinking that to be faithful to one's work is to follow the way ff the Buddha.[8]

Suzuki Shōsan[9] and the Ethics of Work

(1) Fundamental Standpoint

At the very beginning of the modern era in Japan we can find an aspect of Buddhism which would have developed into the spirit of capitalism, if only it had developed. This is the ethics of work propounded by the Zen monk Suzuki Shōsan and his school. I would like to examine the nature of his theory and at the same time enquire into the reasons why it failed to develop into a practical religious and economic movement.

Suzuki Shōsan is a Buddhist whose name is almost unknown in the annals of Japanese Buddhism. If you look up books like *A History of Japanese Buddhism* and *A History of the Japanese Zen Sect,* you can hardly find his name. Even in various large Buddhist dictionaries his name is not listed. And yet in the Buddhism that he propounded we can find many modern elements that ought to claim our attention.

Shōsan belonged to a family of *bushi* (*samurai*)[10] in Mikawa Province (present Aichi Prefecture). He was born in the seventh year of Tenshō (1579) in Mikawa-no-kuni, Higashi-kamo-gun, Norisada-go (Morioka Village) as the eldest son of a Matsudaira[11] vassal named Suzuki. His popular name was Kyūdayū.[12] Shōsan was his secular name, though even after leaving the world he continued to use it. He participated in the battle of Sekigahara[13] and the summer and winter campaigns of Osaka and fought with great distinction. As a vassal of the Shōgun he was an important personage. In the sixth year of Genna[14] (1620), however, he quite suddenly abjured the world and became a monk at the age of forty-two. Before taking this step he had frequently lodged in Buddhist temples and had been on friendly terms with several famous *Zen* monks of his day. It seems that in the ceremony of *tokudo* the officiating

monk was Daigu Oshō of the Rinzai Sect.[15] After this he made pilgrimages to various parts of the country, practicing asceticism. In the ninth
year of Kan'ei (1632) he founded the Sekiheizan Onshin-ji Temple[16] in
his native place. In the first year of Keian[17] (1648) at the old age of sixty-
nine he went all the way to Edo and engaged in educating the citizens.
At the hour of the monkey (4 o'clock in the afternoon) on June 25th
in the first year of Meireki[18] (1655) he died at Kanda in Edo.

The striking feature of his thought as a whole is the intensely critical
spirit. First of all, he consistently took a very critical stand against the
traditional Buddhist sects which had existed until his time. He himself
belonged to the Sōtō Sect, but he used words of violent criticism against
the sayings of Dōgen, the founder of that sect, holding that Dōgen himself had not attained to the most profound enlightenment. Moreover, he
did not recognize the authority of the founders of the various Japanese
Buddhist sects and criticized famous *Zen* masters since the time of Chinese Buddhism one after another.

However, even though he did not recognize the authority of particular
individuals or groups, he advocated a complete turning to the Buddha
heart and soul. "Imagine that the Buddha is alive here and now, and
worship Him with your whole being," he said. While radically denying
the authority of past religious groups and the individuals who established
them, he relied completely on self, and tried to come face to face with
the Buddha.

His non-sectarian character was built upon such a standpoint. In general he devoted himself to the Sōtō Sect, but he had friendly relations
with many teachers of the Rinzai Sect and was inclined to the thought of
the Chinese *Fuke*.[19] Also he recommended the *nembutsu* to the general
laity. He himself was ordained with the Novice Discipline by Discipline
Master Genshun.[20] He was a complete liberalist. In fact he constantly
used the word "freedom", saying that the aim of Buddhist asceticism
was the practice of freedom. Of course, his "freedom" was religious and
spiritual and not political or social, but when he insisted that the work
of the businessman was "the freedom of the world" he used it nearly in
the same sense as that of today. Thus aiming at freedom, he opposed

various kinds of feudalistic ethics existing in his time and attempted at reformation—though it was of little avail. Among other Buddhists of the Tokugawa Period there must be few who were so critical of feudalistic ethics as he was.

Another noteworthy expression of his critical spirit is found in his attack on Christianity, entitled *Yabure Kirishitan*[21] (An Argument against Christianity). While the Japanese of his day simply dismissed Christianity as *jahō*[22] (false teaching), sorcery and magic, he adopted a theoretical criticism of it. While the Buddhists of the time generally only sat idle when confronted with the problem of Christianity, Shōsan took up this problem and, not content with simply slandering and vilifying it, made a logical examination of its teaching. This fact points to his discernment as a thinker.

As a modern exponent of religion, he has left us numerous works, all of which are written only in simple, easily intelligible Japanese. In those days most *Zen* priests, whenever occasion offered, wrote poetry in Kanbun (classical Chinese), but he entirely broke with this practice. Apart from him there was scarcely any Buddhist who wrote only in Japanese. Of course scholars of Japanese classics wrote only in Japanese. But unlike these people, he had not the slightest trace of pedantry in his writings. He was a man of the masses. One could point to many notable characteristics of this progressive thinker. Now I would like especially to examine his theory of the ethics of business.

(2) Virtue in All Walks of Life

The most striking feature of the thought of Suzuki Shōsan is his contention that the way of Buddhahood consists simply in devoting oneself assiduously to the secular business of one's life. In order to make clear this idea he wrote his book entitled *Bammin Tokuyō*.[23] This book is generally acclaimed by his followers to be the greatest of his works. Among most Japanese Buddhists there was a strong inclination to think that the way of the Buddha consisted in separating oneself from the world, secluding oneself in mountains and woods and performing *Zen* meditation or in devoting oneself to the constant recital of the *nembutsu*. For example, even in the city there was a tendency to place the essential character of the life of a monk in separating himself from secular life and living in a monastery. While the generality of lay people engaged in secular pursuits, they thought that the secular life and the life of faith were two different things. Suzuki Shōsan, however, acted against this viewpoint in vogue and tried to practice the way of the Buddha in the middle of the secular life.

> "Buddhist asceticism expiates all sin and removes all suffering. This spirit is the secret of ease of mind and body, and applies to any person whether he be warrior, farmer, artisan or tradesman."

In his opinion, any kind of business was a way of Buddhist asceticism and by means of it anyone could attain to buddhahood.

> "Every profession is a Buddhist exercise. You should attain to Buddhahood through your work. There is no work that is not a Buddhist exercise. You can see this from the fact that every work contributes to the welfare of the world. Man is made in the image of Buddha and is endowed with the Buddha nature. He should never commit the folly of turning aside to the way of evil."

According to him, all occupations were manifestations of the Absolute Being and had their respective social meanings. All occupations, superior and inferior, are holy as they are expressions of the unique and ultimate Buddha.

> "The One and Absolute Buddha benefits the world, making his appearance in millions of beings. But for the smith, the carpenter and every other workman, we could not be provided with the necessities of life. Without the warrior we could not enjoy peace in our country. Without the farmer the world would lack its food. Without the merchant there would not be freedom in the world. There are various other kinds of occupations and everyone of them has some contribution to make to the world. Some investigate things about the heaven and the earth, while others examine the five viscera of the human body and practice medicine. Thus there is an infinite variety of callings, and all of them are of great service to the world. You must realize, however, that all this is the function of the One Buddha."

However, people of the world were not familiar with this reasoning. They felt that business life itself would contaminate and defile them.

"We are endowed with this blessed Buddha nature, but some people do not realize this and disgrace themselves, indulging in evil deeds and turning aside into the path of evil. All such people rightly deserve the name of common mortals full of illusion.

But he insists that each person must rely upon self with the conviction that he is a Buddha, because all living creatures without exception are, in the last analysis, united with the Buddha.

"All the Buddhas of the three temporal worlds have shown us by their very existence that all human beings are Buddhas. We distinguish colors with the eye, hear sounds with the ear, smell with the nose and speak with the mouth, and thus we have freedom to do what we want. But this freedom, whether it be freedom of the hand or the foot is to be attributed to the freedom of the One Buddha. Meanwhile the secret of salvation consists in faith in yourself. If you sincerely wish to attain to Buddhahood, you have only to believe in yourself, and according as your spirit becomes mature, you will naturally reach the supreme point of sincerity, finally getting confident and secure. It is then that you enter into unconsciously into the state where there exists neither self nor others and where you have no notion of space; and the true Buddha hidden in yourself manifests himself. Only have faith in Buddha; again, I say, have faith!

"The true Buddha hidden within yourself" or, in other words, your original self—to rely on this is the real essence of Buddhist teaching; and since any kind of business is an activity of this single Buddha, each person's devotion to his work can be made into a following of the Absolute. Accordingly, Buddhism since it aims at making a contribution to the world is the precious pearl of society. There can be no way of practicing Buddhism other than that of devotion to the worldly life of business.

"Buddhist scripture teaches us that we will certainly be delivered from worldly existence if we have passed through the way of the world. The meaning of this is that *one attains Buddhahood by keeping the laws of the world*. Therefore the laws of the world are at the same time the laws of Buddha. As *The Avatamsaka Sūtra* teaches us, "The laws of Buddha are no different from those of the world; the laws of the world are no different from those of Buddha." You have not the least idea of the spirit of Buddhism if you will not listen to the truth that one can attain Buddhahood in keeping the laws of the world.

Basing his theories on this fundamental position, Suzuki Shōsan maintains that, irrespective of the social and occupational distinctions which were beginning to be established in the feudalistic conditions of the Tokugawa period, each person should strive to put into practice the Buddhist teaching. In his *Bammin Tokuyō* he puts forwardh is own peculiar ethics of business, treating of warriors, farmers, artisans and merchants.

(3) Labor and Farming

In his *Bammin Tokuyō,* the chapter entitled *Daily Life of the Warrior* is followed by another in which he insists that the asceticism of the Buddhist way is automatically perfected by the farmer who devotes himself to agriculture:

"A farmer puts to me the following difficulty: It is very important to pray for happiness after death; but I am fully occupied with farm labor every day. While engaged in this lowly work I feel sad that I shall suffer in the world to come because of my useless life in this world. How can I arrive at the merit of Buddhahood?"

The way of thinking of this farmer is governed by the medieval assumption that religion is something precious, rising above the secular world, while business activity is something mean—"the lowly work of earning one's bread". In contrast to this, Shōsan thinks that devotion to agriculture is a way of Buddhist asceticism.

"Farming is nothing but a Buddhist exercise. If your intention is bad, farming is a lowly work; but if you are deeply religious, it is the saintly work of a Bodhisattva."

Whether farming is a way of Buddhist asceticism or not depends on the interior dispositions of the farmer who devotes himself to agriculture.

Accordingly, in his opinion, the life of farming is no obstacle to the life of faith.

"You are mistaken if you long for leisure to pray for happiness in the next life. Those who have a firm resolution to attain Buddhahoodd lea an ascetic life. Those who pray for happiness in the next world, at the same time filling their minds with desire for pleasure, will never attain Buddhahood even if they keep praying through all eternity. Do hard work in the heat and in the cold; regard as an enemy your own flesh overgrown with evil passions; turn up the soil and reap in the harvest with your plough, your hoe and your sickle. Cultivate the fields with concentrated mind, as though you were doing penance. When you have time to spare, evil passions are apt to grow; when you are engaged in hard labor, sparing no pains whatever, you will never have your mind troubled with evil passions. Thus you can practice Buddhism unceasingly. Why should a farmer want to practice Buddhism outside of his work on the farm? Even the man who prepares to become a monk, devoting himself to pious worship, if he cannot get rid of selfish attachment, shall never be freed from the circle of transmigration, however laudable his achievements."

He attempts to see the religious aspect of the life of farming in the fact that this manual work entails much hardship. The medieval way of thinking that considers farming itself as something degrading was, in his opinion, utterly mistaken.

"If you make the great vow to expiate your sins through farming, and turn up the soil invoking the merciful name of Amida Buddha at each stroke of your plough, you will surely be rewarded with the fruit of Buddhahood."

From of old, manual work as a form of asceticism has been held in great esteem in the Western Church. But as Harnack points out, reverence for work and its "authority" especially from the point of view of morality is not a characteristic feature of Christianity from the beginning nor is it its distinctive note. This point is especially emphasized by modern Puritanism which points the stream of Calvinism, and this is said to have an intimate connection with the establishment of modern capitalism. If it is true that all this is a peculiar feature of the modern (or at least the beginning of the modern) period, one can say that Shōsan's theory of work is equally modern.

After explaining the business ethics of farmers, Shōsan proceeds to that of artisans. The word "artisans" as used here corresponds to *ko* of the four grades *shi–nō–kō–shō*[25] (military, agricultural, industrial and mercantile classes). Here, asked the same questions by artisans, he gives them the same answers.

(4) The Ethics of Merchants

Shōsan finally treats of the ethics of merchants: *The Daily Work of Merchants*. And here he speaks to merchants in the same way as he speaks to farmers and artisans.

"A merchant puts the following question to me. 'Though I have been fortunate enough to receive the gift of life, engaged as I am in the humble way of trade, I am entirely preoccupied with the thought of gain. How sad that I cannot make efforts to attain enlightenment! Please show me how to attain to my end.'

As in the case of the farmer, the questioner is here taking the medieval point of view in regard to business. And in answer Shōsan teaches that the merchant must devote himself squarely to the acquisition of gain.

"My answer is this. Those engaged in trade should first of all learn how to make as much profit as possible.

Here the ethics of the pursuit of gain are openly stated. However, he stresses that the merchant must have great reverence for the virtue of honesty if he is to reap any advantage.

"And how can you bring this about? I suggest that you above all learn to walk the straight path of honesty, abandoning yourself to the way of Heaven. An honest man enjoys Heaven's blessing and is protected from disaster by Buddhas and deities. He naturally increases his wealth and is loved and respected by everyone. All will be well with him. On the other hand, a selfish person who pursues his own interest and devours gain at the sacrifice of others will incur the curse of Heaven and bring calamity on himself. He will be hated and despised by everybody. Everything will go wrong with him.

Because he is speaking as a religious man he uses concepts like "protected by Buddhas and deities" and "the curse of Heaven" in the course of his explanation, but if you take away these religious expressions it is almost identical with the reverence for, and emphasis on "honesty" made by the forerunners of modern capitalism beginning with Benjamin Franklin.

In general, he affirms the ethics of any social position and class existing in the feudalistic society of his day. He teaches that since one's social position, degree of wealth and length of life are all determined by "karma", casting away one's personal interests and passions one should work for the good of the people.

"Whether your social status is high or low, whether you are rich or poor, whether you live a long life or a short one—all these things are predestined in accordance with the deeds practiced in your previous existence. It is useless to pray for fame or for gain; it will do you no good. On the contrary, you will only increase your guilt and be punished for going against the way of Heaven. Be in awe of this, and abandon self-interest. Regard your trade as a gift of Heaven and yourself as an agent who brings freedom all over the country. Leave yourself at the mercy of Heaven, cease to worry about gain, and be honest in business. Everything will go well with you then, for Heaven's reward corresponds to your deeds as naturally as fire burns things dry or water finds its own level.

He seems to recognize determinism, taking the standpoint that everything is fixed, but he attempts to put into practice the freedom of man. "Without the merchant there can be no peace in the world." Here, if you substitute "God" for "Heaven" and "the way of Heaven" and put "the salvation of God" in place of "freedom", can you not find in it the ethics of capitalism of the early period of modern Europe, tracing its foundation to Calvinism?

It is especially to be noted that in a vague way he is expressing the doctrine of utilitarianism. A man who had come down in the world said in the course of conversation: "I am content with poverty, and my heart is at ease." To this Shōsan made the critical answer: "Poverty is no good. It is better to be rich." He expressed this point of view when Buddhists and Confucianists were constantly advocating poverty.

However, he was by no means preaching materialism, much less was he advocating hedonism or epicureanism. He taught that even the man who made gain should not be attached to it. Following the general Buddhist viewpoint, he divides good into two classes: defiled good (one which contains attachment) and pure good (one which does not). The man who considers property to be something stable and clings to it, pursuing it as an end, looks for defiled good. But to be detached from personal desires and to be faithful to one's business on behalf of the people, reflecting that all things are impermanent—this is pure good. The merchant must aim at walking independently in the universe by learning this undefiled good. And this is the condition of Nirvana.

"You should not rejoice at good fortune. You must learn to distinguish what is called "merit with attachment" from what is called "merit without attachment". If you regard this illusory world of ephemeral beings as something substantial and eternal, doing good deeds with a strong attachment to life, such meritorious deeds are called merit with attachment. This merit with attachment is the cause of happiness and prosperity. However, if you become a rich man of high position through your merit with attachment, and enjoy a pleasant life, you will certainly come to the end of your fortune, and then you will have no choice but to degrade yourself in the ways of evil. This can be compared to an arrow shot into the sky, which falls to the ground when it has spent its force. Hence merit with attachment should not be entertained. But good without attachment is the source of enlightenment. Desire of Buddhahood occurs when you meditate on the truth that "All phenomena are transitory; all flesh is bound to die," and pay attention to the saying "There is no peace in this world; it is like a burning house." Good without attachment consists in praying for the divine bliss of Nirvana without any attachment whatever to the inconstant world of perpetual change. Therefore, you should make a vow to do good without attachment in your business of trade and increase your piety, keeping the truth in mind that everything in this world is ephemeral and subject to change. Sacrifice yourself for the world; purely for the sake of your country and your brothers, transmit the products of your district to another district and bring the products of other districts to your district, and convey them to the farthest land. Travel from place to place with a firm intention of promoting the welfare of the public, and realize clearly that your work itself is nothing but practice of Buddhistic discipline in expiation for your sins. You do penance when you go over mountains; you purify your soul when you cross rivers and streams; you learn self-renunciation and chant sūtras when you go sailing over the vast ocean. Reflect that life is only a journey through the transitory world. Cast off any attachment whatever and engage in trade without desire of gain, so that Heaven will protect you and various deities will benefit you. You will then become a man of good fortune yet you will disdain simply to remain a person of wealth. Your faith will become adamant in the end so that you will attain to the state of silentc ontemplation all the time no matter what you may be doing. In this way you will naturally attain enlightenment and taste the divine bliss of Nirvana. The result will be that you will get complete freedom from all obstacles and become independent of the universe. This everlasting joy has no comparison. Bear this carefully in mind, and observe it faithfully."

Here are developed the business ethics of Buddhism. Now "Earnestly seek gain; but having attained to it, do not enjoy it; use it for the people"—these words of Shōsan teach us the following points from the economic point of view: 1) The pursuit of gain, 2) to save one's gain and not to use it as consumer's goods for pleasure, or, in other words, the accumulation of capital, and 3) to circulate capital advantageously. Accordingly, if one analyzes Shōsan's assertion from the economic point of view, the same way of thinking is at work as in the capitalistic ethics of the early period of the modern West. In the assertion that the merchants effect the freedom of the world and "get independent in the universe" we can see the reflection of the thought of the merchant class then on the rise. An attitude of restraint in regard to spending is an outstanding feature in the sermons of the monks of Jōdo Shin Sect to the laity of the day, but this teaching was quite contrary to that of Shōsan which I have quoted.[27] In the case of Ninomiya Sontoku[26] this further developed into the theory of capitalism.

(5) Religion in Business

In another of his writings, Shōsan refers to the vocational ethics of monks, doctors, artisans and hunters. Here I am only attempting to introduce his thought in outline. In the history of Japanese Buddhism he was probably the first to develop an ethics of business on such a large scale.

In Japan, the phrase from a chapter of the Lotus Sūtra which reads, "Any occupation to earn one's livelihood is not inconsistent with Absolute Truth" was much in vogue until then, but this is satisfied with the teaching that there is no contradiction between Buddhism and the secular life. It is beyond dispute that Jōdo Shin Sect, adopting the position of a secular Buddhism, devoted itself to the task of building the life of faith upon the life of business, but in its mode of expression it does not escape from the notion that the secular life is something defiled and of little value. Rennyo[28] also teaches: "Now in my belief one ought not simply to endeavor to subdue the evil thoughts and distracting illusions that occur in the mind. You are free to engage in trade, or to serve your master, or to become a hunter or a fisherman. You have only to trust Amida Buddha firmly whose Original Vow is to save all the despicable creatures like ourselves who are occupied day in day out only in these lowly and sinful actions." But here the secular life of business consists of "lowly and sinful actions". The medieval viewpoint of business has not passed away. On the other hand, the assertions of Shōsan are much more positive, for in this opinion the secular life of business is far from contradicting Buddhism but is Buddhism itself.

Suzuki Shōsan himself believed that he was the first in the history of

Japanese Buddhism to proclaim that the essence of Buddhism is the actual practice of business morality.

"From ancient times there have been many wise monks. Yet they were conversant only with Buddhist doctrines. No one has ever advocated that the laws of the world are applicable to everything. It is possible that such persons existed, but I have never yet heard of them. I assume that I am the first to profess this."

Although leading the life of one who had rejected the world, he continued to use his secular name "Suzuki Shōsan" or "The old man Suzuki Shōsan" when he published his writings.

In this way Shōsan respected secular Buddhism more than monastic one and tried to advise people against their desire to shave their heads and leave the life." While Buddhists in those days generally held that the monk should practice the way of asceticism confined to his room and the layman come to the doorway, Shōsan's contention was exactly the contrary.

Striving to practice Buddhism in the midst of secular life, he rejected the Buddhism of solitude, of mountains and of woods. Previously he had felt nostalgic for the life in the mountains and woods, but now he declared that this was not desirable. "I used to be fond of living in the mountains. The smallest wood was enough to tempt me to build myself a hermitage there. So I have often secluded myself in the mountains. But now I have to realize that this love of a secluded life comes from an ascetic temperament. This attitude is nothing different from that of the secular man who builds a garden or decorates a room."

To practice austerities in the midst of the mountains is not true Buddhist asceticism. They regard people in the world as the vulgar masses and simply build up their own self-complacent ego, "looking down snobbishly on the world." Faced by any chance of fortune, they fall with a crash. He teaches that a good example of it is the hermit Ikkaku who, after twenty years spent in asceticism in the mountains, was seduced by a woman. "It is better to practice Buddhist austerities in the world."

Consequently, Shōsan ended his days as a Buddhist of the city teaching, a form of Buddhism that was suitable for the people. Aiming as he did at a religion of secular life and of the people at large, Shōsan, though a *Zen* monk, ended up by rejecting *Zazen*[29] as a method of asceticism. He believed that it was wrong to exhaust the ascetic by making him practice assiduous *Zazen,* since the aim of Buddhist asceticism was to nourish the spirit. He was probably the first *Zen* monk publicly to dissuade people from practicing *Zazen.*

Now it could be argued that English Puritanism which is derived from Calvinism manifests the most thorough basis for the modern West's attitude toward business. According to Richard Baxter who is one of the most representative figures of this faith, what is valuable for increasing the glory of God is not inaction or hedonism but action. Consequently, the waste of time is, in principle, the greatest sin, and inactive meditation (at least when it is practiced at the expense of business work) is valueless and, in some cases, should be completely rejected. In recent Japanese religion a contention exactly corresponding to it is made by Shōsan.

(6) Significance in the History of Thought

However, a theory like that of Chōsan was never accepted by the feudalistic society of his day.

"I have come through eighty years of hardship and none has ever listened to me. I am rejected by my contemporaries and am left to die and rot. In my sorrow I write this for posterity, hoping that there may be some prepared to read this even though there is no one who pays any attention to it today."[30]

This brings us up against the following problem: If Shōsan spoke in favor of secular Buddhism and preached reverence for action, why did he himself forsake the world? Is this not a contradiction? And to this he answers:

"I shaved my head simply because of my karma. Probably I was predestined to become a monk. It was of necessity that I got my head shaved."[31]

Here he adopts the standpoint of determinism.

It seems to me that we can find a solution to this problem in the following way. Shōsan, when he shaved his head and forsook the world, was sincerely seeking the Buddhist way. It was as a result of great experience that he finally came to stress secular Buddhism, but at this juncture it was already impossible for him to return to his former life in the world. In the centralized feudalistic society of the time, in which one's social position was regulated to the limit, even if a person who had left home and forsaken the world wanted to return to the secular life again, there was no possibility of his being accepted. Every profession was inherited, and it was especially difficult for a person of high position to return to the world. Therefore, Shōsan found himself in the contradictory position of disparaging the rejection of the world on one hand while leading a monastic life on the other. This situation he accepted as his karma. In the social structure of the time this fate was indeed a karma.

The notion that business is a holy thing and that its practice has a religious meaning is one held by the reformers at the outset of Protestantism in the West. It was already in evidence in Luther. At that time a terminology which speaks of business as a "calling" or "vocation" from God came into being. In the case of Calvin this went so far as to be associated with determinism. On this point the ethical theory of business of Shōsan adopts the same stand. Each person's business is part of the One Buddha and is something bestowed by Heaven. However, all the leaders of Western Protestantism got married, had families and carried on the religious direction of people in the world as seculars. But Shōsan, through propounding secular Buddhism, maintained to the end the position of a monk. It is said that his followers consisted of fifty men, and they were all monks. It looks like a contradiction that he who attempted to prevent people from becoming monks should himself take monks as his disciples, but his biography shows that most of them first became monks under the direction of others and later turned to Shōsan and that it was only the rest of them that became monks in order to follow him. In either case, these people became monks of necessity in the feudalistic society because of some extraneous (especially social) circumstances. They felt subjectively that some karma from their previous existence had ripened ("the full development of virtue of a previous existence")[32] and so they became monks. Though he preached secular

Buddhism, the pressure of the feudalistic society of his day did not allow him to become a secular person.

In this way, although the ethical theories of the reformers in the West developed into a real force, those of Shōsan could not succeed in achieving an economic revolution in any concrete form. Max Weber makes the excellent criticism that in the history of Japanese religion the State was not the protector of religion but was only the police for it. The powerful pressure of this police, which caused Japanese religion to decay, succeeded in utterly crushing a Buddhist movement in its embryonic condition, which, if only it had been able to develop into a real force, would have spurred capitalism to evolution.

2. The Science of Philosophies—TOMINAGA Nakamoto (1715–1746) and the History of Philosophies

Philological Method

It is widely believed that Tominaga Nakamoto (1715–1746) championed the "Mahāyāna Non-Buddhist" thesis upon reading a great deal of Buddhist scriptures. Admirers and refuters alike agreed to the effect that he read the entire Buddhist *Tripitaka*. Partly due to the extensive citations from numerous canons and partly due to his career as a proof reader at the printing office of *Tripitaka* at the Obakusan temple, this popular belief was well established. Appraisal of his works by the scholars of National Learning may have had the same function. Motoori Norinaga (1730–1817) wrote, "even the most well learned Buddhist priests would not excell Nakamoto in the amount of learning."[33] Hirata Atsutane (1776–1843) supported it by saying, "Nakamoto with his fathomless learning read every scripture and every commentary of Buddhism."[34] But, upon the ground of careful collation of his citations with the sources he cited,[35] we are convinced that he did not read so many Buddhist scriptures either in the original language or in the Chinese translation. His learning of Buddhism has been overestimated.

That he did not read Buddhist scriptures as originated and recorded in India is verified as follows. Every sentence in Nakamoto's works starting with phrase, "such sūtra says so and so" is found in some commentaries written in Chinese.[36] Many of these citations correspond to the paraphrased citations of the commentaries made in China, but they often are missing in the text. Certainly some of his quotations are locatable in the original text and their Chinese translation, but these are found in some Chinese commentaries without being paraphrased. Besides, Tominaga Nakamoto misunderstood many Buddhist terminologies which he could have correctly understood only if he referred to the context of the texts. These examples indicate positively that he did not read the texts of Buddhist scriptures much.[37]

In spite of this undeniable technical defect, his honor as the prime philologist of this nation is not demeaned greatly. That he could formulate a historical and developmental structure of Buddhist philosophies out of the same materials that the tradition-bound Buddhist scholars made a poor use of is worthy of unlimited attention. The most noteworthy is that Tominaga Nakamoto, an eighteenth century merchant scholar lived in the commercial town of Osaka, framed a developmental history of Buddhist philosophies, while using exactly the same sources out of which the Buddhist scholars of T'ang China constructed an evaluative classification of Buddhist philosophies.

It was not the knowledge or materials but the way of handling the materials or the methodology of research that distinguished TOMINAGA Nakamoto from ordinary Buddhist scholars. It was nothing but the difference in the method that brought about a radically different result from the same materials. The philological method of study, which HIRATA Atsutane praised as a good approach,[38] awarded TOMINAGA Nakamoto an enduring eminence.

Humanism

A personal realization of the ethical principles oriented TOMINAGA Nakamoto to the philological methodology. In the philological studies, he did not commit himself to any traditional discipline, nor did he acquiesce to either Shinto, Buddhism, or Confucianism. He asserted that he was not a devotee of Confucianism, or Shinto, or Buddhism, but that he was a critical observer who maintained a personal viewpoint.[39]

Such was his basic position. Although several philologists were born before him in Japan, none of them ever went beyond the traditional framework of National Learning, Confucianism, or Buddhism. They were in want of the spirit of objective criticism. No one ever declared to be independent from the established doctrines. No one had enough philological ability to present a vital framework among the major philosophies in the context of their history and geography. T MINAGA Nakamoto deserves the name who held the most extensive perspective among the scholars during Tokugawa Japan.

As TOMINAGA Nakamoto did not bind himself with any philosophical or religious school, there was no admitting "heresy" or "heterodoxy" for him. He could see the expressions of the human reason in what the Buddhist and other dogmatists regarded heretic. Rigid doctrinaire position of the Buddhists, for example, defined Brahmanism an abominable and evil heretic. TOMINAGA, however, said, "Who can prove it wrong when none of the critiques read so called Four Vedas and other literature of the tenet? The proponents of Brahmanism did not reach China, either. Then, if the Brahman teaching was correct or wrong was beyond the judgment for the Chinese critiques."[40] TOMINAGA also noted, in reference to the Mahakaccayana school that proclaimed the "being was void,"[41] and to the Chandaka school that advocated the "being in the negation of the void,"[42] that the evaluation of these philosophies by the Tendai philosophers and other scholars of the established doctrines was unduly low, and that it was lamentable. TOMINAGA was the one who rightly assessed the merit of these alien theses.

Thus, every thought, it seemed to TOMINAGA Nakamoto, was the equally valuable expressions of the human spirit. For him, the love of learning (philo-logia) was the way of life. Undoubtedly he was the prime philologist whom alone was this methodology truly realization.

This attitude made him unique among the contemporary philologists. Motoori Norinaga, the most distinguished National Learning philologist, did not attempt to evaluate the contribution of the Indian and Chinese cultures to the formation of the Japanese culture properly.

MOTOORI unequivocally rejected the value of the foreign cultures, while idealizing and applauding the ancient Japanese culture. MOTOORI's definition of learning was that it was the efforts to clarify the ways of the Divine Antiquity. "Scholars must make it his duty to investigate and clarify the ways of the Divine Antiquity. Scholars must not invent a new way. Scholars commit themselves in the consideration and examination of the ways of the old, inform the results to others, and keep them in written forms so that the authorities may avail themselves of these records for ruling when time will come five hundred or a thousand years later."[43]

Scholars of National Learning uncritically rejected Buddhism and Confucianism, and sticked to the attitude of subjecting themselves absolutely to the authority of National Learning. In spite of the fact that National Learning was a new discipline born during Tokugawa Era, it consistently discouraged the students from criticizing their masters and encouraged them to devotional acquiescence to what their masters said. MOTOORI Norinaga's single hearted veneration for KAMO Mabuchi (1697–1769) and HIRATA Atsutane's cathectic reverence in the authority of MOTOORI Norinaga support this comment. By this example is shown that they lacked the spirit of criticism. Scholars of National Learning were thus less realized to the essence of the love of learning than TOMINAGA Nakamoto, who studied Shinto historically and who attempted to systematize it. It was natural that TOMINAGA Nakamoto reproached the National Learning scholars on the ground that they neglected the historical development in Shinto. If we focus upon the degree of realization in the essence of philology as our standard of valuation, we have every reason to locate TOMINAGA Nakamoto above the scholars of National Learning.

Tokugawa Japan gave birth to some critical scholars from the Confucian camps also. ITO Jinsai (1627–1705) and OGYU Sorai (1666–1728) were leading such scholars. Their insight into the historical development of Chinese philosophies, however, was not as deep as NAKAMOTO, and they pursued the traditional method of research that had been customalized among the Sinologists. For these Confucianists, the Way of the Sages retained the absolute authority. Though critical in some measure, the studies of the Confucian classics as vanguard by OGYU Sorai yet found the supreme code of morality in the ancient ways of the Sages. OGYU Sorai wrote, "Whoever benefits others and saves people does good thing, because he does what many people would like to have them done. Of all good things, the way of the early kings is the best. Nothing is more valuable. The best way was stated in the way of the early kings."[44] The statement was the least coming for the position of TOMINAGA Nakamoto. "Recently Jinsai argued that MENCIUS alone inherited the proper philosophy of Confucius, and Sōrai proclaimed that the Way of Confucius was identical with the way of the early kings, while CHU Hsi and MENCIUS misunderstood Confucius. These statements are drawn from the approach fundamentally mistaken."[45]

Among the Buddhist scholars of the day, FUJAKU (1706–1781) and KAIJO (–1805) were distinguished in terms of the critical studies. That they were both Buddhist priests, however, turned out to be a limitation and restricted them from developing a scientific history of Buddhist thoughts. FUJAKU went as far as doubting whether or not Mahāyāna was Non-Buddhistic, but this doubt ended in the attempt of verifying that Mahāyāna also was part of Buddha's teaching.[46] He explained that Mahāyāna was a secret teaching as against the overt teaching of Hinayana, and that thereby it was not known among the common followers. KEISHU Risshi was another champion of such thesis. KEISHU insisted that Buddha had secretly preached the Mahāyāna teaching only for a limited number of disciples, and that only such teachings that were open to the public were recorded as the teachings of Hinayana.[47] KAIJO proposed a hypothesis that the Buddhist scriptures were not necessarily the sermons that Buddha delivered in person, but that some of them were the expressions of enlightenment by those who received the insight from the teaching of Buddha. He presented a view that there must have been many compilers of the scriptures, even though their content should always express the thought of Buddha. KAIJO was thus very close to the "Mahāyāna Non-Buddhist" thesis.[48]

TOMINAGA Nakamoto was distinguished from these contemporary thinkers by the compassionate and sympathetic attitude open to any result of human effort. And he understood the human being aesthetically. TOMINAGA Nakamoto was an observer of the human phenomena, rather than an initiator of a social movement.[49]

Endemic Philosophy

By philological studies TOMINAGA Nakamoto attempted to understand the philosophies of different peoples in the context of the respective historical and endemic setting, and to clarify their mutual relationship.

TOMINAGA Nakamoto payed attention to the endemic conditioning of philosophies, and named it *Fūki*. The Indians' inclination toward mysticism, he said, was reducible to the Indian climate and geography. The reason why the Japanese did not develop an intricate mystical thinking was explained by the climate and geography of Japan quite different from those of India. Additional reference was made to a statement of a Chinese scholar who said that the southern people were agile because of the conditions of the area.[50] Although he did not discuss this topic exhaustively, what he had written contains enough to show us his proposition for the necessity of a science of the climate and geography.

The Way of Truth emphasized that the ethical principles were reflective of historical and endemic background. In the *Historical Survey of Buddhism* (SHUTSUJO Kōgo) TOMINAGA discussed that ethical philosophies ought to be considered in the context of the climatic and geographic conditions. He proclaimed that no philosophy could overcome the circumstantial and ethnic limitations in forming its characteristic. "Therefore in preaching or founding a way, the masters since the Divine Antiquity always made use of the local customs of the places where they would propagate the instructions. No matter how highbrow a way may be, it cannot escape this principle."[51]

TOMINAGA Nakamoto described the climatic and geographic reflections of the spiritual cultures of different nations with compact and appropriate phrases. Some of the illustrations follow.

According to him, Indian culture valued mysticism, Chinese culture valued rhetoric, and Japanese culture valued simplicity. "In terms of the discourse, the Indians favored limitless expressions, the Chinese liked impressive rhetoric, whereas the Japanese inclined to simple and straight-forward expressions."[52] The alle ories of the Indians as "to put the Sumeru Mountain into a seed of opium," or of the Chinese as "flat mountains" or "the three ears of the elephant" were beyond the imagination of the Japanese. These allegorical expressions, which were impossible under natural circumstances, could work effectively and vividly only in so far as there existed literary traditions to support them. The Japanese, on the contrary, did not feel at home with these artificial expressions. The statement that the Japanese used "simple and straight-forward"[53] expressions primarily was made by MIYOSHI Muneaki (–), a merchant from Osaka, and was perfectly agreeable to TMINAGA Nakamoto. It is the most interesting that the intellectuals merchants of Osaka in the 17th century held and brought into conversation such endemic considerations.

TOMINAGA Nakamoto claimed that the vice of the Chinese way of thinking was rhetoric. "The trait of the Confucian argument is the overabundance of rhetoric. Rhetoric is what we call oratory. China is a country which greatly delights in this. In the teaching of the Way and in the education of man, if one lacks proficiency in speech, he will find no one to believe in or follow him. For example, take the word Rites (*ri*). It originally signified simply the ceremonies on the four great occasions in life: coming of age, marriage, mourning, and religious festivals. But as you know they talk now of what is the Rite of a man as the son of his father, what is the Rite of a man as the subject of his sovereign. They speak of it in connection with human relationships. They speak of it in regard to seeing, hearing, speaking, and acting. They also assert that Rites owes its inception to the division of heaven and earth, and embraces the whole universe. Take another example, that of music (*gaku*). The character *gaku* originally meant to be entertained by the music of bell and drum. But then they began to say that music was not necessarily confined to bell and drum. Music, they said, was the harmony of heaven and earth. You can see the way they talk. Take again the character for sage (*sheng*) which originally signified a man of intelligence. They have gradually stretched it to the point where a sage is the highest type of humanity, even capable of working miracles. Thus we know when Confucius talked of humanity, TSENG Tsu of humanity and righteousness, TSU Ssu of sincerity, Mencius of the Four Beginnings and the goodness of human nature, HSÜN Tzu of the badness of human nature, the *Book of Filial Piety* of filial piety, and the *Great Learning* about [what the superior man] loves and hates, the *Book of Changes* about heaven and earth, all of these are just ways of presenting the plainest and simplest things in life with an oratorical florish in order to arouse interest and make people follow them. Chinese rhetoric is like Indian magic, and neither of them is particularly needed in Japan."⁵⁴

The Indian spiritual characteristic was found in their dependence on the magic. Teachers of India, therefore, had to employ magical expressions. "The Indian scholarship constitutes itself upon the magic. Unless the scholarship is supported by miraculous stories, it does not convince the students. The Indians are extremely found of the magic. The magic for the Indians is like the rhetoric for the Chinese. In India whoever preaches a religion or teaches an ethical doctrine must rely on the magic. Whoever one may be, one cannot expect any follower if his stories did not include miracles."⁵⁵ Therefore, TOMINAGA felt, it was only natural for Buddhism that had emerged in India to employ for the purpose of communication the stories of the miraculous and wonderful magics. "Other doctrines at the days of Gautama were unexceptionally magical. When Gautama tried to overcome them by expounding his own doctrine, he had no choice but showing superior magics." Thus it turned out that the very bent toward the magic came to characterize Buddhism.

"The vice of Buddhism is mysticism. Mysticism is what we call the magic. India is a country which greatly delights in this. In the teaching of the Way and in the education of man, if one lacks proficiency in magic, he will find no one to believe in or follow him. Gautama practiced spiritual exercises in mountains for six years. It was solely for the sake of learning the technic of getting into trance, and thus he became good at getting into trance. The divine miracles and the divine powers or knowledge described in various scriptures are expressions in terms of magic. Phrases like 'representation of the universe in the white hair spin on the forehead of Buddha,' 'the strech of one's tongue that reached heaven,' 'Vimalakirti instituting eighty-four-thousand men in a room of ten feet square,' and 'the transfiguration of Sariputta into a woman' are a few of the magical expressions of Buddhism. Magic, then, was the most effective means of communication for the Indians, if they would explicate the causational principle and the existential meaning. Magic was thus a necessity for the Indians, but it is definitely unnecessary for the Japanese."[56]

The entire history of Buddhism appeared to be no more than the repetition of various forms of magical instructions. "When the disciples of Buddha forges theses, they presentfthem as if they were Gautama's teaching. They do so in order to have them authorized by the name of Buddha. Theses in such guise are another type of magic.[57] Most descriptions in the Buddhist literature, therefore, are magic. "Nine out of ten teaching and commentaries in the three sections of the Buddhist scriptures are magic. . . . The most remarkable of the Buddhist scriptures is allegory accompanied with magic. Magic is commonly practiced in India and the Indians like magic."[58]

" 'Divine ability' is another form of Magic. It is the Buddhist term for what non-Buddhists would call magic.[59] The difference[60] is that non-Buddhists expect secular reward from it, while the Buddhists want to get it for the sake of spiritual exercise.[61] Whenever one reads Buddhist scriptures, one must be careful not to lose sight of the context by being dismayed by the unusual expressions. Readers must understand that the magical and miraculous stories are merely conventional measures of instruction. 'The principle of Retribution' that Buddhism teaches is another form of magic, and is not the truth of Buddhist teaching.[62] The traditional Buddhist scholars, TOMINAGA Nakamoto claimed, were not receptive enough to understand the endemic expressions of Buddhism. Therefore, the research of Buddhist doctrines, he urged, needed ample consideration of the ethnic peculiarities of India.[63]

A reference was made to Taoism which, unique among Chinese disciplines, favored magic like the Indians.[64]

To sum, "the vice of Buddhism was magic and the vice of Confucianism was rhetoric,"[65] and not very much were included in the Buddhist or Confucian teachings if magic and rhetoric were removed.[66] "Only if the Buddhist priests knew that Buddha expressed through magic and Confucius through rhetoric, they ought to realize that Buddhism and Confucianism were much simpler."[67]

What view did TOMINAGA Nakamoto hold as to Shinto and the Japanese way of thinking? According to TOMINAGA, Japan's ethno-endemic trait was, above all, the custom of "secret transmission," which was well represented in Shinto.

"The vice of Shinto is secrecy, devine secrets, and secret and private transmission, such that every thing is kept under the veil of secrecy. Hiding things leads to lying and theft. Magic and oratory are interesting to see or to listen to—they thus have some merit. But this vice of Shinto is of the lowest sort. In olden times people were simple, and so secrecy may have served certain educational purposes, but the world today is a corrupt world in which many people are addicted to lying and stealing, and it is a deplorable thing for Shinto teachers to act in such a way as to protect and preserve these evils."[68]

This characteristic was prevalent in every sphere of the daily life of the Japanese people.

"Even in such lowly things as Nō drama and the Tea Ceremony, we find them all imitating Shinto, devising method of secret transmission and authentication and attaching a fixed price to the transmission of these 'secrets' for selfish gain and benefit. It is truly lamentable. If you ask the reason why they devise such practices, their answer is that their students are immature and untried, and must not be granted to ready an access to their teachings. It sounds plausible, but any teaching which is kept secret and difficult of access, and then is imparted for price, can not be considered in accord with the Way of Truth."[69]

Thus TOMINAGA Nakamoto noted and rebuked the Japanese tradition of overestimating the lineage and of staying within the closed human relationship. TOMINAGA, born among the free merchants of Osaka, was a free thinker. He believed that this pre-modern characteristic of the Japanese people had to be amended.

Historical Relativism

TOMINAGA Nakamoto payed attention to the historical development of the philosophical traditions.

Whenever a philosophy was being formed, according to his discourse, it developed as a partial addition to the preceding philosophical basis while willing to overcome the predecessor. "Anyone who teaches a philosophy or founds a school of philosophy has a certain preceding authority upon which he relies. And he attempts to overcome it while comparing his thesis with it. It often happens that scholars of later years overlook the relationship between the predecessor and the latecomer."[70] In the history of philosophy, new theses appear consequentially.[71] "A new thesis is an addition to the existing theses."[72]

If such a frame of reference was taken, the students should come to consider the historical aspect of philosophy necessarily. Nakamoto denounced the traditional scholars on the ground that they little considered this feature of philosophy. This claim was revolutionary at the time of TOMINAGA Nakamoto, though students of humanities today may take it for granted. From this view point, the religious geniuses of the old times were seen as the human who cumulated much knowledge throuhg the years and who were bound with the past philosophies, if they attempted to transcend them. They were not the super-man whom the God gave special previleges. Now that religious heroes were the historical and the human beings.

In this thought is a humanist view point comparable to the view point of the modern western humanists. In the western hemisphere, humanism has existed not only in the modern times, but also in Classical Greece, Cicero being an example. What characterizes the modern humanism and was absent in Cicero is its growth through the struggle against Christianity and the Christian idea of life. Christianity, in fact, intervened the classical humanism and its modern renaissance. In[73] spirit TOMINAGA's historical study of Buddhist thoughts correspond exactly to the modern western humanism. It is his emphasis of historical observation that helped him organize a systematic history of Buddhist philosophies and that made him a distinguished figure among the Japanese philosophers.

In the research of the history of philosophies, TOMINAGA Nakamoto depended mostly on language analysis, holding a systematic opinion upon the nature of the discourse. Namely he proposed three "things" and five "categories" as critieria for textual criticism.

Three "things" were explained as follows. "My method of study emphasizes three things by which all human discourse can be properly understood. As long as one's approach is made through these three things, there is no discourse which defies clear understanding." Each of the three "things" was explained individually in detail.[74]

(1) "Discourse has man behind it." This meant that "as one man or one group of men differs from another, so does discourse." TOMINAGA illustrated this by showing how terminology employed in the various Buddhist scriptures reflected the different language and outlook of various authors. The terms thus specifically used by certain men or certain group of men showed their contention.

(2) "Discourse has time behind it." This meant that as each age had its own characteristics, so the pronunciation and spelling of discourse partook of it. TOMINAGA, showing that the different Chinese translations of Buddhist literature employed different rendering, explained that the same vocabulary was spelled and enunciated differently at different times. As the scholars by these days believed that the spelling and pronunciation of discourse were solid and immovable, this view sounded revolutionary at his time, though it is a common sense today. The accustomed use of the well established Chinese characters which survived the same symbol for a few thousand years had provided the scholars with the belief that the language was immovable. "Those who value the new translation claim that the old translation committed mistransliteration. But the fact is that the discourse and procunciation differ at different times. They are different but both correct rendering from the sources of different times."

(3) "Discourse falls into different categories." These categories had particular reference to the ways in which different teachings or truths were further developed or modified in the hands of others.

a. Assertion or expansion, including exaggeration and metaphor.

This category was expressed in the character for the wave swelling up and luging forward. "Yuima-gyo (*Vimalakirti nirdesa sūtra*) says, 'Learning the law of universe is the academy.' Zenyo-kyo says,' Natural departure from the craving is the academy.' These statements show the example of expansion or exaggeration. The academy is the academy, not identical with learning. Shintoists also make this fort of statement. For example, they say, 'The body of a man is the world in heaven.' In the mean time, Zo-ichi-agon-gyo (*Ekottarāgama, Tseng-i-a-han-ching*) and Kise-kyo speak of the four kinds of food. Only one of the four, *Dan-jiki,* is included in the ordinary concept of food. The rest, *Koraku-jiki,* implying clothes, houses, perfume, and furniture, *Nen-jiki,* implying thinking, imagination and conception, and *Shiki-jiki,* implying the matters which human eyes and ears recognize, are not ordinarily regarded as food, though the sutra says they are. These, we must say, are the expansion of the discourse, 'food.' " *Jiki* originally meant the food edible by men through mouth only. Later other things came to be included in the word, which he called expansion. "People say metaphorically, 'to *eat* a hitting by a club,' or 'to *eat* a punch.' Dai-chido-ron (*Mahaprajnaparamitōpadesa, Ta-chih-tu-lun*) regards scriptures as the relics of the Buddha. But relics are relics. They are not written scriptures. These are examples of expansion. If scholars learn this, many questions become much simpler." These illustrations suggest us that TOMINAGA, with steady and scholastic perspective, attempted to investigate the truth behind the rhetorical exaggeration.

b. Generalization.

This category was expressed in the character for the wave spreading out. This category, it seems, referred to the general discourse, while covertly holding the particular reference behind the overt general expression. "The original meaning of Tathaga as applied to the Buddha was 'He who comes thus.' As the storehouse of the Mind, however, it was described in the Ryoga (*Lankavatara Sūtra*) as 'the source of good and evil,' and in the Hannya (*Prajna Paramita Sūtra*) 'All creatures from Heaven to Hell are embraced in the storehouse of the Tathagata.' " The expressions of this sort belonged to this category.

c. Collision or contradiction.
This category was expressed in the character for the wave breaking against the shore.[75] This seems to have implied such expressions that emphasized and extracted part of the general form of discourse. "It is said, in Shoman-gyo (*Srimālā-devi-simhanāda-sūtra, Sheng-man-ching*), 'The Buddha's Truth-body (*Dharmakaya*) does not exist apart from the world of passion,' and in the storehouse of Tathagata, 'The Tathagata is found amidst all the passions of the sentient world.' These are cases of collision."

d. Reversion or inversion.
This category was expressed in the character for the wave washing back. This was the case of using a discourse in the opposite of the original meaning. The Chinese expression "to follow one's own bent" as a translation for the Sanskrit *pravarana* was an example. "To follow one's own bent" originally had the bad connotation of lacking restraint; here it takes on the good one of acting spontaneously in accord with one's true nature."

e. Transformation or modification.
This category was expressed in the character for the wave turning away. This referred to the turning and elevating of the meaning of the original discourse. *Iccantika* in Sanskrit, for example, meant the most wicked villain without any help. Fa-Hsien, who traveled in central Asia, India and Ceylon between 399 and 414, said 'Everything has Buddha nature except *Iccantika*,' in the first translation of *Mahā-parinirvāna-sūtra, Nieh-p'an-ching*. Whereas the sūtra's later translation,

known as *Ta-pan-heh-p'an-ching* described the comparable statement as, 'Even the *Iccantika* with no merit possesses the Buddha nature.' TOMINAGA stated, "I would believe that *Iccantika,* originally considered to be lacking a Buddha nature, should an aftlef' creature capable of spiritual conversion possess the seed of Buddhahood, because the transformation or modification of the idea of potentiality for Buddhahood derives from the possession of spiritual self hood rather than from one's status among men."

When TOMINAGA proposed "Discourse has three things," his attention seems to have been paid the most heavily upon the personal particularity of the discourse. "As the frame of reference of my research, I say, discourse has three things. Different terms for a concept in different Buddhist scriptures reflect the different wording in the different schools or denominations of Buddhism. The unique wording of a school or a denomination is comparable to the trade mark of the merchants. Students of later years often forget the historical situation, and try to explain the terms independently and for their own sake, thus missing the links and the intentions of the original. This is the mistake in which later scholars often fall."[76]

Along with the process of diversification of Buddhist schools and denominations, every discourse attained many implications. The Chinese thought that "The diversity of meaning of the Sanskrit discourse cannot be compared to that of any other language," and they referred to the six different meanings for the word, *bhagavat.* But the vocabulary with diverse meanings was not the preoccupation of the Sanskrit. "The Chinese discourse contains many implications. Consult a dictionary, and you will notice many footnotes under every heading. They show the diversity of the Chinese discourse." TOMINAGA did not forget to mention that the Japanese discourse was not an exception. "Not only the Chinese, but the Japanese discourse implied many things."

TOMINAGA's study of the language has so far been covered. He explained his theses quite simply. We may have to mention that the theses were not clear enough in the present standard of philological criticism.

Yet it remains the most remarkable that he accomplished a synthetic and systematic philosophy of language with the historical perspective at the time when he lived.

The Way of Truth

TOMINAGA Nakamoto was the first who studied all the major philosophical systems of India, China, and Japan *historically*. A study of the history of philosophies or ethical thoughts is impossible without the student's own philosophical convictions. Without some ethical retrospection, a student can never systematize the ethical thoughts that appear before him. Then we ought to understand what the position accorded with his own conviction was, as long as we would expect a thoruough understanding of his history of philosophies.

The ethical philosophy of TOMINAGA Nakamoto was presented in a book titled the *Testament of an Old Man (Okina no Fumi)*. TOMINAGA claimed that he transcended Shinto, Confucianism, and Buddhism, and, upon synthesizing them, advocated the Way of Truth, or the way of the ways. "Departing from the three teachings of Buddhism, Confucianism, and Shinto, he advocates what he calls the Way of Truth."[77] But if we analyze the teachings of the Way of Truth, we cannot find any revolutionary idea in them. The items of popular morality of his day constitute the Way.

"If you have a master, serve him well. If you have children, educate them well. If you have retainers, manage them well. If you have an elder brother, show him every respect. If you have a younger, show him every sympathy. Toward old people, be thoughtful; toward young people, be loving. Do not forget your ancestors. Be mindful of preserving harmony in your household. When associating with men, be completely sincere. Do not indulge in evil pleasures. Revere those who are superior, while not despising the ignorant. What you would not have done to yourself, do not do to others. Be not harsh; be not rash. Be not obstinate or stubborn. Be not demanding or impatient. Even when you are angry, do not go too far. When you are happy, be so within bounds. You may take pleasure in life, but do not indulge in sensuality. Be not lost in sorrow; whether you have enough or not, accept your lot as good fortune and be content with it. Things which you ought not take, even if they seem insignificant, do not take; when you ought to give, do not hesitate to do so even it means giving up all, even your country. As to the quality of your food and clothing, let it conform to your station in life and avoid extravagance. Do not be stingy, do not steal, do not lie. Do not lose yourself in lust, be temperate in drinking. Do not kill anything that does no harm to mankind. Be careful in the nourishment of your body; do not eat bad things; do not eat too much."[78] "In your free time study the arts of self-improvement; try to be better informed."[79] To sum, this was the way to teach to be virtuous.[80]

The Way of Truth was thus a concrete teaching by means of which men realized their ways in daily life. It was not an abstract concept. The way as the cause of human phenomena was "being done." If it was not realized in the world, it was not the way at all. The way was present in the phenomena of the world. It was not a product of imagination or thinking.

The world where the way functioned was composed of space and time. Therefore the way was necessarily bound by chronological and spatial limitations if it was to be realized in the world. Second characteristic of the Way of Truth was a derivative of the chronological limitation, namely, the Way ought to be in accord with the "present" necessities. Third was derived from the "spatial" limitation. The Way of Truth ought to be the way of "Japan." It was strongly held that the Way as the law of causality among the human beings was conditioned by the historical and endemic situations. The awareness of the importance of the historical and endemic elements in the human phenomena, if otherwise not much different, made the Way of Truth unique among the philosophies of the day.

Then the question was what the "virtue" was.

TOMINAGA simply explained that to do virtue was in accord with and to do evil was against the Way of Heaven, Earth, and Nature,[81] and did not deeply investigate the nature of the virtue. In the claim of doing virtue, TOMINAGA argued, the three established religions agreed completely.

"The way of Confucius and the way of Buddha are the same. Both demand to do virtue."[82]

The question was whether the teaching of the three religions and that of the Way of Truth were identical or not. Enumerating the items of virtuous and moral actions, TOMINAGA admitted that "All of these things are already mentioned in Confucian and Buddhist writings, and do not need to be made a special point of,"[83] Then, why did he reject the three religions? Why did he champion the Way of Truth anew? Why did he distinguish the Way from the other ways?

He emphasized "the Way of Truth," primarily because it was the way "that is practicable in the present Japan."[84] This phrase illustrates the three concepts by means of which the Way of Truth was defined. Firstly, it ought to be practicable. "The phrase the way of the ways was derived from the fact of its being done. So the way which is not realizable is not the Way of Truth."[85]

Shinto, Confucianism, and Buddhism, or more precisely, Shinto as sponsored by the scholars of National Learning, Buddhism as explained by the contemporary priests, and Confucianism as lectured by Neo-Confucianists, were all "the ways ill approved by the Way of Truth," mainly because they neglected the historical and endemic traits of the human being. They were not the ways that should be practiced in Japan of the day. TOMINAGA pointed out how the customs and habits were different at different places and times.[86] Even the Buddhist priests and Confucian scholars in Japan could not rigorously observe the prescriptions of behavior as given in Buddhist or Confucian scriptures.[87] Imitation of the Indians or the Chinese was not only impossible, but meaningless.

The Buddhists' devotional adoration of the Indian culture, Nakamoto commented, was by no means plausible. "Buddhists learn the teaching of the Indians, attempt to practice the teaching, and dare to communicate the teaching to other Japanese. But none ever used nor any audience learned Sanskrit. Make a house and furnish it in the complete imitation of the Indian fashion, and you would learn it impractical. In India it is a good manner to reveal one's shoulder when saluting. Even the exhibition of one's thighs is an acceptable manner in India. There are ample such examples in the Buddhist literature. What should happen, then, if the Buddhists should imitate these alien habits?"[88] "Buddhist scriptures had it, 'Even if I should tell you something, you need not follow it in case it did not apply the custom of the place where you are. If my instruction do not cover what you want to know, do whatever is good at the place," and "Buddha did not teach for everybody to imitate the customs of India."[89] The true intention of Buddha in these words, TOMINAGA lamented, were not correctly understood by the contemporary Buddhists of Japan.

TOMINAGA Nakamoto insisted that the Confucianists' adoration of the Chinese culture was not practical either.

"In China meet is important food. If the Confucianists were to follow whatever ways Confucius had taken, they should store beef and mutton, and live on them, . . . They should converse in Chinese and use Chinese characters. Out of several variations, they should choose the pronunciation of Lu area and of the Chou period, and use the characters as used in the classics."[90]

The uncritical devotion to and the foolish imitation of the Chinese culture, TOMINAGA said, was meaningless and was contrary to the truth of the Confucian teaching. "Confucianists say, 'Do as the aliens do if you are in the alien community.' Also is it said, 'The Rite follows the local customs.' Then it is not that the Confucian scholars demand everybody to imitate the Chinese manners and customs. It is against the truth of Confucian teaching that the Confucianists of Japan would blindly practice what are alien to the Japanese, in the desire to imitate everything Chinese."[91]

TOMINAGA Nakamoto rejected the position of the contemporary Shinto also. Although his "Mahāyāna non-Buddhist" thesis was highly appreciated by the Shintoists because it provided a powerful means for the Shintoists to attack the Buddhists, TOMINAGA did not refrain from rebuking Shinto position for the lack of historical perspective. In spite of the continuity, Japan today and Japan in the Divine Antiquity had different manners and customs, and the thorough revivalism to antiquity would inevitably result in the most absurd confusion.

"In early Japan, the salutation of meeting was to crap hands toward the person and to bow four times; rice was ate on a leaf of a tree; at mourning, people sang songs and wept aloud; when mourning was over, people went to a river and bathed in order to be released from pollution." Students of Shinto deliberately follow these customs, provided that they would conform to the ancient ways. As money did not exist in the Divine Antiquity, the students of Shinto should refrain from using money no matter how important it is today. They shall not wear the contemporary clothing as the style is a recent introduction during Wu times. They shall learn the ancient language and naming. For example, they shall address their father *kazo,* their mother *iroha,* etc."[92]

The vice of Shinto was that it neglected the historicity. "The practice of Shinto today is not the truth of Shinto. It advertizes curious and meaningless behavior while taking its model in the ancient customs."[93]

Ethics ought to be relevant to the particular chronological and spatial condition in which the specific person was located. "We must realize that it is very difficult and absurd to attempt to imitate the customs of China and India or to try to revive the practice of the Divine Antiquity, when the customs differ within the distance of ten or twenty miles and when the event of five or ten years ago is hardly remembered. The imitation, if it should happen to be perfect, is meaningless because the background differs. These three religions, therefore, are not the ways to be practiced in Japan today."[94]

TOMINAGA emphasized the contemporaneity of the meaning of history. "To write with the present-day script, to use present-day vernacular, to eat present-day food, to dress in present-day clothes, to use present-day utensils, to live in present-day houses, to follow present-day regulations, to mix with present-day people, to do nothing bad, to do all good things —that is the Way of Truth. That is the Way which is practicable in present day Japan."[95]

It is not that TOMINAGA rejected the truth involved in the three religions, but that he opposed the attitude of the people that were blindly involved in one of the three teachings and that could not reflect on the

historical and endemic situation of the human being. He did not agree
with the people who attempted to apply the ethical principles of other
countries or of different ages to the present-day Japan. "I am not demanding the abolishment of the three religions. What I mean is to emphasize
the truth in them."[96] That is, TOMINAGA wanted to eliminate such situation that "the ways practiced today are superficial plays around Shinto,
Confucianism or Buddhism losing sight of the truth in Shinto, Confucianism or Buddhism."[97] Neither was he a popular syncretist of the three
religions. He intentionally rejected the thesis of some Chinese Buddhists
that all the religions were uniform, because he did not think that the
syncretists grasped the ultimate reason in the individual religions.

The most noteworthy feature of his thought is that he transported the
cause of morality from the Divine authority to the human existence.
Denying the traditional manner of authetication, he said, "The Way of
Truth is ngt come from either India or China. Nor is it an invention of
the Divine Antiquity which we have revived. It is not come from the
heaven or the earth either. It is the question of the present day people.
It is the common sense in our daily life. If it is done, others are pleased
and the doer is pleasant, and everything goes well. If it is not done, others
are irritated and the idle is unpleasant, and everything goes ill. Therefore
it is done naturally from the experience of daily life. It is not an artificial
product with particular intention."[98]

In the west, the humanism of early modern period was born from the
realization of the human dignity and the struggle of its detachment from
the yoke of the traditional authorities. TOMINAGA's humanism was an
oriental counterpart of it. Only upon such humanist realization he could
initiate the philological studies of the classical literature.

Whether ethics may stand only upon the ground of humanism or not
is problematic, and yet his contention as such has the importance that
does not allow us to overlook it.

TOMINAGA pursued the study of the general history of philosophies,
or the general history of ethical thoughts with the consciousness such as
described above. There is no denying that Japan had competent philol-
ogues before and after him. All of them, however, were either Buddhist,

Confucianist or Shintoist, and were bound by the dogma of respective disciplines. TOMINAGA alone could clarify independence from any discipline. He declared, "I am not a disciple of Confucianism, nor of Shinto, nor of Buddhism. I am an observer of all the philosophies and discuss them from my own standard."[99] He was the first who wrote a systematic history of oriental philosophies with the new historic and endemic perspective. The *Historical Survey of Buddhism* (出定後語) was so excellent a dissertation that the contemporary studies of the history of Buddhism go along the line that TOMINAGA opened so many years ago. His treatise on the history of Chinese philosophies the *Failings of the Classical Philosophers* (説蔽) is unfortunately lost, but its outline is surmised from another remaining work, the *Testament of an Old Man* (翁の文). TOMINAGA never thought any philosophy was absolute, and endeavored to clarify the meaning of each system in the historical and the endemic context.

We have sketched the Way of Truth of TOMINAGA Nakamoto. We would classify this "way of the ways" as "an ethical philosophy of ethical philosophies."

Particularism

Thus the ethical philosophy of TOMINAGA Nakamoto was the best characterized by the emphasis upon the historic and endemic particularity. The valuation of the particular, however, has been traditional in the way of thinking of the Japanese people in general. The earliest of such example, as far as we can trace, was the text criticism of the Japanese Buddhists during the Heian Period (794–1192). The Tendai critics emphasized the importance of the matters (*ji*), while its Chinese counterpart the T'ientai scholars mainly worked on the principle (*ri*). The matters were the specific or particular being bound by the spatial and timely conditions. This trend was the most clearly revealed in the text criticism of Nichiren (1222–1282) who constructed his thesis on the ground of the Japanese Tendai doctrine. Nichiren proposed to classify the Buddhist teachings into five categories, which he called "the five religious dimensions," "the five levels of understanding," or "the five phases of Buddhism." The five categories were the content of the teaching in the scripture, the spiritual quality of the people whom the teaching was addressed, the need and the situation of the time at which the teaching was delivered, the particularity of the land where the teaching was preached, and the religious or philosophical conditions prior to the evangelization by the teaching. The proposition was that the teachings were to be evaluated and given order in reference to these five categories. Saichō (767–822), the founder of Japanese Tendai, had already discussed the importance of the elements of time and land, but he did not go to the extent of defining them the spinal code of the sect. Nichiren was the one who advanced the thesis to the maximum. And he was the first to introduce the category of the religious or philosophical conditions. The philosophical current of emphasizing the matters which found its ultimate expression in Nichiren was never developed either in India or in China. The Tendai and Nichiren way of criticizing other philosophies showed much in common with the way of criticism of TOMINAGA Nakamoto.

The same type of contention was recognized among the Confucianists of Japan. NAKAE Toju (1608–1648), who held that the Confucian teaching was the absolute way applicable universally, considered that the way appeared differently in accordance with the difference of the time, the space and the social position in which each man was placed.

"As Confucianism is the eternal way of God, the way of Confucius is alive wherever there is a human being, wherever boats and carts reach, wherever heaven covers and earth holds, wherever the sun and the moon shine and wherever there is frost or mist. But the rites and the manners prescribed in the book of Confucius need not and cannot be practiced at different times, or at different places, or by different men."[100]

Toju taught to "practice the rites and manners according to the way as accepted by the practice of the native community."[101] He believed that the Japanese observed the ternal way of God by following the way of Shinto. KUMAZAWA Banzan (1619–1691) thought similarly. According to him, there existed only one single way, the way of gods of heaven and earth. The way, however, appeared in different forms at different places. The monosanguinous lineage of the Emperors of Japan and the occasional revolutions of the dynasties of China must not be taken as the two different ways, but they should be regarded as the different expressions of the same way. "In Japan there are innate merits of merits of Japan alone."[102] KUMAZAWA then could revere Shinto as the way of Japan while remaining a Confucianist. "The way of God of heaven and earth is the Great Way, whose expression in Japanese land and water is Shinto." "Shinto at the Japanese land and water cannot be stored here or there, nor is it rentable somewhere."[103]

The way of thinking of these Confucian scholars came very close to that of the traditional Japanese Buddhist philosophers in the emphasis of the particurality over the universality of the truth. The only difference was that the Confucianists spoke of the endemic particularity whereas the Buddhists emphasized the historical particularity, eschatology being an example of the latter.

We are not sure if TOMINAGA was influenced by the thoughts of Tendai philosophers and Nichiren, or NAKAE Toju and KUMAZAWA Banzan. But we are convinced that TOMINAGA and others developed their theses toward the same direction of recognizing the value in the particular.

The most exhaustive "philosophy of philosophies" ever constructed by the Japanese, we would presume, was the theory of consciousness by Kūkai (774–835). We must also pay attention to the philosophies of text criticism developed among the Tendai scholars. They were, however, the additions to or diviations from the text criticism of the Chinese Buddhism. They were, we should understand, the Japanese versions of the Chinese text criticism that came to being as the Chinese metamorphosis of the Indian way of thinking. Shintoists, on the other hand, did not formulate anything similar to a philosophy of philosophies by the medieval period, in spite of the efforts to fuse the continental philosophies into native way of thinking. In addition, the exclusive National Learning of Tokugawa Japan invited the sterility of such activities. Therefore we would commend the thought of TOMINAGA Nakamoto as the unique example of Japanese philosophy of philosophies.

The criticism of and the evaluation of all the world views from such a viewpoint as TOMINAGA had taken, i.e. that of historically specified "present-day Japan," had never been attempted either in India or in China. We recognize in this the typically Japanese outlook on the world.

Such outlook on the world or such philosophy of philosophies, in criticizing and evaluating all the philosophies from the view point of the present-day Japan, would eventually arrive at ethno-centrism or state-centrism at the extreme of spatial specification, and to opportunism or conventionalism at the extreme of chronological specification. This means that this view point includes the danger to neglect the universal law breaking through the chronological and spatial divisiveness. This view point is at the opposite extreme of the Indian outlook of the world.[104]

It is said that the first "philosophy of philosophies" or "philosophy of histories of philosophies" was made known by the works of HEGEL. But it is true only so long as the history of philosophies in Europe originating from Greece is concerned. If we turn our attention to cultural areas other than Europe, e.g. India, we immediately recognize a good number of works achieved along the line. We must also recognize that the Indian way of dealing with this field of learning has been quite different from the modern European way. The modern Germanic and the medieval Indian views of the world must be distinguished. We must also distinguish the TOMINAGA view of the world from either of these. We would deem it necessary to classify it in the independent type, the Japanese view of the world.

HEGEL stated that there was no realization of the individuality but that there was all-embracing universalism in the Orient. The statement described well the characteristics of the Indian way of thinking. We would admit that the Indian have dealt with and evaluated the conflicting philosophies or outlooks of the world in terms of the universally applicable principle. The Japanese scholars as represented by TOMINAGA Nakamoto, however, showed a radically different approach to the question. We would not, therefore, agree with the statement of HEGEL above, if it meant to be applied to all the oriental philosophies.

1 Religionssoziologische Schriften, II, S. 296–297.

2 淨土眞宗.

3 Ibid., S. 304–305.

4 Ibid., S. 303.

5 気分 Ibid., S. 304.

6 口伝法門, 天台 *kuden hōmon*: "esoteric teaching by oral tradition."

7 宗要抄.

8 OGATA Michinori, *"Chuko Tendai no Keizai Rinri Kannen"* 中古天台の経済倫理観念 (The Concept of Economical Ethics in Medieval Tendai). *Indogaku Bukkyōgaku Kenkyū* 印度学仏教学研究 (Study on Hindu and Buddhist Thought), 1958, March, VI, No. 2, pp. 110–111. See also the same author's *"Kuden Hōmon no Jissen Rinri"* 口伝法門の実践倫理 (Practical Ethics of Kuden Hōmon), *Nihon Bukkyō* 日本仏教 (Japanese Religion), 1958, October, No. 2, p. 44.

9 鈴木正三.

10 武士.

11 三河国東加茂郡則定郷 (盛岡村), 松平.

12 九太夫.

13 関ヶ原の役.

14 元和六年.

15 得度, 大愚和尚, 臨済宗.

16 寛永, 石平山恩真.

17 慶安.

18 明暦.

19 曹洞宗, 道元.

20 普化.

21 玄俊.

22 破吉利支丹.

23 邪法.

24 万民徳用.

25 士農工商.

26 The Japanese translation of Robert N. BELLAH, *Tokugawa Religion, Nihon Kindaika to Shūkyō Rinri* 日本近代化と宗教倫理 (Japanese Modernization and Religious Ethics), translated by HORI Ichirō 堀一郎, IKEDA Hidetoshi 池田英俊, Miraisha, 1962, p. 179, p. 191, p. 207.

27 二宮尊徳.
28 蓮如.
29 座禅 umbilicular contemplation.
30 SUZUKI Shōsan, *Roankyō* 驢鞍橋, 1660, II, 89.
31 Ibid., III, p. 19.
32 All the quotations are taken from Shōsan's works or his memoirs which are compiled in *Zemmon Hōgoshū* 禅門法語集 edited by YAMADA Kōdō 山田孝道 and MORI Daikyō 森大狂, *Kokubun Tōhō Bukkyō Soshō* 国文東方仏教叢書 by WASHIO Junkei 鷲尾順敬 and *Suzuki Shōsan Dōjin Zenshū* 鈴木正三道人全集 by SUZUKI Tesshin (Sankibō Busshorin 山喜房仏書抹, 1962 and others).
  This paper is written on the basis of the author's *Kinsei Nihon ni Okeru Hihanteki Seishin no Ichikōsatsu* 近世日本に於ける批評的精神の一考察 (A Study of the Critical Spirit in Modern Japan) Sanseidō, 1949 (also in *Gendai Bukkyō Meicho Zenshū* 現代仏教名著全集, Ryūbunkan 隆文館, Tokyo, 1960. II).
  33 *Tamakatsuma*, 8
  34 *Shuttei Shogo*, 3
Social History of Buddhism
  35 See 中村元, "Critical Spirit of Pre-modern Japan" 1965:『出定後語註解』pp. 255–303,『翁の文註解』pp. 305–307.
  36 E.g.「集解標旨鈔」
  37 E.g.「法苑珠林」,「大乗義章」,「法苑義林章」「天台三大部」, 」華厳五教章」,「翻訳名義集」
He may have read part of *Tripitaka*. Some of his quotations correspond to the *Tripitaka* of Ming edition, while different from other editions. In reference to the legend that TOMINAGA stayed at Obakusan which published the *Tripitaka* of Ming edition, it could have been possible that he had occasions to read it. But this surmise is not strong enough to repudiate our thesis that he did not read it much.
  38「出定笑語」巻3.
  39「出定後語」第24 (*Historical Survey of Buddhism*)
  40 Ibid., 第22.
  41「大智度論」第18巻 (大正蔵25巻 192頁) (*Mahāprajnāpāramitopadeśa*)「摩訶止観」6上 (大正蔵 46巻 73頁) (*Mo-ho-chih-kuan; Various Aspects of Meditation*)
  42「天台四教義」(大正蔵46巻 724頁) (*T'ien-t'ai-ssū-chiao-i; Four Fundamental doctrines of the T'ien-t'ai Sect*).
  43「うひやまぶみ」 (*Essays of Motoori Noringa*)
  44「弁名」上 善良三則 (*Discourse on Name*).
  45「翁の文」第11節 (*Testament of an Old Man*).
  46「顕揚正法復古集」第 I 巻 in 村上専精「大乗仏説論批判」84 頁以下「香海一滴」in 前田恵雲「大乗仏教央論」278–280頁
  47 敬首律師「真如祕稿」
村上 48 p. 116 ff. 前田 pp. 281–283.
  49 He was not an observer of the commandments. He did not think drinking was prohibited. See「出定後語」第 14–16.
  50「出定後語」第 8
  51 Ibid.
  52 Ibid.
  53 Based on the *Analects*.

54「翁の文」第15節　(Translation in Theodore DE BURY ed. *Sources of Japanese Tradition* (1958) p. 487–488).

55「出定後語」第8

56「翁の文」第14節

57「出定後語」第8

58「出定後語」第8
第25「異却幻変の説」
第10「無量劫を以てする者は幻の幻なり」

59「出定後語」第8

60「翁の文」註　神通は修行より出る」

61「出定後語」第25

62「出定後語」第24

63「出定後語」第15, 25

64「出定後語」第24

65 Ibid.

66 Ibid.

67「出定後語」第8

68「翁の文」第16節　(DE BURY, p. 488).

69「翁の文」第16節　(DE BURY, p. 488).

70「翁の文」第9節

71「出定後語」第9

72 Ibid., 第6

73 H. A. KORFF. *Humanismus und Romantik* (1924, S. 10.

74 Quotations below otherwise specified are from Chapters 11 and 25 of the *Historical Survey of Buddhism*.

75 Mecius.「親之過小而怨，是不可磯也」
Chao Chih.「磯激也」
Chu Hsi.「磯水激石也，不可磯言微激之而遽怒也」

76「楽律考」[TOMINAGA Nakamoto, *Discourse on Music*].

77「翁の文」序 (DE BURY. Op. cit., p. 483).

78 Ibid. (Ibid., p. 484–485).

79 Ibid. (Ibid., p. 485).

80「出定後語」雑　第25

81 Ibid., 戒 第14

82 Ibid., 三教 第24.

83「翁の文」第6節 注 (DE BURY, p. 485).

84 Ibid., 第6節 (Ibid., p. 484).

85 Ibid., 第5節

86 Ibid., 第1節 (DE BURY, pp. 483–484).

87 Ibid., 第2, 3節

88 Ibid., 第1節

89「五分律」第2, 3巻 (大正蔵22巻 153頁).

90, 91「翁の文」第2節

92, 93, 94, 95 Ibid., 第5節

96, 97 Ibid., 第8節

98 Ibid., 第7節

99「出定後語」三教 第24

100「翁問答」下巻之末 (藤樹先生全集 第 3 巻 248-249頁).

101 Ibid., 第94問 (Ibid., 251頁).

102「三輪物語」(蕃山全集 第 5 巻 67).
(See FISHER, GALEN. "Kumazawa Banzan. His Life and Ideals." *Translations of the Asiatic Society of Japan,* 2nd ser., XVI (1938), 221-58).

103 比屋根安定「日本宗教史」943頁

104 中村元「哲学的思索の印度的展開」(1949), 1-68頁

CHAPTER VII

PROBLEMS OF JAPANESE PHILOSOPHICAL THOUGHT

1. Basic Features of the Legal, Political and Economic Thought
    The legal, political, and economical thought of a people cannot be
discussed without taking the chief basic philosophical concepts of the
people into consideration. Professor NORTHROP says: "In fact, the philosophy of any society is but the name for the basic concepts and assumptions agreed upon by its people for organizing the data of their experience
and ordering their relation to nature and to one another."[1] Among the
main features of Japanese ways of thinking we must note the following
three:

   (1) *Acceptance of actuality.* (1) Apprehension of the absolute in the
phenomenal world; (2) "this-worldliness"; (3) acceptance of natural
human qualities; (4) the spirit of tolerance; (5) cultural stratification; and
(6) weakness of the spirit of direct criticism.

   (2) *Tendency to emphasize a particular social nexus.* (1) Emphasis on
human relations; (2) human relationships of greater importance than
the individual; (3) absolute view of limited social organization; (4) reverence for family morality; (5) emphasis upon hierarchical relations of
status; (6) the supremacy of the state; (7) absolute obedience to a particular person; (8) emperor worship; (9) closed character of sects and
cliques; (10) protection of the particular social nexus by force; (11)
emphasis on activity in society; (12) sensitivity to moral introspection;
and (13) lack of self-consciousness in religious reverence.

   (3) *Non-rational tendencies.* (1) Non-logical tendencies; (2) weakness
in ability to think in terms of logical consequences; (3) intuitional and

emotional tendencies; (4) lack of ability to form complex representations; (5) fondness for simple, symbolical representations; (6) weakness in knowledge of objective processes.[2]

Esteem for Human Nature

In general, the Japanese are inclined to search for the absolute within the phenomenal world or in what is actual. Among all the natures that are given and real, the most immediate to man is the nature of man. Hence the Japanese tend to esteem highly man's natural disposition. So, as one of the most prominent features of traditional Japanese ways of thinking, we may point out the emphasis on the love of human beings. This might be described as the naturalistic view of life.[3] This tendency has been conspicuous among Shintoists. Buddhist idea have also been taught with close reference to matters of love, and even sexual love is considered to be not incompatible with religious matters. The tendency to esteem man's nature gave rise to the love of human beings in reality.

The tendency toward humanitarianism has been traditional among the Japanese; yet it has generally escaped the attention of scholars. The love of others in its purest form is called "benevolence" (Sanskrit: *maitri, karuna*). This idea was introduced into Japan with the advent of Buddhism. The attempt to realize universal religions in politics caused rulers to deal with people affectionately and compassionately, as in the case of Asoka, who said: "All people are may children."

Prince Shōtoku (574–622) asserted: "As the disease of infatuation among the common people is endless, the compassionate measures taken up by bodhisattvas also are endless. . . . Common people are of less beatitude; we teach them to do meritorious deeds. . . . Properties are what can save people from poverty and affliction. So Buddhas save living beings in various areas with the Four All-Embracing Virtues, the Four Virtues of Infinite Greatness, and the Six Perfections." Prince Shōtoku emphasized "harmony" or "concord" in human relations. With deep self-reflection, he advocated such concord in the first article of his Constitution: "Above all else esteem concord; make it your first duty to avoid discord. People are prone to form partisanship, for few persons are really enlightened. Hence there are those who do not obey lords and parents, and they come in conflict with their neighbors. But when those above are harmonious and those below are friendly, there is concord in the discussion of affairs, and right views of things spontaneously gain acceptance. Then what could not be accomplished?"

Some scholars say that the conception of concord (wa) here was adopted from Confucianism, for the word wa is used in The Analects of Confucius. But the term "wa" was used in connection with propriety or decorum in that work,[4] and concord was not the subject there. Prince Shōtoku, on the other hand, advocated concord as the principle of human behabior.[5] His attitude seems to have derived from the Buddhist concept of benevolence, which should be distinguished from the Confucian.

The Constitution of Prince Shōtoku esteems the welfare of the people and is sympathetic toward them. The fifth article teaches sympathy with suffering people in law suits. Other articles also contain such admonitions as: "Such are the kinds of men who are never loyal to the lord, nor benevolent toward the people. All this is the source from which grave civil disturbances occur." (Article VI) "Provincial governors and district administrators should not levy exacting taxes on their respective peoples." (Article XII) In the Constitution common people came to have some significant role in the consciousness of the ruling class. This role could not be destroyed in later history, and the trend might be regarded as the first step in the gradual development of democracy.

King Asoka also endeavored greatly to promote cultivation of medical herbs. "Wherever medical herbs, wholesome for men and wholesome for animals, are not found, they have everywvere been caused to be imported and planted. Roots and fruits, wherever they are not found, have been caused to be imported and planted." Prince Shōtoku also, together with his officials, carried on a "hunt for medical herbs," and established dispensaries.

The spirit of benevolence was preached not only by the Buddhists; it also made its way into Shintoism, and was tied up with one of the three divine symbols of the Japanese Imperial Family, which claimed to rule on the spiritual basis of benevolence. The Tokugawa Shogunate inherited this attitude. Benevolence also came to be regarded as one of the principal virtues of the *samurai,* who asserted that it was not sufficient for them to be physically brave and strong, but that they should be compassionate with the common people.[6] Japanese Confucian scholars of politics also lay special emphasis upon the love of others. KUMAZAWA Bansan, a famous Confucianist of the Tokugawa Period, called Japan "the land of benevolence."[7] These facts give ample testimony to the assumption that the ruling class of Japan aimed at benevolence as their principal ideal.

In pre-Buddhist Japan, cruel punishments were not lacking; emperors killed their subjects arbitrarily.[8] On the occasions of the interment of emperors, their retainers were buried alive around their graves.[9] Such customs were eventually abolished, and after the advent of Buddhism there existed in Japan hardly any punishment that could be called cruel. During the Heian Period, capital punishment was not practiced for about three hundred and fifty years. Since crucifixion appeared for the first time in Japanese history during the Age of the Civil Wars, it was probably introduced after the advent of Christianity and suggested by it.

The love of human beings seems to be closely connected with the love of the beauties of Nature, which is as old as the Japanese people themselves. CHIANG Monlin describes the Asian way of knowing nature as follows: "The Chinese people are devoted to nature, not in the sense of finding the natural laws but in the sense of cultivating the poetic, artistic, or moral sense as lovers of nature." This holds true for the Japanese attitude also.

The features pointed out here give us some clues to the basic concepts of Japanese legal, political, and economic thought.

The Spirit of Harmony or Concord

The unanimous moral solidarity of a community has been aimed at as the social ideal, on an island scale, in Japan. This was felt intuitively in the spiritual atmosphere of the primitive society of Japan. Later, when the centralized state was established after the conflicts among various tribes had ended, what was stressed in the first place as the principle of the community was "concord." According to the Sixteen Article Law (as set forth in the *Chronical of Tibet*); "Whosoever quarrels, is punished severely." (Article 1) Asoka also stressed the spirit of concord (*samavāya*). In the same way, men are apt to be bigoted and partial. Inside a community or between communities, conflicts are sure to occur. One should overcome such conflicts, and concord should be realized, so that a harmonious community may be formed in an ideal way. The spirit of concord was stressed throughout all the articles of the Constitution. Concord between lord and subject, between superior and inferior, among people in general and among individuals, was taught repeatedly. This concord is essentially nothing but concord, not obedience.

Prince Shōtoku did not teach that the people should merely follow or obey, but that discussion should be carried on in an atmosphere of concord or harmony, so that one might attain right views. Earnest discussion was most desirable.

King Asoka said: "Let us cease from wrath, and refrain from angry looks. Nor let us be resentful just because others oppose us. Every person has a mind of his own; each heart has its own learning. We may regard as wrong what we hold as right. We are not unquestionably sages, nor are they assuredly fools. Both of us are simply ordinary men. Who is wise enough to judge which of us is good or bad? For we are all wise and foolish alternately, like a ring which has no end. Therefore, although others may give way to anger, let us on the contrary dread our own faults, and though we may be sure that we are in the right, let us act in harmony with many others." (Article X)[10]

If we discuss affairs with this feeling of harmony—desisting from anger —difficult problems will be settled spontanuously and in the right way. In this way alone is it possible that decisions can be reached at conferences.

King Asoka also asserts the necessity for self-reflection: "(A person) seeth the good deed only (saying unto himself:) 'This good deed has been done by me.' In no wise doth he see (his) sin (saying unto himself:) 'this sin have I committed,' or 'this, indeed, is a depravity.' But this certainly is difficult to scrutinize. Nevertheless, it should certainly be looked into thus: 'these (passions), indeed, lead to depravity, such as violence, cruelty, anger conceit, envy and by reason thereof may I not cause my fall.' "

The democratic way of managing a conference was realized in the remote past. In the mythology which reflects the primitive society of Japan, deities convened in divine assembly in the bed of a river. This tradition was followed and developed by later monarchs.

Setting forth multifarious mental attitudes of rulers and officials, Prince Shōtoku, in Article XVII, denounced dictatorship and stressed the necessity of discussing things with others: "Decisions on important matters should generally not be made by one person alone. They should be discussed with many others. But small matters are of less importance, and it is unnecessary to consult many persons concerning them. In the case of discussing weightly matters you must be fearful lest there be faults. You should arrange matters in consultation with many persons, so as to arrive at the right conclusion."

This represents the beginning of Japanese democratic thought, for Article XVII corresponds to the first Article, to the effect that discussion should be carried on in the spirit of concord.

This trend developed into an edict after the Taiki Innovation (645), which thus denounced the dictatorship of a sovereign: "Things should not be instituted by a single ruler."

Whence has the denunciation of dictatorship been inherited?

The ancient way of ruling represented in Japanese mythology is not dictatorship by a monarch or by the Lord of All, but a conference of gods in a river bed. Where public opinion was not esteemed, a conference could not have been held successfully: hence the spirit of primitive Shintoism must have been inherited and developed by later rulers.

On the other hand, it is possible that the rules of the Buddhist order influenced the thought of the Prince, rules set forth in full detail in the scriptures, including the rules of decision by majority. The fact that consultation with many others was not explicitly encouraged by Asoka, nor by Sontsan-Gampo, but by Prince Shōtoku, is noteworthy. This ideal was preserved in the days when the emperors were in power: Japanese monarchy or the Emperor Institution developed as something different from dictatorship.

Professor Northrop observes that when a dispute arises among Asians, one does not settle it by recourse to determinate legal principles, but pursues the "middle way" of mediation between the determinate theses of the disputants, by fostering the all-embracing intuitively felt formlessness common to all men and things.[11]

This emphasis upon mediation rather than legal codes and litigation is the way to settle disputes in pre-Western Confucian China, Buddhist countries, and India. Prof. NORTHROP explains: "This does not mean that Buddhist . . . India, Thailand and Confucian China do not have codes. They do. But the attitude toward them is entirely different from that of the West. The proper way is not to use codes, but mediation. The code is regarded as an evil to be used as a last resort for settling disputes between immoral men when the moral way to the settling of disputes by intuitive feeling and mediation fails."[12]

CHIANG Monlin writes: "Modern legal sense as the West understands it is not developed in China. Avoid the courts if you can. Let us settle our disputes without going to law. Let's compromise. Let's have a cup of tea and sip together with friends and talk things over." This is exactly the situation we find among the countrymen of Japan also. There is a well-known Japanese proverb which is understood by everybody in practice: "In a quarrel both parties (the two) are to blame." This is not due to lack of esteem for law on the part of Japanese people, but to financial and other reasons. If people should go to court, they will lose much time; it may take them several years to settle even one case. They have to employ lawyers and spend much money. Even if they should win at court, they will eventually obtain very little. Hence resort to legal measures very often impairs (taking everything into account) the happiness and welfare of the people concerned and others around them. Barristers-at-law are not always respected, but very often abhorred, by the common people of Japan, from fear that they may take advantage of the people's lack of legal knowledge in order to make money. The writer personally knows some Japanese intellectuals who claim to be businessmen at home, but to be lawyers when they go abroad: They want to conceal their status as lawyers while they work among the Japanese.

But this does not mean that Japanese laws are applied partially. The Japanese give the same meanings for the expression of definite laws or codes, for all men and occasion; there is no difference at all. Yet they do not always want to resort to legal measures.

As the objective causes which brought about such a tendency in the Japanese people, we may cite the social life peculiar to their land and climate. The primitive Indo-Europeans, being nomadic and living chiefly by hunting, were in contact with alien peoples. Here, human relations were marked by fierce rivalry. Peoples were in great migration; one race conquered another, only to be conquered by still another. In such a society, struggles for existence were based not on mutual trust but on rational plan and strategem.

Japanese society, on the other hand, developed from small localized farming communities. The Japanese did away with nomadic life early, and settled down to cultivate rice fields. People living on rice must inevitably settle permanently in one place. In such a society *families* continue on, generation after generation. Genealogies and kinships of families through long years become so well known by their members that the society as a whole takes on the appearance of a family. In such a society individuals are closely bound to each other and they form an exclusive human nexus. Here an individual who asserts himself will hurt the feelings of others and thereby do harm to himself. The Japanese learned to adjust themselves to this type of familial society, and created forms of expression suitable to life in it. Here grew the worship of tutelary gods and local deities. Even today there is a strong tendency in the Japanese social structure to settle closely around such tutelary gods and local deities. This tendency is deeply rooted in the people and has led to their stressing of human relations, especially the spirit of harmony or concord. The Japanese have learned to attach unduly heavy importance to the human nexus in disregard of the individual.

The Concept of Law

Professor Northrop says: "There is never a legal, political or economic society except when all the facts of that society are ordered by certain common normative or, in other words, ideological principles. Law and its political institutions, and one may add also economics and its business institutions, are effective only as they correspond to express this ideological or normative inner order."[13]

It seems that his opinion holds true for the Japanese also, when we consider that the Japanese people were brought to the form of a nation only at a time when laws, or at least normative forms, were established among the people.

Law-giving was not lacking even in the genuinely Shintoistic, pre-Buddhistic age. To illustrate, it is said that Emperor Seimu determined the frontiers and civilized the country, and that he issued laws. He reformed surnames and selected given names.[14] The laws of the primitive Japanese, as of all ancient peoples, were those of customs. Though their details have been lost, it is likely that the two fundamental principles—Imperial sovereignty and the family system—were firmly established even in those days. No positive law, however, is known to us from those days. It is with Prince Shōtoku that we first come to know something of laws in the modern sense.

Prince Shōtoku, the real founder of the centralized state of Japan, proclaimed the Seventeen-Article Constitution in 604. This was the first legislation in Jaean, a characteristic expression of the original and creative development of the Japanese in those days—adopting the civilizations and thought of China and India, chiefly based upon the spirit of Buddhism. This is, so to speak, the *Magna Charta* of Japan. The Constitution prescribed the rules of conduct which the officials of the Imperial government should obey, thereby perchance revealing how badly needed such rules were. The Constitution was proclaimed about forty years prior to the Taika Innovation (Reform of 645).

It has been confirmed by scholars that there is a close connection between the spirit of Shōtoku's Constitution and the political regime established by the Taika Innovation, which accomplished the unified state of Japan.

In connection with Prince Shōtoku's Seventeen-Article Constitution: King Songtsan-Gampo, the founder of the centralized state of Tibet, proclaimed a Sixteen-Article Law of similar purport at nearly the same time; while, going back to antiquity, we find that King Asoka published many Rock and Pillar Edicts which proclaimed various precepts whose number was not fixed. The characteristic common to all of these documents is that they are approximate to moral precepts in the form of representation, and that they were different from positive laws in practice. The Tibetans were especially conscious of this point. According to them, the Sixteen-Article Law was men's Law (*mi-chos*) which was different from Gods' Law (*tha-chos*). The former was an ethical law, whereas the latter was a religious one; both constitute the System of Laws (*chos-lugs*). King Asoka classified them both under the name of "Law" (*dharma*).

Based upon such fundamental laws, practical laws were instituted. The Tibetans called them "Laws of Ruling" (*rgyal-khrims*). Songtsan-Gampo is said to have instituted laws to punish murder, theft and adultery. These correspond to the laws and rules since the Taika Innovation. The laws which were in practice in the Maruyan age around Asoka seem to have been incorporated into the *Arthasāstra* of Kautlya. Due to later interpolations in the work, however, it is very difficult to identify those which were composed in the Maruyan age. Nevertheless, there is one difference: Ongtsan-Gampo's Law taught popular morals meant for common people, whereas Shōtoku's Constitution proclaimed the "Ways of the Public", i.e., mental and moral attitudes of officials concerning state affairs. The edicts of Asoka were mostly meant for common people; some, for officials. This difference betrays the fact that bureaucracy was very strong even at the outset of the centralized state of Japan, and it foretells the supremacy of bureaucrats in later-day Japan.

Positive-laws were officially promulgated later. In 671, a code of laws, said to have consisted of twenty-two volumes, was collated; but the entire code was lost, and its contents are unknown. In 701, the work of codification was cōmpleted. This entire code, known as the Taiho Code, consisting of eleven volumes of general law concerning government organization, administration, and private relations, and six volumes of criminal law, was promulgated and enforced. Revised in 718, these Taiho laws, with many subsequent revisions and supplements, governed the nation for about five hundred years, until 1190.

With the establishment of a feudal regime, the individual Shoguns issued laws. As the authority of the Shoguns increased, the territory within which the Taiho laws were enforced decreased. In the Age of Civil Wars (1467–1585), many feudal lords issued their own regulations or family laws. The Tokugawa Shogunate (1603–1868) tried to govern the country according to already existing customs and, as far as possible, avoided the making of written laws. Contact with Western nations and a study of their civilization after the Meiji Restoration showed the necessity for laws in harmony with the modern world. In 1882, the criminal code was promulgated. This was followed in 1889 by the proclamation of a Constitution and, in 1900, by the civil code. Up to the end of World War II, Japanese law was characterized by the two fundamental principles mentioned earlier; the sovereignty of the Emperor, and the patriarchal family system. In 1946, after the surrender of Japan, a new constitution was promulgated, and the preceding principles were legally abolished, although they still exist in practice.

Professor NORTHROP says: "Only by mastering also this basically Western scientific and philosophical way of conceptualizing nature in terms of laws and concepts which are universals will they understand and apply effectively the Western type of political constitution, economic system and legal processes. For only through this form of knowledge is it possible for men to find the values transcending family loyalty necessary to make these Western social forms effective.[15]

The move to conceptualize human affairs in terms of laws and concepts which are universals has been effected by the Japanese to some extent. In the Rock and Pillar Edicts proclaimed to the subjects in general, freedom of thought is expressed, and no effort is made to teach that Buddhism alone should be esteemed. However, in an edict (the *Bhabru* inscription) issued to a Buddhist order, it is said that the monarch places faith in the Three Jewels, i.e., Buddha, the Law, and the Order. "King Priyadarsin of Magadha, having saluted the Sangha, wishes them good health and comfortable (bodily) movement. Ye know, Reverend Sirs, how great are my respect and kindliness towards Buddha, Dhamma, and Samgha."

"The ordering of a theoretically directed world by means of legally drawn contracts, constitutions or charters is alien to the Asian of the villages,"[16] says Professor NORTHROP. He adds: "Truly the Greco-Roman Christian concept of moral, spiritual and legal man as an instance of universal law protects as well as presupposes liberty. This idea came to expression in the Middle Ages as much as in modern times. What is the Magna Charta but the thesis that even the King is subject, just like anyone else, to the law? His title to kingship is valid only if he accepts the divine logos as superior to himself."[17]

They why had the Japanese in those days to resort to Buddhism?

The concept of universal law came into existence very early in the time of Prince Shōtoku, when he said: "Sincerely revere the Three Treasures. The Three Treasures, viz. the Buddha, the Law, and the Congregation, constitute the final ideal of all living beings and the ultimate foundation of all countries. Should any age or any people fail to esteem this truth? There are few men who are really vicious. They will all follow it if adequately instructed. How can the crooked ways of men be made straight, unless we take refuge in the Three Treasures?"[18] Here we find the concept of a universal law which is something beyond laws based on the inductive status of the individual in the joint family and of the family in its respective tribe or caste. According to the Prince, the "Law" is the "norm" of all living creatures; the "Buddhas" is in fact "the Law embodied", which, "being united with reason," becomes the *sangha*. So, according to his teaching, everything converges in the one fundamental principle called the "Law".

The Empress Suiko issued an Imperial edict to promote the prosperity of the Three Treasures in the year 594. It is said that, at that time, all the Ministers vied with one another in erecting Buddhist temples for the beatitude of their lords and parents. Thus the Buddhist culture came to take root, grew and blossomed. A new epoch in the cultural history of Japan began.

It is likely that other Asian kings who adopted Buddhism thought in the same way. Asoka, however, resorted to *dharma,* which is valid for various religions, and not necessarily Buddhism alone. Buddhism was nothing but one of many religions which received protection from him, just like Brahmanism, Jainism and the Ājīvikas, although it is certain that Asoka particularly patronized and supported Buddhism.

Things being so, it may seem that there was a fundamental difference between Asoka and other Asiatic monarchs, including Prince Shōtoku. Investigating the fundamental ideas which transformed these historical facts into reality, however, we find there was not much difference. In the case of Prince Shōtoku, there was only one philosophical system which taught universal laws—Buddhism. It was natural that the Prince should term Buddhism "the final ideal of all living beings and the ultimate foundation of all countries." In the case of Asoka, however, many religious systems had already become highly developed, and there were many other religions which claimed to be universal philosophical systems, so he had to take up many religions. When we examine matters more deeply, we find that according to the Prince the quintessence of Buddhism consists in acknowledging the universal laws taught by all religions and philosophies, as is evidenced in early and Mahāyāna Buddhism. Therefore we are led to the conclusion that there is no fundamental legalistic difference in outlook between King Asoka and Prince Shōtoku. In this respect they had this in common: that they wanted to found their kingdoms on the basis of universal laws or the truth of the universe.

Due to this characteristic of Buddhism, neither Prince Shōtoku nor King Songtsan-Gampo, not to mention Asoka, suppressed the indigenous faiths of their respective peoples, although they both esteemed and revered Buddhism. That is why Shintoism in Japan and the Bon religion in Tibet have been preserved up to the present. In Burma, the faith of Nats is prevalent even now among common people. Taking into consideration such an attitude we shall be able to understand why the following edict was proclaimed in the reign of Prince Shōtoku: "In my reign, why shall we be negligent of practicing the worship of Shintoist gods? All my officials should worship them sincerely." Both Shintoism and Buddhism have been given protection by the government throughout history. When we compare these facts with the situation in the West, we find a fundamental difference.

Christianity gradually came to the fore in spite of various persecutions. Freedom of faith was finally assured by Emperor Constantine with the edict of Milan in the year 313. Christianity became the state religion on the occasion of the unification of the state by Emperor Theodosius. The Eastern Roman Emperor Justinian, in 529, forbade the worship of heathen gods except the Christian God. These measures characterized the later theological development of Western culture.

Prince Shōtoku, on the other hand, established a new official organization, reforming the old regime under which the higher court ranks were hereditary. Under the new regime anyone could attain promotion according to his ability and merit without distinction of birth. This new system of appointment was called the Twelve Court Ranks (603). The same measures seem to have been taken up by the Mauryan dynasty, on the advice of Kautilya. As it was the officials who acted as the central figures in the newly established centralized states, their morale had to be firmly maintained.

Some Western intellectuals say that Eastern peoples make no distinction between good and bad, right and wrong. But Prince Shōtoku taught that the spirit of esteeming good and hating bad should be cherished: "Punish the vicious and reward the virtuous. This is the excellent rule of antiquity. Do not, therefore, let the good deeds of any person go concealed, nor the bad deeds of any go uncorrected, when you see them. Flatterers and deceivers are like the fatal missile which will overthrow the state, or the sharp sword which will destroy the people. Likewise sycophants are fond of telling their superiors the errors of their inferiors; to their inferiors, they censure the faults of the superiors. Such are the kind of men who are never loyal to the lord, nor benevolent toward the people. All this is the source from which grave civil disturbances occur."

(Article VI) This spirit can be traced in the case of King Asoka of old, who deplored that good deeds are difficult to effect, whereas bad ones are easy to do: "Good is difficult to perform. He who initiates good does something difficult to perform. Hence by me much good had been done. If my sons, grandsons, and my descendants after them, until the aeon of destruction, follow similarly, they will do what is meritorious, but in this respect he who abandons even a part (here), will do ill. Verily, sin is easy to commit."[19] In the scripture of early Buddhism it is also taught: "Evil deeds, deeds which are harmful to oneself, are easy to do. What is beneficial and good, that is very difficult to do."[20] Moreover, the Prince wrote: "Light crimes should be embraced by our power of reforming influence, and grave crimes should be surrendered to our power of strong force."[21] He did not avoid resorting to force in order to punish the severely wicked.

In "Bushidō," or "the Way of Knights," which developed in later times as the peculiarly Japanese "way", and which was regarded as the actual political philosophy of the Japanese, the distinction between good and bad was extremely stressed and strictly observed. "Bushi" or Knights should do nothing mean or despicable even at the cost of their lives.

Considering these historical facts, the assertion made by some scholars that Westerners are keen in the rigid distinction between good and bad, whereas the Eastern peoples are not, is untenable.

"In hearing judicial cases of common people judges should banish avaricious desires and give up their own interest. Deal impartially with the suits brought by the people. Of the cases to be tried, there are a thousand each day. If so many in one day, there will be immense numbers of disputes to be settled in a series of years. Nowadays it is alleged that some judges seek their own profit, and attend to the cases after having taken bribes, which as given rise to the saying: 'The suits of the rich men are like the stone cast into the pond, whereas the suits of the poor men are like water thrown upon a rock.' Hence the poor people do not know where to betake themselves. Such a state of affairs, if brought about, would mean a deficiency in the duty of officials." (Article V)

King Asoka also taught the officials that they should aim at the happi-

ness and welfare of people, and that for that purpose they should observe the utterances, ordinances, and instructions of *dhamma*. He esteemed forbearance and lightness of punishment.[22] "Each person has a
duty to perform; let not the spheres of duty be confused. When wise and
capable persons are entrusted with high offices, there will arise a unanimous voice of pleased approval; but when wicked persons hold high
offices, disasters and disturbances are multiplied. In this world there are
few who are endowed with inborn wisdom; sainthood is the goal attained after long self-discipline. All matters of State, whether great or
small, will surely be well ordered, when right persons are in the right
positional in any periods, whether critical or peaceful, all affairs will be
peacefully settled, when wise men are secured. In this way will the State
be lasting, and the realm be free from dangers. Therefore the wise
sovereigns of ancient times sought good men for high offices, and not
good offices for favored ones." (Article VII) "All officials, high and low,
should beware of jealousy. If you are jealous of others, others in turn
will be jealous of you and so is perpetuated the visious circle. So if we
find others excel us in intelligence, we are not pleased; if we find they
surpass us in ability, we become envious. Really wise persons are seldom
seen in this world—possibly one wise man in five centuries or one sage
in ten centuries. Without securing wise men and sages, wherewith shall
the country be governed in good order?" (Article XIV)

Nationalism and Imperial Prestige

It has been often pointed out that the basic social and moral principles
of Asian peoples consist essentially of filial piety. Professor NORTHROP
says: "The basic social and moral principle of this joint family is filial
piety—where by filial piety is meant not merely loyalty to one's father
and mother, but loyalty to this joint family. Hinduism and Buddhism
may not feature the concept of filial piety as do Confucian Asian families,
but the fact is nonetheless there."[23]

With regard to the Japanese, this feature holds true to some extent, but
not wholly. In Japan, loyalty to lords in the days since the Meiji Restoration have been much stronger.

The peculiarly Japanese conception of the prestige of the Emperor and the Emperor Institution bear a close relation to the traditionally fundamental conception of harmony. The atmosphere of "harmony" which has prevailed between the Emperor and his subjects has enabled the Emperor Institution to last as long as the institution which has been characteristic of the political history of Japan. In other countries dynasties changed. But in Japan there has been only one ruling dynastry or royal family; it has no specific family name, thus evidencing the remote antiquity of its rulership. This dynasty has never been broken during its long history of more than two thousand years. In the past, the Emperor was looked at as a child of the Sun Deity, but not with awe. In olden days, the prestige of a deity was superior to that of an Emperor. In the genuinely Shintoistic, pre-Buddhistic Japan, as Emperor who was compassionate with the people was respected with affection as an ideal monarch (as illustrated in the person of Nintoku).

In the case of the Prince an intention which was hardly shown in the cases of monarchs of other countries is expressed, until in later days the prestige of the Emperor came to be closely connected with the hierarchical order of Japanese society.

"When you receive the orders of the Sovereign, you should listen to them reverentially. The lord is like the heavens and the subjects are like the earth. With the heavens above and the earth below united in performing their functions loyally in their respective positions, we shall see the world ruled in perfect good order as in harmonious rotation of the four seasons. . . . If the earth should attempt to supplant the heavens, all would simply fall in ruin. Therefore when the lord speaks, let his subjects listen and obey; when the superiors act, the inferiors comply. Consequently when you receive the orders of the Sovereign you should be attentive in carrying them out faithfully. If you fail in this, ruin would be the natural consequence." (Article III)

The intention of having his edicts observed among the common people was very strong in the case of Asoka also. Having the edicts inscribed on the stone pillars erected by him, or on the polished surface of rocks, was aimed at their being read by the common people. Asoka said: "Since

I was consecrated twelve years, I have caused Edicts of *dhammas* to be written for the welfare and happiness of the people, so that without violation thereof, they might attain to this and that growth of *dhamma*."

It is needless to note that those who could read and understand the edicts must have been lkmited only to the classes of rulers and intellectuals in those days. However, those who were impressed by the sentences of the edicts must have amounted to a considerable number. Moreover, Asoka urged people to propage the *dhamma*. "Relatives should propagate (the teaching) appropriately to their own relative." He saw to it that the edicts were recited on fixed days and that their purport was clarified. "This document should be heard on the Tishya day every for-monthly season; and, indeed, on every festive occasion in between the Tishya days it may be heard even by one (official). By acting thus, endeavor to fulfill (my instructions)." But, in the case of Asoka, any intention of emphasizing the prestige of the monarch from his quality as a sovereign is not found. His words were claimed to be esteemed for the reason that they expressed universal laws. Nor in the Sixteen-Article Law of Songtsan-Gampo is loyalty to the monarch taught at all.

What *was* stressed by Prince Shōtoku, however, was the relation between lord (Emperor), officials, and the common people in the centralized state.

Officials rule common people in compliance with the command of the Emperor. The principle of governing the state is propriety, morale or morality in a wider sense. If the superiors are lacking in morality, the common people cannot be ruled; if the common people cannot be ruled; if the common people are lacking in morality, many crimes and delinquencies will happen, however much an endeavor may be made. Management by officials should therefore be based upon propriety or morality.

The relationship between the Emperor, the officials, and the common people was expressed after the model of ancient China, formulated in State Confucianism, but implanted on the soil of Japan. It seems that this conception was closely connected with the abolition of ownership of land and people by big clans on the occasion of the Taika Innovation.

This development firmly established the basis for the Emperor Institution.

The thought of esteeming the prestige of the Emperor is especially conspicuous in the Constitution. "Provincial governors and district administrators should not levy exacting taxes on their respective peoples. In a country there should not be two lords; the people should not have two masters. The people of the whole country have the Sovereign as their sole master. The officials appointed to administer the local affairs are all his subjects. How can they levy arbitrary taxes on the people in the manner of public administration?" (Article XII) This Article is assumed to bespeak the centralized administration in the territory under the Imperial Court, and to presage the abolishment of ownership of land and people which occurred later on a nation-wide scale; the rights and power entrusted to officials were going to diminish. The preceding clauses of Article XII also herald the absolutism of the later Emperor Institution, which was characteristic of Japan. Such a way of esteeming the prestige of the Emperor can hardly be illustrated from the abundant classical literature of India and China; while in the West, where Christianity was the predominant factor, it would also be difficult to find a counterpart.

To quote from Professor NORTHROP: "Admiral PERRY confronted the Japanese leaders with Western nationalism and the power of modern Western military weapons. Western nationalism requires, as its name suggests, primary loyalty to the nation rather than to the Asian joint family. Shintoism contributed exactly this. For it is of the essence of Shintoism that the Japanese people are the descendants of a sun goddess."[24]

The ultimate form in which the Japanese concept of emphasis upon a specific, limited human nexus manifested itself was ultranationalism, which appeared after the Meiji Restoration. But Japanese ultra-nationalism did not suddenly appear in the post-Meiji period; its beginning can be traced to the very remote past.

The notion of Japanese superiority is most boldly expressed in the concept of the Divine Nation. We find the following statement by KITA-BATAKE Chikafusa, a Shintoist writer (1293–1354): "Our Great Nippon is a Divine Nation. Our Divine Ancestors founded it; the Sun Goddess let her descendants reign over it for a long time. This is unique to Our Nation; no other nation has the like of it. This is the reason why Our Nation is called a 'Divine Nation'."[25] This concept of a "Divine Nation" was adopted by some Buddhists, such as the Nichiren and Zen masters.

Confucianism, which the Chinese had earlier adopted as their official theory of the state, was accepted by the Japanese with hardly any trouble. (The only controversial point was the problem of changing unsuitable Emperors; even this, however, caused no special friction.) When Confucianism was introduced into Japan, the ruling class studied it so that they could "become government officials and Confucians, and serve the country."[26]

This attitude toward Confucianism was to persist among the ruling classes, and in the Tokugawa Period Confucianism was taught with special reference to the concept of the state (*kokutai*) by almost all the schools and individual scholars of Confucianism including ITŌ Jinsai, YAMAGA Sokō, YAMAZAKI Ansai, and the Mito school. Japanese Confucianism, associated with the nationalism or the authority-consciousness of the Japanese people, asserted its own superiority over foreign systems of thought.

But since the Confucian concept of the state was formulated in accordance with the needs of Chinese society, it naturally contained a number of principles with which the more thorough-going Japanese nationalists could not agree. The state as conceived by Chinese philosophers was an idealistic model state; while the state that the Japanese nationalists had in mind was the actual Japanese state. This was the reason that Japanese nationalism—nurtured, so to speak, by Confucianism—had ultimately to deny the authority of Confucianism. YOSHIDA Shōin, the most influential leader of the movement to establish the modern state of Japan, declared in his criticism of Confucius and Mencius: "It was wrong of Confucius and Mencius to have left their native states and to have served other countries, for a sovereign and a father are essentially the same. To call one's sovereign unwise and dull, and forsake one's native state in order to find another sovereign in another state, is like calling one's father foolish and moving from one's house to the next house to become the son of a neighbor. That Confucius and Mencius lost sight of this truth can never be justified."[27]

A similar tendency can easily be dicerned in the process of assimilation of Buddhism. Japanese Buddhists carefully picked out such doctrines as would be convenient for, or not inconsistent with, their nationalism.

The *Suvarpaprabhāse-sūtra* and some later scriptures of Mahāyāna Buddhism, unlike those of early Buddhism, advance the theory that a monarch is a son of divine beings (*tenshi, devaputra*) to whom has been given a mandate from Heaven, and whom Heaven will protect. This theory, which became greatly cherished in Japan, had its origin in the Brahmin law-books, which regulated the feudal society of medieval India. Later, Indian Buddhists came to mention this theory merely as a prevailing notion of society. Although not characteristic of Buddhism, this idea came to be especially stressed by the Japanese.

The attitude which Indian Buddhism assumed toward the state was, from the time of its origination, one of caution. For instance, it placed monarchs in the same category with robbers; both were thought to endanger people's welfare. According to Buddhist legend, the people in remote antiquity elected a common head who would see to it that the people were protected, good people rewarded, evil people punished. The sovereign originated from this (*cf.* social contract). The Buddha Sākyamuni is said to have praised the republic of the Vajjis as the ideal state form.

But the Japanese, who accepted Buddhism on a large scale, refused nevertheless to adopt its concept of the state which to them appeared to run counter to the native idea of "state structure" (*kakutai*). We thus had a writer named KITABATAKE Chikafusa who was ready, on the one hand, to accept Buddhism in general, but eager, on the other, to emphasize the importance of the Japanese Imperial Family in the following way: "The Buddhist theory (of the state) is merely an Indian theory; Indian monarchs may have been the descendants of a monarch selected for the people's welfare, but our Imperial Family is the only continuous and unending line of family desceinding from its Heavenly Ancestors."[28]

HIRATA Atsutane, a fanatic Shintoist leader, discredits the whole Indian theory of the origin of the state as a mere explanation of the origin of "Indian chieftains."[29]

It is evident from the references in historical documents to the purpose of the adoption of Buddhism that considerations of protection for the state by means of prayers and religious rites constituted a dominant factor in Japanese Buddhism from the very beginning. Most Japanese monasteries in those early days were state-operated. Protection of the state, a prime concern in the Japanese mind, was thus firmly established in religion, and became the slogan of nearly all the Buddhist sects.

So far we have dealt with the problem of nationalism from the viewpoint of philosophy and religion. The outstanding features of Japanese nationalism may be summed up as follows:

In the past, the Japanese people dedicated a large and important part of their individual life to the state—to an extent never attempted by other Eastern peoples. The extent of such dedication is itself the first feature of Japanese nationalism.

The second feature is that Japanese nationalism was developed from concern for the particular state of Japan. There are different ways in which nationalism is applied in practice: We know that it has, many times, been expounded by thinkers in India and China, as well as in the West. But their nationalism was theoretically concerned with the state in general, and not with their particular state. Nationalism tends, by its very nature, to be applied to a state in particular. In Japanese nationalism, by way of contrast with the above-mentioned states, the particular entity of Japan came to be the sole standard upon which all judgments were based. This fact, without doubt, hashed a close relationship with the general tendency in Japanese thinking, especially in the past, to overlook the universal and to lay stress upon an exclusive human nexus. In the opinion of this writer, the natural basis for Japan's exclusive concern with herself is isolated from the continent by water. The Japanese have only rarely experienced a real fear of alien peoples; they have known the existence of foreign nations only indirectly, except in the case of World War II.

The dominance of the state over individual life was, in a sense, a condition extremely favorable to Japan's start as a modern state, if only in form, in the Meiji era. One imagines that it would have been difficult for her to become the modern state that she is today so quickly, had it not been for the strong consciousness the people have had for the state. As the modern history of the West has shown, the formation of the state is a necessary condition for the active progress of peoples. Japan, in this sense, may be said to have been more favorably conditioned for modernization than other nations of the East which were not so unified.

Certain apprehension may, however, be felt here by some. They may ask: Is not Japan's state-consciousness already a thing of the past? Is she not being rapidly modernized? Has not the experience of defeat in World War II brought the Japanese people to consider themselves as individuals making up their society and participating in the sovereignty of the state, rather than "subjects" of the Emperor?

We are inclined to offer only a tentative "yes" to these questions. For, although it is true that changes are being made in these directions, it is also true that it is no easy task for the Japanese to do away with their inherent thinking. We must remember that the country is overflowing with people, with a network of tightlyformed village communities covering the land. The nation's economy is such that the state must still exercise controls over a large portion of individual life. Above all, since distant antiquity the nation's progress has always had its motivation in the Imperial Family, although it is now not so powerful as before. Furthermore, the Japanese sentiment toward the Imperial House has been friendly rather than hostile, as in some other foreign countries, and the ruling class were often quite benevolent in their dealings with the people. All in all, an atmosphere of family-like intimacy pervaded by Westerners, and even by Indians or Chinese, as self-contradictory. The Japanese, however, felt no inconsistency in the term, but found it good and valid. In view of these factors, would it really be possible to put an end to the Japanese way of thinking about the State? This is not something we can take pride in before other nations; but, just as religion was the basis of the practical morals of the Chinese, so the state was the basis of all thought

among the Japanese.[30] The Japanese way of thinking is undergoing a
change, but their thinking is an inheritance, a tradition. We feel that it
is our part to see to it that this tradition never again gives rise to an in-
human ultra-nationalism, but to a world-wide solidarity in the future.

Economic Activities in This-Worldly Life

It is a problem worthy of study why the Japanese alone among the
many Asiatic countries came to be far advanced several decades ago in
adopting modern civilization. In respect to this, we should like to point
out the emphasis upon social activities as one of the features of the Japanese way of thinking. This feature can be traced back even to the thought
of Prince Shōtoku.

The phenomenalistic way of thinking that asserts reality itself to be
emergent and in flux has been traditionally prevalent among Japanese.
This emergent and fluid way of thinking is compatible with the inclination of thinking that emphasizes a particular human nexus—another way
of thinking which is traditionally conspicuous among Japanese. These
two factors have combined to bring about an emphasis upon activities
within a concrete human nexus.

It is a well-known fact that primitive Shintoism was closely tied up
with agricultural rituals in agrarian villages, and that Shintoist gods have
been symbolized, till now, as gods of production.

Coming into contact with foreign cultures and becoming acquainted
with Chinese philosophies and religions, the Japanese adopted and absorbed Confucianism in particular, which teaches a way of conduct appropriate to a concrete human nexus. The thoughts of LAO Tzu and
CHUANG Tzu are inclined to a life of seclusion in which one escapes from
a particular human nexus and seeks tranquility in solitude. Such was not
to the taste of the Japanese at large. In contrast, Confucianism principally
determines rules of conduct according to a system of human relationships. In this respect, Confucianism never came in conflict with the existing Japanese thought patterns at the time of implantation.

In the case of Buddhism, however, some problems arose. Buddhism
declared itself to be a teaching of other-worldliness. According to Bud-

dhist philosophy, the positive state of "other-worldliness" is arrived at after one has transcended "this world." The central figures in Buddhist orders have all been monks and nuns, who have freed themselves not only from their families but from any specific human nexus. They were not allowed to become involved in any economic or worldly activities. It is likely that in olden days there existed social reasons that prompted a great many people to become monks.

In addition, the topographical characteristics of Japan, vastly different from India, require men to serve humanity within a specific human nexus. The doctrine of early Buddhism was not compatible with such requirements, so early Buddhism and traditional conservative Buddhism, which inherited the former teachings, were despised and rejected under the name of Hinayāna, and Mahāyāna Buddhism was particularly favored and adopted. Mahāyāna Buddhism was a popular religion that came to the fore after the Christian era. Some schools of Mahāyāna Buddhism, if not all, advocated the finding of the absolute truth within secular life. In accepting Buddhism, the Japanese selected in particular the form which had such characteristics; even in accepting those doctrines which were originally devoid of this nature, they deliberately bestowed such a character upon them. The stereotyped phrase, "Japan is the country where Mahāyāna Buddhism is practiced",[31] can be understood solely by reference to these basic facts.

Such an attitude in accepting Buddhism is clearly shown in the case of Prince Shōtoku. His "Commentaries upon Three Sūtras" are those upon the *Shōman (Srimaladevisimhanada)-sūtra,* the *Yuima (Vimalakirtinirdesa)-sūtra,* and the *Lotus (Saddharmapundarika)-sūtra.* The selection of these three Sūtras out of a multitude was entirely based upon the Japanese way of thinking. The *Shōman Sūtra* was preached, in compliance with Buddha's command, by Madame Shōman (Srimāllā), who was the queen and a lay believer. The *Yuima Sūtra* has a dramatic composition, in which *Yuima (Vimalakirti),* lay believers, reversed the usual order and give sermons to *priests and ascetics.* In the first two *sūtras,* they commend the idea of grasping the truth in secular life; while, according to the last, all laymen who faithfully follow any of the teachings of Buddha are expected to be redeemed.

The Crown Prince himself, all through his life, remained a lay believer. It is said that he called himself "*Shōman*, the Child of a Buddha".[32] The intention of Prince Shōtoku was to place emphasis upon the realization of Buddhist ideals within the concrete human nexus of people retaining in secular life. He sought absolute significance within the practical conduct of everyday life, and asserted: "Reality is no more than today's occurrence of cause and effect." He added: "Ten thousand virtues are all contained in today's effect."[33] Such an interpretation has something in common with the doctrine of the *Tendai* and *Kegon* sects, but the particular expression "today's" makes it distinctly Japanese. For those who have gone through Buddhist reflection, this world of impurities and sufferings in itself turns out to be a place of blessings, as the doctrine attaches great importance to action. "Since I wish to enlighten mankind, I regard life and death as a garden."[34] All the good deeds practised in the world of life and death are eventually turned into the causes that lead men into the rank of a Buddha. "Uncountable ten thousand good deeds equally lead to becoming a Buddha."[35]

It is worth noting that the ultimate state of religion is not bestowed upon men by divine entities that transcend them, but is realized through practice within the human nexus. "The result of becoming a Buddha originates from ten thousand good deeds."[36] Mahāyāna Buddhism stressed altruistic deeds; Prince Shōtoku assigned special emphasis to them and considered that Buddhas and Bodhisattvas should serve all living beings. That is the reason for occasional distorted interpretations given to phrases in the Buddhist scriptures.[37] According to the Lotus Sūtra the advice is given "to sit always in religious meditation." This sentence was revised by Prince Shōtoku to mean: "Do not approach a person who always sits in religious meditation."[38] The meaning is that unintermittent sitting in meditation enables a man to practice altruistic deeds.

A similar idea underlies the later teachings of Japanese Buddhism. According to Saichō (Master Dengyō), both priests and laymen attain the self-same ideal (the consistency of clergy and laity). According to Kūkai (Master Kōbō), the founder of Japanese Vajrayāna, absolute reason should be realized thIough actuality. (Reality is revealed in accordance with phenomenal things.) "Pure Land" Buddhism also developed along that line. The idea that he who believes in the true wish of *Amitabha* will be redeemed, staying as he is in a lay condition, persisted through all the later periods. The *Jōdo-Shin* Sect emphasized not only that all living creatures are saved on account of their religious faith (the turning towards the Pure Land), but also that the Great Benevolence saves all those who are lost (the returning from the Pure Land). During the Tokugawa Period, the most famous itinerant merchants of Ōmi Province, who peddled assiduously all around the country, were devoted followers of the *Jōdo-Shin* Sect who travelled with the spirit of service to others.

Buddhist morals were also metamorphosed. The Indians considered alms-giving, a virtue of principal importance for Buddhists, as something to be strictly observed. Most of the Buddhist scriptures extol the deeds of those who abandoned not only their country, castle, wives and children, but also their own bodies, and gave most generously to other human beings (or even to animals).[39] Such a life of abandoning everything and possessing nothing was an ideal life for the Indian ascetics. Recourse to such drastic oeasures, however, was not allowed for the Japanese, who attached more importance to the concrete human nexus· Prince Shōtoku, therefore, confine the meaning of "alms-giving" to "the abandonment of properties other than one's own body".[40] In this manner, the inclination of the Indians to go imaginatively beyond the ethics of the mundane human relationship underwent a revision when Buddhism was accepted by the Japanese.

The emphasis upon the human nexus ran parallel to the stress upon all the productive activities of men. In a country like India, where the intensity of heat, the abundance of seasonal rainfall, and the fertility of the soil together bring forth a rich harvest, without much human labor needing to be exerted on the land, the ethics of distribution rather than of production are naturally emphasized. That is a reason why ō ms-giving comes to be considered most important. But in a country like Japan, by way of contrast, production is of vital importance; hence stress is placed upon the ethics of labor in the various professions.

The *Lotus Sūtra,* the most important of all the Japanese Buddhist scriptures, was accepted by the Japanese as something that gives a theoretical basis for such a social and economic demand.

This sūtra states that, if one preaches with comprehension of the true purport of the *Lotus Sūtra*: "When one preaches various teachings, they all coincide with the true purport and nothing will contradict the True Aspect of Reality. When one elucidates secular treaties, the words of this-worldly government, or the deeds of production, they all accord with the True Doctrine."[41] This sentence was interpreted by the Japanese to mean that everything is true as long as it comes from a man who has once comprehended the truth of *Lotus Sūtra*. The same sentence was further interpreted by the Japanese, however, to mean that all activities in the fields of politics and economics were to be subjected to the Absolute One. SHŌSUI Shiei explained the sentence thus: "The One Mind, the Eternal Truth, and the aspect of appearance and disappearance are no separate things. That they are one is revealed in accordance with that they are three; that they are three is discussed in accordance with that they are one. Government and production, therefore, could be in no contradiction to the True Aspect of Reality."[42] This idea of Chōsui came to be taken by the Japanese to be the original idea of the *Lotus Sūtra*.

Government and production, therefore, could not be in contradiction with the True Aspect of Reality. Some Japanese Buddhists were thus led to recognize the particularly sacred significance of physical labor. It is an historically well-known fact that the Buddhists endeavored to go directly to the people through various welfare activities.

This feature can be noticed even in Japanese *Zen* literature. Dōgen, the founder of *Sōtō Zen,* thought that Buddhism could be realized within the professional lives of the secular society. SUZUKI Shōsan, a *Zen* master, found absolute significance in the pursuit of one's own profession, whether warrior, farmer, craftsman, merchant, doctor, actor, hunter, or priest. Because it is the essence of Buddhism, according to him, to rely upon the original self or upon "the true Buddha of one's own," and because every profession is the function of this "One Buddha," it amounts to the fact that to pursue one's own profession is to obey the Absolute One. So he teaches farmers: "Farming is nothing but the doings of Buddha." To merchants he teaches: "Renounce desires and pursue profits single-heartedly. But you should never enjoy profits. You should, instead, work for the good of all the others." Since the afflictions of this world, it is said, are predetermined in former lives, one should torture oneself by working hard in one's own profession, in order to redeem the sins of the past. It is noteworthy that immediately after the death of Calvin, an idea similar to his happened almost contemporaneously to appear in Japan. The fact, however, that it never grew into a capitalistic movement of great consequence ought to be studied in relation to the underdevelopment of the modern bourgeois society in Japan.

Such a theory of religion also leds itjelf to religious movements outside of Buddhism in Japan. To illustrate, NINOMIYA Sontoku's movement inclines to be practical and activistic. Sectarian Shintoism assumes a similar tendency. The founder of the *Tenri* religion teaches: "Keep your hear pure, busy yourself with your profession, and be true to the mind of God." The other new sects of Shintoism mostly fall into a similar pattern.

Respect for labor in professional life resulted in high esteem for things produced as the fruits of labor. Reverence for foodstuffs is especially manifest. Dōgen, the *Zen* master, for example, recognizes the sacred significance of food and says that each item of foodstuffs should be labelled with honorifics. The tendency to teach the taking of good care of all the products of labor, however trivial they might be, is also manifest among the *Jōdo Shin* Sect, which is diametrically opposed, in other respects, to *Zen* Buddhism.

The precept that we should take good care of economic products, the fruits of human labor, is not necessarily confined to Japanese religions only, but seems common to most universal religions. In India or South Asian countries, however—where men are not required to labor too hard in order to produce daily necessities—relatively little has been said against waste. The fact that the preservation of economic products is particularly emphasized should be considered in the light of the topological peculiarity of Japan.

The form in which Chinese thought was accepted was also tinged with an activist tendency in interpreting the ways of human beings. Itō Jinsai (1627–1705), in particular, understood what is called the Way as being active and as representing the principle of growth and development. On that basis he rejected the nihilism of LAO Tzu. OGIU Sorai (1666–1728), a peculiarly Japanese Confucianist, positively advocated activism, rejecting the static tendency of the Confucianists of the Sun Period of China. Quiet sitting, with reverential love in one's heart, was the method of metal training extolled by the Confucianists of that period, which was thus ridiculed by Sorai: "As I look at them, even gambling appears superior to quiet sitting and having reverential love in one's heart." A necessary conclusion drawn from such an attitude was the recommendation, as made by Sorai, of practical learning, useful in practical life. Such was the mental climate which nurtured the economic theory of Dazer Shundai and the legal philosophy of MIURA Chikkei. Whereas Chinese Confucianism surpassed Japanese Confucianism in thinking upon metaphysical problems, Japanese Confucianism directed its attention to politics, economics, and law—the practical aspects of human life.

That Japan alone made rapid progress in modernization during the years just before World War II, while the other Asian countries were generally slow in this process, may be attributed partly to the emphasis laid by the Japanese upon practical activities within the human nexus.

A great danger lies in the fact that the religious view of the Japanese may easily degenerate into the sheer utilitarianism of profit-seeking activities, in case it loses sight of the significance of the absolute, which underlies the productive life of professions. But at the same time credit should be given to the tendency to esteem the human nexus. If the religion of Japan is enhanced to such a height that religious truth may be realized in accordance with the human nexus (which is at once universal and particular, transcending every specific nexus ant at the same time embracing all of them), then and only then will it achieve universal significance.

2. Buddhist Ifluence upon Japanese Ways of Thinking

Introductory Remarks

It is a well-known fact that Japanese thought in general has been greatly influenced by Buddhism. Buddhist philosophy itself is an elaborate system of thought, and the traces of its influence upon the Japanese can be found in many aspects of their life. For thorough investigation of all of them, even a life-time would scarcely be enough. Now as a humble student of Indian and Buddhist thought, I should like to discuss some features of the Japanese way of thinking related to Buddhist thinking.

Rennyo, a great propagator of Pure Realm Buddhism, said: "It was in the reign of Emperor Kinmei that the Buddhist Gospel was introduced into our country. Before that time the teaching of Buddhism was not propagated here, and there was nobody who attained enlightenment. Due to some good causes (i.e., merits) in the past lives, we have had the fortune to be born in a time when Buddhism is flourishing, and good to hearken to the teaching for salvation."[43]

There are so many traces of Buddhist influence upon the Japanese way of thinking. In the following, three conspicuous features will be discussed.

1) humanitarianism
2) moral self-reflection
3) tolerance.

Humanitarianism

The problem of humanitarianism has been discussed by many scholars from different points of view. I should like to add some comments upon this problem from the standpoint of a student of Indian and Buddhist philosophy.

As one of the most prominent features of Japanese ways of thinking, we may point out the emphasis on the love of human beings.

In ancient Japan a man asked a *Zen* priest: "The sūtra says one could not be a Bodhisattva[44] unless one serves Buddhas by burning one's own body, elbows, and fingers. What is the meaning of this?" Answer: "The burning of one's body, elbows, and fingers is metaphorically used to mean the elimination of the three sorts of ignorance, of the branch, the leaf, and the root. . . . If one eliminates these three darknesses, one becomes a Bodhisattva. . . . If one should try to serve the Buddhas by burning one's actual body, would any Buddha receive it?" Here the practices actually followed among the Buddhists both in ancient India and China were completely denied by the Japanese Buddhists.

The Japanese put special emphasis upon the love of others. Among many sects of Japanese Buddhism, the Pure Land Buddhism (Jōdo sect) a religion which typically emphasizes benevolence, enjoys great popularity. The Pure Land Buddhism preaches the benevolence of Amitābha Buddha, who saves even bad men and ordinary men. Most of the high priests of the sect have especially benign looks. The emphasis upon the deeds of benevolence is recognizable also in other sects. The Japanese accepted the practice of the strict disciplines handed down from primitive Buddhism in the form of the "Ritsu sect". This sect originally followed a seclusionist method of ascetic practices. Later, however, with its development into the Shingon-Ritsu sect, a priest like Ninsho (1217–1303) launched upon such social welfare works as helping the suffering and the sick. He dedicated his whole life to the service of others. For this he was even criticized by his master, "he overdid benevolence." It was a breach of the ancient disciplines to dig ponds or wells or to give medicine and clothing to the sick or to accumulate money for them, but he never let himself be influenced by this.

Needless to say, the idea of benevolence had an important significance in Chinese Buddhism. *Zen* Buddhism, however, developed as a Chinese people's Buddhism, did not seem to emphasize the idea of benevolence so much. To confirm this, there is not a single reference made to the word "benevolence" in such well-known scriptures as *"Shin-jin-mei"* (the Epigram of Faith), *"Shodo-ka"* (the Song of Enlightenment), *"Sando-*

kai" (Compliance with the Truth), and *"Hokyozammai"* (Precious-Mirror Mediation). To go back still further, nothing is said about it in what is supposed to be the teachings of Bodhidharma.[45] It is probable that the Chinese *Zen* sect, under the influence of Taoism and other traditional ideologies of China, was inclined to seclusion and resignation, and neglected the positive approach of practicing deeds of benevolence. Such is my general impression, though a final conclusion cannot be drawn until we have made a thorough study of the general history of the Chinese *Zen* sect. At the time the *Zen* sect was brought into Japan, however, it came to emphasize deeds of benevolence, just as the other sects in Japan did. Eisai, who introduced *Rinzai-Zen,* put the idea of benevolence to the forefront. In a reply to the question whether the *Zen* sect was not too much obsessed by the idea of the void, he says: "To prevent by means of self-discipline the evil from without and to profit others with benevolence within—this is what *Zen* is." As for the rules for ascetics of the *Zen* sect, he teaches: "You should arouse the spirit of great benevolence—and save mankind with the pure and supreme disciplines of the Great Bodhisattva, but you ought not to seek deliverance for your own sake." SOSEKI (MUSO Kokushi), SUZUKI Shōsan, SHIDO Munan, and other *Zen* priests represent a positive repulsion against the seclusionist and self-satisfied attitude of the traditional *Zen* sect. They stress, instead the virtue of "benevolence" overtly, chooses for instruction the phrase, "speak kingly to others" (words of affection) from among the various Buddhist doctrines of the past. "Speaking words of affection means to generate the heart of benevolence and bestow upon others the language of affection, whenever one sees them. To speak with the heart, looking at mankind with benevolence as though they were your own children, is to utter words of affection. The virtuous should be praised, the virtueless pitied. To cause the enemy to surrender, or to make the wise yield, words of affection are most fundamental. To hear words of affection in one's presence brightens one's countenance and warms one's heart. To hear words of affection said in one's absence goes home to one's heart and soul. You should learn to know that words of affection are powerful enough to set a river on fire." In addition, he puts emphasis upon the virtues of giving, altruism and collaboration, at the bottom of which flows the pure current of affection.

The spirit of benevolence was not only preached by Buddhists, but it also made its way into Shintoism, and tied up with one of the three divine symbols of the Japanese Imperial Family. It also was popularized among the general public and came to be regarded as one of the principal virtues of the *samurai*. The love of others by no means comes out of self-complacency. On the contrary, it goes with a humble reflection that I, as well as others, am an ordinary man. This had already been stressed by Prince Shōtoku at the beginning of the introduction of Buddhism into Japan.

"Forget resentment, forsake anger, do not become angry just because someone opposes you. Everyone has a mind, every mind comes to a decision, and decisions will not always be alike. If he is right, you are wrong; if you are right, he is wrong; if you are not quite a saint, he is not quite an idiot. Both disputants are men of ordinary mind; who is decisively capable of judging an argument between them? If both are wise men or both foolish men their argument is probably a vious circle. For this reason, if your opponent grows angry, you had better be all the more cautious lest you too are in error. Although you might think you are quite right, it is wiser to comply with the other man." (The Precepts of Prince Shōtoku X) Out of this emerged the spirit of tolerance, which we shall discuss later.

The problem remain whether or not this tendency to stress love is inherent to the Japanese people. That there is no god of love in Shintoism was once criticised by a famous Buddhist scholar, caused a great sensation among the Shintoists. They presented some counter-evidence, which seemed far from convincing. This issue cannot be settled as yet, but requires further investigation. But the general impression is that the spirit of benevolence was introduced into Japan probably with the advent of Buddhism and exerted a renovating influence upon the mental attitude of the Japanese. Within this limit, it may be asserted that there exists a certain element of humanitarianism in the thinking of the common man in Japan.

Moral Self-Reflection

The second conspicuous feature of Buddhist influence upon Japanese ways of thinking is the acuteness of moral self-reflection. I do not mean that the Japanese are more keen on moral problems than other nations, but that the moral attitude of the Japanese is to a great extent due to Buddhist influence.

In pre-Buddhist Japan people rejoiced in this-worldly life without acute self-reflection. Their actions were aimed at physical or sensual pleasures. Princes held frequent festivals; they became easily intoxicated with liquor. They composed love songs in a joyful mood. They were rather passionate. Incest was prevalent throughout the people. They were enjoying happy days simple-mindedly just like children. Sins were regarded as something material. The ancient Japanese thought that they had only to get rid of them by means of simple practices of religious or physical purifications (e.g. invocation of formulae, ablution, etc.)

The advent of Buddhism caused the Japanese to open their mental eye to the spiritual or metaphysical realm. Owing to Buddhist influences, the Japanese in general have come to hold the notion that good deeds (merits) bring forth good results, just as in the Western proverb: "Sow virtue, and the harvest will be virtue."

The consciousness of sin came to be most conspicuous in the case of St. Shinran.

Pure Land (Realm) Buddhism, introduced from China, reached the zenith of its development with Shinran, in whom the working of moral self-reflection was extremely strong. "Truly I have come to realize, and it is deplorable, that I, am an idiotic vulture, am drowned in the boundless sea of carnal desire, lost in the enormous mountains of worldly ambitions, not being pleased with becoming entitled to be saved, and taking no pleasure in approaching the True Evidence. Shame on me; woe is me!" Moral self-reflection as acute as Shinran's seems not to be shown in the Buddhist literature of other countries. Monks who broke their vows in India appear to have held the notion that sins could be expiated by reciting magical formulae (dhārani). Little has been said about the pangs of conscience of renegade monks in China either. Shinran, on the contrary, could not but face the shameful reality of man. Shinran, who looked into the deeper self of man, turned to the Buddha, the absolu," one. He was thus led to advocate "the discipline of non-disciplinete which was based on self-reflection of great moral intensity.

The motivation for the ascetics of India and China to enter the priesthood was, in most cases, the realisation of the impermanence of the phenomenal world rather than the realisation of man's sinfulness. In the case of Shinran, in contrast, little is said about the impermanence of this world. The controlling motivation for Shinran is the sense of the sinfulness of man. It is not that man is simply changeful. A more fundamental thing about man is that he is a sinner, obsessed with afflictions, yielding to evils. Realising as he does that things are impermanent, he still clutches at these impermanent things. Man is so deeply immersed in sins that he could never be saved but for the miraculous power of the vow of Amitabha. Such was Shinran's doctrine.

It is noteworthy that profound religious self-reflection, based upon the Pure Realm doctrine, was professed by some of the emperors.

"Though the mind's moon shines
To show the way to the Pure Land,
Woe be to the clouds still uncleansed." (By Emperor Gotoba)

This poem means that ardent as my desire is to be reborn into the Pure Realm trusting and relying upon the vow of Amitābha, the sins I have committed weigh so heavily upon my heart that I am haunted by doubts about the vows; and how far beyond comprehension, the poem laments, is the state of the salvation.

Religious and moral self-reflection as profound as that stated above is not confined to Japanese Pure Realm Buddhism. The form of accepting the *Zen* doctrine in Japan, as in the case of Dōgen, reveals a profound moral self-reflection. He attaches great importance to the act of making confession. "Should you confess in this manner, the assistance of the Buddha will assuredly be yours. Make a confession to the Buddha with your soul and body and the power of the confession will eradicate all the roots of your sins." He commends good deeds, and preaches that one will be able to become a Buddha through one's good acts. "Quite an easy way there is to become a Buddha. Not to do evil deeds, not to be obsessed with the matter of life and death, but to take pity upon mankind, to revere the gods, to be considerate to inferiors, and to keep one's mind free from hatred, desires, afflictions and anxieties is exactly what is called being a Buddha. One should not seek Buddhahood anywhere else." He emphasizes the observance of injunctions.

The emphasis upon the introspection among Japanese priests, is apparent also among laymen. For example, MINAMOTO Sanetomo, the medieval feudal lord, says:

> "There's no way out
> Of this agonizing hell,
> Whose empty vault
> Only flames can fill.
> The founder of a temple,
> The erector of a tower,
> For their acts get credit;
> But none gets merits
> So rewarding as a repentant sinner."

On the whole, when and only when one reflects upon one's deeds sincerely enough, is one awakened to one's sinfulness.

It was also reported by the European missionaries who came to Japan at the early stage of the modern period, that crimes were relatively few, and reason reigned among the Japanese.

In any case, although they may be weak in sin-consciousness in its religious sense, the Japanese are sensitive in shame-consciousness in its practical and moral sense.

For the Japanese in general, whether or not one infringes religious disciplines is a matter of little consequence. A matter of vital importance for them is whether or not one conforms to the morals of the particular human nexus to which one belongs.

The listing of virtues after the fashion of Indian Buddhism, however, was not to the liking of the Japanese in general, who looked for the one central virtue directly posited. It is the virtue of *"honesty* (sincerity)", which was originally adopted from Buddhism, that emerged from such a demand, and come to be generally recognized as the central virtue by the Japanese. Ancient imperial rescripts state: "the honest heart to be the virtue that all the subjects should observe." Probably influenced by them was the doctrine of the Ise Shrine, according to which the Sun Goddess was supposed to have said: "Divine protection is based upon honesty." During the Muromachi Period, the virtue of "honesty" as the doctrine of the Ise Shrine came to prevail among the entire country. It was generally recognized by the Japanese of those days that the virtue of "honesty" in Shintoism originated from Buddhism.

Tolerance

The Japanese are said to be destinguished from other ancient nations by their spirit of tolerance. Although there must have been inter-racial conflicts in prehistoric Japan, there exists no evidence, as far as archaeological remains are concerned, that their armed conflicts were too violent. According to the classical records also, the Japanese treated the other peoples, whom they had conquered, with the spirit of tolerance. As for tales of wars there are many, but there is no evidence that the conquered peoples were made into slaves *in toto*. Even the prisoners were not treated as slaves in the Western sense of the word. Although there remains some doubt as to whether or not there existed a so-called slave-economy in ancient Japan, since the percentage of slave-servants was very small in the whole population, it may be safely said that the labor-power of the slaves was never used on a large scale. Such a social condition gives rise to the tendency to stress the dominance-control-by-power relationship. This is not to deny entirely the presence of the latter type of relationship in the Japanese society since olden days. The social restrictions and pressure upon the individual might have been indeed stronger than in many other countries. Nevertheless, in the consciousness of each individual Japanese, the spirit of conciliation (harmony) and tolerance is preeminent.

The spirit of tolerance of the Japanese made it impossible to cultivate deep hatred even toward sinners. In Japan there existed hardly any punishment that was cruel. Since crucifixion appeared for the first time in Japanese history during the age of civil wars, it was presumably started after the advent of Christianity, and suggested by it. Burning at the stake seemed to be in practice during the reign of Emperor Yuryaku, but it went out of practice afterwards to be revived occasionally during the modern period.

In the medieval West, condemnation at the stake took place under religious authority, which never happened in Japan. During the Heian Period, capital punishment was not practiced for three hundred and fifty years. It was not revived until the War of Hogen took place. Although this may be attributed to the influence of Buddhism, there has hardly been any period in any other country marked with the absence of the death penalty.

For the Japanese, full of the spirit of tolerance, eternal damnation is absolutely inconceivable. A Catholic priest, who forsook Christianity under the persecution of the Tokugawa Government, condemned the idea of eternal damnation preached in Christianity. He said, concerning rewards and punishments in the other world, that if God were the Lord of Benevolence, He ought to condemn Himself rather than condemn human beings and punish them for their sins. From among the doctrines of Christianity the idea of eternal damnation was especially hard for the Japanese to comprehend. Dr. M. Anesaki, commenting on this point, says: "This is the outstanding line of demarcation between Judaism and Buddhism." The Japanese also found it difficult to understand the idea of "being beyond deliverance for ever." The *Hosso* Sect, a school of Buddhist Idealism, based upon the philosophy of Dharmacla, advocates "the difference of five predisposition." Among men there are five types, the man who is predisposed to become a Bodhisattva,[46] the one predisposed to become an *Enkaku* (pratyekabuddha, one who attains self-complacent enlightenment), one predisposed to become a *Shōmon* (srāvaka, and accetic of Hinayāna Buddhism), one who is not predisposed, and one who is beyond deliverance. Such an idea of discrimination was not generally accepted by the Japanese Buddhists. Prevalently accepted, instead, was the view, "All of mankind is predisposed to become Buddhas."

A question may be raised here. Is not the spirit of tolerance prominent among the Japanese an influence of Buddhism rather than an intrinsic native characteristic? Before the advent of Buddhism the Japanese also resorted to atrocities. Are not the Emperors Buretsu and Yūryaku described as violent and ruthless? The reason why the death penalty was not meted out during the Heian Period was that the ideal of Buddhism was realized in politics.

Even in present-day Japan, statistics proves that in the districts where *haibutsu kishaku* (the abolition of Buddhism by villence immediately after the Meiji Restoration) was committed, cases of the murder of one's close relatives are high in number, whereas they are relatively low in number where Buddhism is vehemently supported. The reverse, however, may also be true, that because the Japanese were inherently tolerant and conciliatory, the infiltration of Buddhism into the people's lives was rapid. It is often pointed out by cultural historians that the Chinese people as a whole are inclined to ruthlessness and cruelty, in spite of the fact that the history of Buddhist influence in China is longer than it is in Japan. In Tibet, despite its being the country of Lamaism flying the banner of Buddhism, the severest of punishments are still in practice. So it may be concluded that the Japanese originally possessed the spirit of tolerance and forgiveness to some extent, which was much strengthened by the introduction of Buddhism, and was again weakened in recent years by the aggrandizement of the secular power on the one hand and by the decline of faith in Buddhism on the other. The fact that the Japanese are richly endowed with the spirit of tolerance and conciliation, while they are lacking in the intense hatred of sins, transformed the Pure Realm Buddhism. According to the eighteenth vow of Amitābha Buddha, he saves the whole of mankind on account of his great benevolence, the only exceptions being "those who committed five great sins and those who condemned the Right Law (Buddhism). Shan-tao (Zendo) of China interoreted this statement as meaning that even the great sinners, under the condition that they do converted, could be reborn into the Pure Land. Introduced into Japan, these exceptions were later considered as problematic, and came to be completely ignored by St. Hōnen. "This (salvation) includes all that are embraced in the great benevolence and the real vow of Amitābha, even the ten evils and five great sins not being excluded, and these who excel in those practices other than that of invocation of Amitābha being also included. Its meaning is to believe in what is revealed in the invocation of Amitābha for once and also for ten times." "You should believe that even those who have committed ten evils and five great sins are eligible for rebirth into the Pure Realm, and yet you should yourself refrain from the slightest of sins."

As far as the surface meaning of the sentence is concerned, Hōnen is diametrically opposed to the Indian men of religion who compiled the *Dai-mu-ryō-ju-kyō* (*Sukhāvativyūha*-Sūtra). Out of such an inclination of thinking was formulated the so-called "view of the eligibility of the evil ones for salvation" (the view that the evils are rightfully eligible for salvation by Amitābha Buddha). This may not be what Shinran really meant. But the fact that such a view was generally considered to be the fundamental doctrine of the Sin Sect can not be denied.

What are the rational basis for such a spirit of tolerance and conciliation? The tendency to recognize the absolute significance in everything phenomenal is conspicuous among the Japanese. It leads to the acceptance of the *raison d'etre* of any view held in the mundane world, and ends with the adjustment of any view with the spirit of tolerance and conciliation. Such a way of thinking appeared from the earliest days of the introduction of Buddhism into Japan. According to Prince Shōtoku, the Lotus Sūtra (The *Sadharmapundarika*-Sūtra), supposed to contain the ultimate essence of Buddhism, preaches the doctrine of the One Great Vehicle and advocates the theory "that any once of ten thousand goods leads to the one thing, the attainment of Enlightenment."

According to the Prince, there is no innate difference between saint and the most stupid men. Everyone is primarily and equally a saint and the most stupid man. Everyone is primarily and equally a child of the Buddha. Prince Shōtoku regarded the secular moral teachings as the elementary gate to enter Buddhism. His interpretation of Buddhism is characterized by its all-inclusive nature. Only by taking into consideration such a philosophical background is one able to understand the moral idea of the Prince when he says: "Concord is to be honored." It was this spirit that made possible the emergence of Japan as a unified cultural state. Prince Shōtoku's philosophical standpoint is represented by the expressions, "The One Great Vehicle" and "The Pure Great Vehicle," which are supposed to have originated from the Lotus Sūtra. Ever since Saichō (Master Dengyō) introduced the Tendai Sect, based upon the Hokke Sūtra, this sūtra has come to constitute the basis of Japanese Buddhism. Nichiren said "Japan is single-heartedly the country of the Lotus Sūtra", and "For more than four hundred years since Emperor Kanmu all the people of Japan have been single-heartedly devoted to the Lotus Sūtra." These words of Nichiren are not necessarily to be regarded as self-centered. Considering that the Pure Realm Buddhism and the *Zen* Sect even, not to mention the Nichiren Sect, are evidently under the influence of Tendai doctrine, there is much truth in these assertions of Nichiren. Among the poems composed on Buddhism, by successive emperors the subject matter is overwhelmingly on matters concerned with the Lotus Sūtra. The thought tendency characteristic of the Lotus Sutra, which tried to accept the raison d'être of all the practices of Buddhism, led to an extremely tolerant and conciliatory attitude to various ideas.

Owing to such a spirit of tolerance and conciliation, the development on a single continuum of various sects was possible within Japanese Buddhism. In India today, there is no Buddhist tradition extant. In China uniformity was established in Buddhism; the *Zen* Sect fused with the Pure Realm Buddhism is the only remaining religious sect, whereas the traditions of all the rest of the sects almost went out of existence. In Japan, on the contrary, there still exist many tradition sects which can no longer be found in China or India.

In spite of the highly sectarian and factional tendency of the various religious sects keeping their traditional difference intact, the contempt of other sects was mutually prohibited by Japanese Buddhists. Even Rennyo of the Jōdo-Shin Sect, which is supposed, to be inclined toward monotheistic Amidism and exclusionist, warns: "You ought not make light of shrines," and "You ought not slender other sects and other teachings."

SUZUKI Shōsan ordains: "In this monastery the right and wrong of the world or the relative merits of other sects ought not to be talked about." Jiun admonished his disciples: "The right and wrong or the high and low of the teachings of other sects should not be discussed."

Such an attitude of tolerance might have been handed down from Early Buddhism. It is noteworthy that, despite the sectarian and factional tendency of the Japanese, they did not want to dispute with their theoretical opponents. Realistically speaking, the amalgamation of Shintoism and Buddhism might have very well been an expedient measure taken in order to avoid friction between the traditional religion, and the incoming Buddhism which came to be accepted as a national religion. It may also be said that it was a political consideration that made Honen and Rennyo warn against rejecting sects other than their own.

But the attitude of tolerance determined the all-inclusive and conciliatory nature of Japanese Buddhism. The ascendency of Buddhism in Japan in the course of more than ten centuries was entirely different from that of Christianity in the West. Buddhism tolerated various primitive faiths native to Japan. A clear notion of paganism was absent in Japanese Buddhism. The gods in the native Japanese popular religion, who should have been considered as pagan gods from the standpoint of Buddhism, were reconciled with Buddhism as temporary manifestations (incarnations avatāra) of the Buddha. Along this line of thought a theory, called *honji-suijaku-setsu* was advanced, in which the Shintoist gods were maintained to be temporary incarnations of the Buddha. Emperor Yōmei is said to have "believed in Buddhism and at the same time to have worshipped the gods of Shintoism."

What "Shintoism" precisely means in the above question needs to be clarified, since in the Nara Period the idea of the reconciliation of Shintoism and Buddhism had already come to the fore. According to this school of thought, the god rejoices in the Law of the Buddha and defends Buddhism, but since the god is an entirety in the mundane world just as other human beings are and is not free from affliction, he also seeks salvation. The Nara Period saw many a shrine-temple built. The Imperial message of 767 stated that auspicious signs appeared, thanks to the

Buddha, the Japanese gods and goddesses of heaven and earth, and spirits of the successive emperors.

Thereafter, during the Heian Period, there were few shrines that did not have shrines built in their confines, where Buddhist priests performed the morning and evening practices of reciting sūtra, and served shrine gods and goddesses together with Shintoist priests.

Indeed, deep-rooted was the belief among the common men in the native gods and goddesses was then enhanced to such an extent that they were entitled Bodhisattvas.

The gods and goddesses were thus exalted from the status of deluded mankind to that of persons who were on their way toward enlightenment, or to the status of those who save mankind.

The idea that the Japanese native gods are the temporary manifestations of the Buddha first appeared in the classical writings of the years of Kankō (1004–1012), in the middle of the Heian Period. After the reign of Emperor Gosanjō, the question was raised as to what the fundamental basis was whose manifestations were these native gods and goddesses. During the period of the civil wars between the Genji and Heike Clans, each god or goddess was gradually allotted to his or her own Buddha, whose incarnation he or she was supposed to be, until at last during the Shokyu years (1218–1222), the idea was established that a god and the Buddha were identical in the body. "There is no difference between what is called a Buddha and what is called a god."

What is the way of thinking that made such a reconciliation of Buddhism and Shintoism possible? The influence of the traditional character of Buddhism cannot be denied, and it is particularly important to point out the influence of the idea of the One Vehicle manifested in the Lotus Sūtra. The imperial Rescript of November, the third year of Shōwa (836) says: "There is nothing superior to the One Vehicle to defend Shintoism." It goes without saying that Nichiren, who expressed absolute allegiance to the Lotus Sūtra, also showed his genuine loyalty to the Japanese gods and goddesses. Even the Jōdo Shin Sect, which was originally opposed to the gods and goddess. Even the Jōdo Shin Sect, which was originally opposed to the gods and goddesses of Shintoism, calmed down their opposition into a more conciliatory attitude. The theoretical basis for such a rapprochement was provided not by the triple-sūtras of Pure Realm Buddhism but by the Tendai doctrine based upon the Lotus Sūtra.

The Japanese native gods, exalted as they are from natural religious deities, kept their own distinctive existences intact. In this respect they differ completely from the Occidental counterpart, such as the ancient German religion, a trace of which is maintained in the form of the Christmas festivities within Christianity. The Japanese never considered it necessary to repudiate their religious faith in the native gods in order to become devoted followers of Buddhism. In this manner they brought about the conception of "God-Buddhas." It is generally seen even today that the ardent Buddhist is at the same time a pious worshipper of Shintoist gods. The majority of the Japanese pray before the shrines and at the same time pay homage at the temples, without being conscious of any contradiction. We may say that such a tendency has some merits on the one hand and demerits on the other. Critical comments will be given on other occasions. Anyhow, it is seen beginning with the reception of Buddhism in Japan.

Perhaps social scientists will in the end furnish us with statistical proof for my suggestion that the Japanese are a tolerant race. My own impression comes, as I have shown, from the study of documents and from personal observations.

1 *F. S. C. Northrop,* The Taming of Nations, 1952, Macmillan, p. 5.

2 *These features were discussed in the author's work:* Tñyōjin no Shii Hōhō (The Ways of Thinking of Eastern Peoples), vol. 1, Tokyo, 1948. *A new edition is to be published by Shunju-*

1 F. S. C. NORTHROP, *The Taming of Nations,* 1952, Macmillan, p. 5.

2 These features were discussed in the author's work: *Tōyōjin no Shii Hōhō* (The Ways of Thinking of Eastern Peoples), vol. 1, Tokyo, 1948. A new edition is to be published by Shunjusha (Tokyo).

3 The author treated the naturalistic view of life in an essay: "Some Features of the Japanese Way of Thinking" (in *Monumenta Nipponica;* vol. XIV, Nos. 3–4, Tokyo, 1958–59, pp. 31–72).

4 *The Analects of Confucius, 1, 12:* 'In practicing the rules of propriety, a natural ease is to be prized." Here "a natural ease" is the translation of the Chinese word *wa.* (*Confucian Analects. Dr. Legge's Version.* Edited with Notes by OGAERI Yoshio, Tokyo; Bunki Shoten, 1950, p. 4).

5 In the Chinese versions of Buddhist scriptures such words as *wakei* (wakyo) or *wago* are frequently used.

6 The details are mentioned in the author's work: *Jihi* (Compassion), Kyoto, Heirakuji-Shoten, 1956, pp. 258–271.

7 *Shugi-washo,* vol. 10, p. 1a (an old printed text, presumably to be found in the libraries of the University of Tokyo.)

8 See, for example, the stories of *Mie no Uneme* and the Emperors Kensō and Keitai; *Kojiki* (Records of Ancient Matters), translated by Basil Hall CHAMBERLAIN, supplement to vol. X, Translations of the Asiatic Society of Japan, Tokyo, 1906, pp. 402, 419, 424.

9 Ibid., pp. 213, 215.

10 Pillar EDICT III (D. R. BHANDARKAR: *Asoka,* 3rd ed., University of Calcutta, 1955, p. 302.)

11 Op. cit. pp. 61–62.

12 Ibid., p. 62.

13 Ibid., pp. 4–5.

14 Yerragudi Edict.

15 Op. cit., p. 133.

16 Ibid., p. 64.

17 Ibid., pp. 215–216.

18 *Separate Kalinga Edicts,* II. (D. R. BHANDARKAR, op. cit., p. 329.)

19 *Pillar Edict V* (D. R. BHANDARKAR, op. cit., p. 270.)

20 *Dhammapada*, v. 163. (The Dhammapada with introductory essays, Pali text, English translation and notes by S. RADHAKRISHNAN. Oxford University Press, London, 2nd impression, 1954, p. 113.)

21 Prince Shōtoku's *Shomangyo-gisho*, ed. by HANAYAMA Shinsho, Iwanami, Tokyo, 1948, p. 34.

22 *Rock Edicts, XIII.*

23 Op. cit., p. 117.

24 Ibid., p. 137.

25 In the introductory manifesto of *Jinno Shōtō-ki*, p. 585.

26 *Kanke bunso*, vol. 3 (*Kitano bunso*, vol. 2, p. 24; in Kitano-shi).

27 Cf. *Komo toki*, vol. 1 (in *Yoshida Shin senshu*, vol. 2, p. 263), ed. by Yamaguchiken-Kyoikukai, Iwanami, Tokyo, 1934.

28 *Jinnō-shōtōki*, Kōchū Nippon Bungaku Taikei, vol. 18.

29 *Shutsujo-shogo*. Ed. and pub. by Kokumin Tosho Kabushiki Kaisha, Tokyo, 1925, p. 592.

30 Indians will be Indians; Chinese will be Chinese. We do not look down upon them or criticize them for being what they are.

31 According to legend, when Shinran paid a visit to the mausoleum of Prince Shōtoku at the age of nineteen, the Prince appeared in his dream and conferred upon him a verse in which is the phrase: "Japan is the country where Mahāyāna Buddhism is practiced." (Goten Ryōkū: *Takeda Shinran Shōnin Seitōden*, vol. 1, in *Shinshū Zensho Shidenbu*, p. 337. Cf. Hōkū: *Jōgū Taishi Shūiki*, in *Dainihon Bukkyō Zensho*, vol. 112, p. 142).

32 MIYAMOTO Shoson: *Chūdō-shisō oyobi sono Hattatsu*, Kyoto, Hozokan, 1944, pp. 888, 889.

33 HANAYAMA Shinsho: *Hokke Gisho no Kenkyū*, Tokyo, Oriental Library, 1933, p. 469.

34 *Yuimakyō Gisho*, in *Dainihon Bukkyō Zensho*, p. 141.

35 *Hokke Gisho, inihon Buddo Zenshō*, p. 46.

36 Ibid., p. 28a. Similar expressions are found here and there. Cf. ibid., pp. 5a, 28a; 34a, and HANAYAMA: *Hokke Gisho no Kenkyū*, pp. 469, 489.

37 The phrase 得一切衆生殊勝供養 was interpreted "to make (Buddhas and Bodhisattvas) worship all living beings of distinction." It is needless to say that this is a twisted interpretation. An altruistic idea is introduced here. (Cf. HANAYAMA: *Shomangyo Gisho no Kenkyū*, pp. 434–437.)

38 HANAYAMA: *Hokke Gisho no Kenkyū*, pp. 386ffi%.

39. The famous story of abandonment of Prince Vessantara (*Jataka* No. 547), for example, is a good illustration.

40 HANAYAMA Shinsho: *Shōmangyo Gisho no Kenkyū*, p. 432.

41 This sentence is very famous and highly esteemed among Japanese. The original Sanskrit test runs as follows: "And the sermon he preaches will not fade from his memory. The popular maxims of common life, whether sayings or counsels, he will know how to reconcile with the rules of the low." *The Saddharmapundarika* or the *Lotus of the True Law*, translated by H. KERN, Oxford, 1909. See vol. 21, p. 351. Cf. also the edition by H. KERN and B. NANJIO, St.-Petersbourg, Imprimerie de l'Academie Imperiale des Sciences, 1912. Bibliotheca Buddhica 10, p. 372; and the edition by WOGIHARA Unrai and TSUCHIDA C., Tokyo, Seigo-kenkyūkai, 1934, p. 315. Here we find no mention of the words "politics" or "economics".

42 Chosui's *Commentary on the Sūragama-sūtra,* vol. 1a.

43 *Jōgai Ofumi* (帖外御文 Extra-canonical letters, No. 52).

44 A Bodhisattva is a future Buddha who wants to save all living beings.

45 Founder of Chinese *Zen* Buddhism.

46 "Being destined for enlightenment," i.e. a candidate for enlightenment, in order to bring salvation to all mankind.

So far I have pointed out some important problems and salient features of Japanese philosophical thought. I hope the readers have come to notice that in the long history of Japanese thought nearly the same philosophical problems were discussed as in other traditions of the world even before the over-all introduction of Western civilization, but in a different setting.

However, I regret that my explanation has not been clear enough to solve these philosophical problems and to evaluate them as should have been done in such a way as is worth while, because my stock of knowledge is limited and the space assigned by the *Kokusai Bunka Shinkokai* is also limited. I must admit that many works by ancient Japanese should be investigated, and that they have been unfortunately been neglected by Japanese intellectuals. This fact might strike foreigners as a strange, but there have been some reasons.

After the Meiji Restoration it was encouraged by the authorities to cut off our own religious tradition to replace it with nationalism and Emperor worship which were exceedingly forced till the end of World War II. Intellectuals have paid attention to the West alone. Western, chiefly German, philosophy alone was taught among philosophers. Whenever a philosophical work is published in German or in French, it is immediately translated into Japanese. It is said jokingly, therefore, that philosophical books written in German sell more in Japan than in Germany itself. There has been no Japanese philosopher who claims to specialize in Japanese thought.

It is true that Japanese tradition was exceedingly esteemed in the past, but it was done by ultra-nationalists, generals and high officials, and not by intellectuals. The latter have been mostly antagonistic to the movements of the former, although not successfully. The studies carried on by some nationalist scholars were forced, twisted and not convincing.

In Japanese national universities there is no chair for Japanese philosophy. Those chairs established for it before the war were abolished, and any project to newly establish one is met by strong opposition on the part of professors who are very watchful of the movement to recover nationalist influence. But I think Japanese philosophy in the past should be examined apart from nationalistic interest.

In Japan Buddhist studies are now flourishing, but most scholars are engaged in philological approaches to them and not in philosophical ones. Works by medieval Buddhist theologians are new resources to be exploited. They contain a lot of absurd explanations when we check them closely with their Sanskrit originals, and so capable scholars are looking down upon them with contempt. They may represent, say, seventy percent absurd and arbitrary sayings, but the remaining thirty percent will exhibit us sayings of philosophical value, just as medieval theological works by Christian, Islamic and Hindu theologians will do. It is a pity that only sectarian-minded theologians of the present time read them and scholars of modern approach do not read them. These works will assure us with great amount of philosophical insight. Things are more or less the same with Shinto and Confucian studies in Japan. Their ways of explaining things are highly twisted and far-fetched, but in most of the cases we can find the necessity for that because they are urged by the need of philosophical consistency and the sociological needs of the day.

Japanese Buddhist logicians have left a huge amount of logical works which are commentaries on Chinese-translated Indian treatises. I do not know how to deal with them adequately; few modern studies have been made in this field. These treasures are left to future investigations by rising scholars.

A BIBLIOGRAPHY OF WORKS ON JAPANESE
THOUGHT IN WESTERN LANGUAGES

I General Works

As regards the books on purely philosophical thought of pre-Meiji period not many works exist. But among works on religion, ethics and aesthetics, there are some references or clues to philosophical thinking of Japan.

Gino K. PIOVESANA. *Recent Japanese Philosophical Thought 1862–1962. A Survey*. Tokyo, Enderle Bookstore, 1963. Reviewed by M. SCALIGERO, EW. vol. 15, 1965, pp. 381–383.

Japanese Religion and Philosophy: A Guide to Japanese Reference and Research Materials. Compiled by Donald Holzman, with Moto-MOTOYAMA Yukihiko and others. Edited by J. K. YAMAGIWA. Ann ARBOR, the University of Michigan, Center for Japanese Studies, Bibliographical Series, No. 7, 1959. This is an introduction to works written in Japanese.

II Japanese Culture

Wm. Theodore DeBARY, Donald KEENE and TSUNODA Ryūsaku. *Sources of the Japanese Tradition*. New York, Columbia University Press, 1958.

Japan in the Chinese Dynastic Histories. Translated by TSUNODA R. Calif., South Pasadena, Calif., P. D. and I. PERKINS, 1951.

TSUCHIHASHI P. Yachita. *Japanese Chronological Tables*. Sophia University, 1952.

Japan: Its Lands, People and Culture. Compiled by The Japanese National Commission for UNESCO, 1959.

Translations from Early Japanese Literature. By Edwin O. REISCHAUER and Joseph K. YAMAGIWA. Harvard University Press, 1951.

Religions in Japan at Present. The Institute for Research in Religious Problems.

Proceedings of the IXth International Congress for the History of Religions, 1958. Tokyo, Maruzen, 1960.

Religious Studies in Japan. Edited by Japanese Association for Religious Studies and Japanese Organizing Committee of the Ninth International Congress for the History of Religions. Tokyo, Maruzen, 1959.

Transactions of the International Conference of Orientalists in Japan.
No. I–V, 1956–1960. Tokyo, Toho Gakkai (Institute of Eastern
Culture).

III Japanese Religion in General

ANESAKI Masaharu. *History of Japanese Religion.* London, Kegan
Paul, Trench, Trubner, 1930. Reprinted by Tuttle Company.

ANESAKI Masaharu. *Religious Life of the Japanese People.* Revised by
KISHIMOTO Hideo. Tokyo, Kokusai Bunka Shinkokai, 1961.
Agency: East-West Center Press, Honolulu.

Wilhelm GUNDERT. *Japanische Religionsgeschichte: Die Religionen
der Japaner und Koreaner in geschichtlichem Abriss dargestellt.* Tokyo-
Stuttgart, 1935. Reviewed by H. DUMOULIN, Monumenta Nipponica, vol. 1, 1938, pp. 282–283.

Heinrich DUMOULIN. *Östliche Meditation und christliche Mystik.*
Freiburg/München, Verlag Karl Alber, 1966.

IV Japanese Buddhism

a) General Outline

(Recent Works)

E. Dale SAUNDERS. *Buddhism in Japan, with an Outline of Its
Origins in India.* Philadelphia, University of Pennsylvania
Press, 1964.

HANAYAMA Shinsho. *A History of Japanese Buddhism.* Tr. by
YAMAMOTO Kosho. Tokyo, the CIIB Press, 1960.

ISHII Mamine Shimpo. *Japanese Buddhism.* Tokyo, Zojoji Press,
1959.

WATANABE Shoko. *Japanese Buddhism: a Critical Appraisal.*
Tokyo, Kokusai Bunka Shinkokai, 1964.

Kenneth W. MORGAN. *The Path of the Buddha.* New York,
Ronald Press, 1956, pp. 307–400.

(Earlier Works)

Sir Charles ELIOT. *Japanese Buddhism.* London, Edward Arnold
& Co., 1935. The most detailed outline in English even in
the present.

SUZUKI D. T. *Japanese Buddhism.* Tokyo, Board of Tourist

Industry, Japanese Government Railways, 1938.

J. B. PRATT. *The Pilgrimage of Buddhism.* New York, 1928, pp. 436–671.

A. K. REISCHAUER. *Studies in Japanese Buddhism.* New York, 1925.

Robert Cornell ARMSTRONG. *Buddhism and Buddhists in Japan.* New York, 1927.

ANESAKI Masaharu. *Quelques pages de l'histoire religieuse du Japon:* conferences faites au College de France. Paris, 1921.

ANESAKI Masaharu. *Katam Karaniyam:* Lectures, Essays and Studies by ANESAKI Masaharu. Tokyo, 1934.

Otto ROSENBERG. *Die Weltanschaung des modernen Buddhismus im fernen Osten.* Heidelberg, O. Harrassowitz, 1924.

TAKAKUSU Junjiro. *The Essentials of Buddhist Philosophy.* Honolulu, The University of Hawaii Press, 1947. A reliable work as an introduction to Japanese Buddhism, although this may not be so easy for foreign readers to read.

Marimum Willem de VISSER. *Ancient Buddhism in Japan: Sūtras and Ceremonies in Use in the Seventh and Eighth Centuries A.D. and Their History in Later Times.* 3 vols. Leiden, 1935.

SUZUKI D. T. *Buddhist Philosophy and Its Effects on the Life and Thought of the Japanese People.* Tokyo, Kokusai Bunka Shinkokai (The Society for International Cultural Relations), 1936.

Rev. James SUMMERS. *Buddhism, and Traditions Concerning Its Introduction into Japan.* TASJ 1907.

Arthur LLOYD. *Formative Elements of Japanese Buddhism.* TASJ. Tokyo, 1908.

Arthur LLOYD. *The Creed of Half Japan: Historical Sketches of Japanese Buddhism.* London, 1911.

Dwight GODDARD. *Buddha, Truth, and Brotherhood: an Epitome of Many Buddhist Scriptures.* Translated from the Japanese. American ed. Santa Barbara, California, 1934.

  b) Buddhism and Japanese

NAKAMURA Hajime. *Ways of Thinking of Eastern Peoples: India-China-Tibet-Japan*. Edited by Philip P. WIENER. Honolulu, East-West Center, 1964. pp. 343-587.

NAKAMURA Hajime. *The Ways of Thinking of Eastern Peoples*. Published by the Japanese National Commission for UNESCO. Tokyo, 1960. (out of print)

TAMURA Y. *Living Buddhism in Japan*. Tokyo, International Institute for the Study of Religions, 1961.

Japan and Buddhism. The Association of the Buddhajayanti, Tokyo, 1959.

NAKARAI, WADA Toyozo. *A Study of the Impact of Buddhism upon Japanese Life as Revealed in the Odes of the Kokin-shū*. Greenfield, Indiana, 1931.

Georges BONNEAU. *La sensibilite japonaise*. 3 ed. Tokyo, 1934.

Kogoshui, Gleanings from Ancient Stories. Tr. by KATO Genchi and HOSHINO Hikoshiro. 4th ed. Tokyo, Meiji Japan Society, 1937.

HANAYAMA Shinsho. *The Way of Deliverance: Three Years with the Condemned Japanese War Criminals*. New York, Charles Scribner's Sons, 1950.

YAMAMOTO Kosho. *The Udumbara: Tales from Buddhist Japan*. Tokyo, the CIIB, Tsukiji-Hongwanji, 1959.

Courses on Religion in Universities. Tokyo, The International Institute for the Study of Religions, Incorporated.

ASAKAWA. *Social Reactions of Buddhism in Medieval Japan*. (In Panama-Pacific Historical Congress, 1915. The Pacific Ocean in History—ed. by Morse STEPHANS and Herbert E. BOLTON. New York, 1917.)

J. M. JAMES. *Descriptive Notes on the Rosaries (jiu-dzu) as used by the Different Sects of Buddhists in Japan*. TASJ. Tokyo, 1905.

ANESAKI Masaharu. *Buddhist Art in Its Relation to Buddhist Ideals, with Special Reference to Buddhism in Japan*. Boston and New York, 1915.

ICHIKAWA Sanki. *Japanese Noh Dramas*, 3 vols. Tokyo, The

Nippon Gakujutsu Shinkokai.

c) Prince Shōtoku

ANESAKI Masaharu. *Prince Shōtoku, The Sage-Statesman and His Mahasattva Ideal.* Tokyo, The Boonjudo Publishing House, 1948.

ANESAKI Masaharu. *Prince Shōtoku, The Sage-Statesman of Japan.* Nara, Hōryūji Temple.

Friedrich HEILER and NAKAMURA H. *My Impression in front of the Mausoleum of Prince Shōtoku.* Osaka, Eifukuji Temple, 1961.

MOCHIZUKI Kazunori. *The Mausoleum of Prince Shōtoku.* Osaka, Eifukuji Temple, 1958.

MOCHIZUKI Kazunori. *A Treatise on Prince Shōtoku.* Tokyo, New Educational Research Institute, 1959.

ANESAKI Masaharu. *The Foundation of Buddhist Culture in Japan. The Buddhist Ideals as Conceived and Carried Out by the Prince-Regent Shōtoku.* Monumenta Nipponica, vol. 6, 1943, Nos. 1–2, pp. 1–12.

BOHNER Herman. *Shōtoku Taishi.* Tokyo, Deutsche Gesellschaft fur Natur- und Völker Kunde Ostasiens, 1940.
This is a voluminous book in German amounting to 1003 pages. Reviewed by C. von WEEGMANN, *Monumenta Nipponica,* vol. 5, 1942, pt. 2, pp. 279–285.

d) Sanron Sect

Richard A. GARD. Why did the Mādhyamika decline? *Journal of Indian and Buddhist Studies,* vol. 5, No. 2, March 1957, pp. 619–623.

e) The Kegon Sect

Serge ELISSEEFF. *The Bommokyo and the Great Buddha of the Todaiji.* (HJAS. Vol. I, 1936, pp. 84–96)

f) Tendai Philosophy

UI Hakuju. A Study of Japanese Tendai Buddhism. *Philosophical Studies of Japan,* published by Japan Society for the Promotion of Science, Tokyo, vol. I, 1959, pp. 33–74.

g) Shingon Sect

Kobo Daishi (The Mikkyo Bunka: The Quarterly Reports on
the Esoteric Buddhism.) 1949–1957. Koyasan University.

TAJIMA Ryujun. *Les deux grands Mandalas et la doctrine de l'eso-
terisme Shingon.* Tokyo, Comite de publication de l'ouvre
posthume du Rev. Tajima, 1959.

Hermann BOHNER. *Kōbō Daishi.* Monumenta Nipponica, vol.
6, 1943, Nos. 1–2, pp. 266–313. In this article the writer
examines various biographies of Kōbō Daishi (in German).

Helmuth von GLASENAPP. *Die Stellung der esoterischen Sekten
Japans in der Geschichte der buddhistischen Überlieferung. Osta-
siatische Studien,* Berlin, Akademie-Verlag, 1959, S. 81–84.

Sangō Shīki (三教指歸)

HAKEDA Y. S. The Religious Novel of Kūkai. Monumenta
Nipponica, vol. 20, Nos. 3–4, 1965, pp. 283–297.

Some important works by Kūkai or Kōbō Daishi were translated
into English by the Translation Institute in Kōyasan University:

1) *Sokushin Jōbutsugi* (即身成佛義 The Doctrine of Attaining
Buddhahood While Living in Human Body). *The Mikkyō
Bunka,* vol. 27, pp. 1–12; vol. 28, pp. 13–22; vols. 29–30,
pp. 23–32; vol. 31, pp. 1–12; vol. 32, pp. 1–10; vol. 33,
pp. 1–14; vol. 34, pp. 1–10; vol. 38, pp. 1–19, 1954–1956.

2) *Unjigi* (宇字義 The Doctrine of the Syllable Hūm). *The
Mikkyō Bunka,* vol. 17, pp. 1–10; vol. 18, pp. 11–20; vol. 19,
pp. 21–32; vol. 20, pp. 33–42; vol. 21, pp. 43–54; vol. 22,
pp. 55–62; vol. 23, pp. 63–72; vols. 24–25, pp. 73–82,
1951–1953.

3) *Shōji Jissōgi* (聲字實相義 A Treatise on the Meaning of
Voice and Syllable and Reality). *The Mikkyō Bunka,* vol. 7,
pp. 1–10; vol. 8, pp. 1–10; vols. 9–10, pp. 1–12; vol. 11,
pp. 1–12; vol. 12, pp. 1–12; vol. 13, pp. 1–12, 1948–1950.

h) Pure Realm Buddhism

YAMAMOTO Kosho. *An Introduction to Shin Buddhism.* Ube,
Yamaguchi-ken, Karinbunko, 1963. This is a detailed and

comprehensive introduction.

H. COATES and ISHIZUKA. *Honen, the Buddhist Saint, His Life and Teaching.* 6 vols. Kyoto, the Society for the Publication of Sacred Books of the World, 1949.

Paul CARUS. *Amitabha.*

FUJIMOTO R. *An Outline of the Triple Sūtra of Shin Buddhism,* vol. I, 1955. Kyoto, Honpa Hongwanji Press.

UTSUKI Nishu. *The Shin Sect, a School of Mahayana Buddhism, Its Teaching, Brief History, and Present-day Conditions.* Publication Bureau of Buddhist Books, Honpa Hongwanji, Kyoto, Japan, 1937.

Selections from the Nippon Seishin (Japanese Spirit) Library. Edited by AKEGARASU Haya. Kososha, Kitayasuda, Ishikawa-ken, Japan, 1936.

James TROUP. On the Tenets of the Shinshu or 'True Sect' of Buddhists. *TASJ.* 1907.

Rev. NAKAI Gendo. *Shinran and His Religion of Pure Faith.* Kyoto, The Shinshu Research Institute, 1937.

Guide Book to the Buildings of the West Hongwanji. Kyoto, West Hongwanji.

(Texts)

The Kyogyoshinsho or the 'Teaching, Practice, Faith, and Attainment.' Translated by YAMAMOTO Kosho. Tokyo, Karinbunko, 1958.

The Shinshu Seiten. The Holy Scripture of Shinshu. Honolulu, The Honpa Hongwanji Mission of Hawaii, 1955. The scriptures other than the *Kyogyoshinsho* are translated.

UTSUKI Nishu. *Selected Texts of Shin Buddhism.*

YAMAMOTO Kosho. *The Private Letters of Shinran Shonin.* Tokyo, Okazakiya, 1946.

Tannishō. A Tract Deploring Heresies of Faith. Kyoto, Higashi Hongwanji Shumusho, 1961.

Shinran-shōnin's Tanni-shō with Buddhist Psalms. Tr. by INAGAKI Saizō. Eishinsha, 510, Nishikubo Takagi, Nishinomiya City,

1949.

KANAMATSU Kenryo. *Naturalness*. Los Angeles, The White Path Society, 1956.

MIKOGAMI Eryu. Outline of the Notes Lamenting Differences. Published in *Journal of Ryukoku University*. Kyoto, 1953.

IMADATE Tosui. *The Tannishō (Tracts on Deploring the Heterodoxies)*. Kyoto, 1928.

i) The Nichiren Sect

ANESAKI Masaharu. *The Buddhist Prophet*. Harvard, 1916.

SATOMI Kishio. *Japanese Civilization, Its Significance and Realization. Nichirenism and the Japanese National Principles*. London, 1923.

Nichiren's *The True Object of Worship*. Tr. by MURANO Senchu. The Young East Association, 1, 3-chome, Tsukiji, Chuo-ku, Tokyo, 1954.

j) Zen Buddhism

1) Outline

There are many works on Zen in English by Japanese authors, but they represent one branch or tendency or another, and cannot help but being one-sided. Strange to say, a rather objective, overall historical sketch was given by a German Catholic father.

Heinrich DUMOULIN. *Zen. Geschichte und Gestalt*. Bern, Francke Verlag, 1959.

Heinrich DUMOULIN. *A History of Zen Buddhism*. New York, Pantheon Books, 1963.

2) Chinese Zen Buddhism in General and Rinzai Sect

John BLOFELD. *The Zen Teaching of Huang Po, on the Transmission of Mind*. An Evergreen Original, New York, the Grove Press, 1959.

SUZUKI Daisetz Teitaro. *Living by Zen*. The Sanseido Publishing Company, Kanda, Tokyo, 1949.

SUZUKI Daisetz Teitaro. *The Zen Doctrine of No-Mind*. London, 1949.

SUZUKI Daisetz Teitaro. *An Introduction to Zen Buddhism* (2nd ed., London, Rider and Co., 1957).

SUZUKI Daisetz Teitaro. *Essays in Zen Buddhism,* First Series (2nd ed., New York, Harper and Bros., 1949).

SUZUKI Daisetz Teitaro. *Essays in Zen Buddhism,* Second Series (2nd ed., London, Rider and Co., 1957).

SUZUKI Daisetz Teitaro. *Essays in Zen Buddhism,* Third Series (2nd ed., London, Rider and Co., 1953).

SUZUKI Daisetz Teitaro. *A Manual of Zen Buddhism* (2nd ed., London, Rider and Co., 1957).

SUZUKI Daisetz Teitaro. *The Training of the Zen Buddhist Monk.* (1st American ed., New York, University Books, 1959).

SUZUKI Daisetz Teitaro. Zen Buddhism. *Monumenta Nipponica,* vol. 1, 1938, pp. 48–57. He discusses the thought of Zen masters of China who were influential in Japan.

SUZUKI Daisetz Teitaro. *Zen and Japanese Buddhism.* Tokyo, Japan Travel Bureau, Charles E. Tuttle Co., 1958.

SUZUKI Daisetz Teitaro. *Zen Buddhism: Selected Writings of D. T. Suzuki.* Ed. by William BARRETT (A Doubleday Anchor Book). New York, Doubleday, 1956.

SUZUKI Daisetz Teitaro. *The Ten Oxherding Pictures.* Sekai Seiten Kanko Kyokai, No. 496. Hanatatecho, Kamigyo-ku XII, Kyoto, 1948.

SUZUKI Daisetz Teitaro. Buddhist Symbolism, Published in *Symbols and Values: An Initial Study.* Thirteenth Symposium of the Conference on Science, Philosophy and Religion. Ed. by L. BRYSON, L. FINKELSTEIN, R. M. MACIVER, and R. McKEON. Harper and Brothers. New York and London, 1954.

SUZUKI Daisetz Teitaro. The Philosophy of Zen, *published in Philosophy East and West.* Vol. I, No. 2, 1951.

SUZUKI Daisetz Teitaro. Zen: A Reply to HuShih. Published in *Philosophy East and West.* Vol. III, No. 1, 1953.

Buddhism and Culture: Dedicated to Dr. SUZUKI Daisetz Teitaro in Commemoration of His Ninetieth Birthday. Edited by YAMAGUCHI Susumu. Kyoto, Suzuki Foundation, 1960.

R. H. BLYTH. *Zen in English Literature and Oriental Classics.* Tokyo, Hokuseido, 1948.

R. H. BLYTH. *Zen and Zen Classics,* vol. I. Tokyo, Hokuseido.

H. DUMOULIN and Ruth F. SASAKI. *The Development of Chinese Zen after the Sixth Patriarch in the Light of Mumonkfin.* The First Zen Institute of America, New York, 1953.

Alan W. WATTS. *The Spirit of Zen.* (The Wisdom of the East Series.) London, 1936.

Alan W. WATTS. *Zen.* Stanford, California, 1948.

Alan W. WATTS. *The Way of Zen.* (A Mentor Book). New York, Pantheon Books, Inc., 1957.

Erich FROMM, SUZUKI Daisetz Teitaro, R. de MARTINO. *Zen Buddhism and Psycho-analysis.*

Ruth Fuller SASAKI. *Rinzai Zen Study for Foreigners in Japan.* Kyoto, the First Zen Institute of America in Japan. (107 Daitokuji-cho, Murasakino, Kyoto, 1960); The First Zen Institute of America, Inc., 156 Waverly Place, New York 14.

3) Soto Sect of Zen Buddhism

MASUNAGA Reiho. *The Soto Approach to Zen.* Tokyo, Layman Buddhist Society Press, 1956. This work includes translations of some chapters of *Shōbōgenzō.*

MASUNAGA Reiho. *Zen for Daily Living.* Tokyo, Shunjusha, 1964.

Heinrich DUMOULIN. Die religiöse Metaphysik des japanischen Zen-Meisters Dōgen, *Saeculum* XII, Heft 3, S. 205–236.

This is one of the rare works dealing with philosophy as such.

Zen. The Way to a Happy Life. Compiled and published by
the Headquarters of the Soto Sect, Tokyo, n.d. In this
work new methods such as measurement of waves in
electroencephalographic studies are applied.

Ernest S. HUNT. Gleanings from Soto Zen, 1957. Honolulu,
Soto Mission.

NUKARIYA Kaiten. *The Religion of the Samurai. A Study of
Zen Philosophy and Discipline in China and Japan.* London,
1913.

Sokei-An (alias SASAKI Shigetsu). *Cat's Yawn.* New York,
First Zen Institute of America, 1947.

FUJIMOTO Rindō. *The Way of Zazen.* Cambridge, Mass.,
Cambridge Buddhist Association, 1961.

*Sōbōgenzō-Zuimonki. Wortgetreue Niederschrift der lehrreichen
Worte Dōgen-Zenzis über den wahren Buddhismus.* Aus-
gewählt, übersetzt und mit kurzer Biographie sowie
einem Anhang versehen von IWAMOTO Hidemasa. Tokyo,
Sankibo, 1943.

(Texts)

Dōgen's Fukan Zazengi (普勧坐禅儀 Teachings to Promote Meditation) was translated into German by H.
DUMOULIN, *Monumenta Nipponica,* vol. 12, Nos. 3–4,
1956, pp. 183–190.

Shushōgi (修證義). Prinzipien der Ubung und Erleuchtung.
Eine Zenschrift fur Laien. Translated into German by
ISHIMOTO K. and P. E. NABERFELD. *Monumenta Nipponica,*
vol. 6, Nos. 1–2, pp. 355–369.

Keizan (1268–1325)'s Zazen Yōjinki (坐禅用心記) was
translated into German by Heinrich DUMOULIN, *Monumenta Nipponica,* vol. 13, Nos. 3–4, 1957, pp. 147–167.
Then in his *Östliche Meditation und christliche Mystik.*
Freiburg/München, Verlag Karl Alber, 1966, S. 291–307.

4) Obaku Sect of Zen Buddhism

SHIBATA Masumi. *Le Sermon de Tetsugen sur le Zen.* Tokyo,

Tisōsha, 1960.

5) Contemporary Zen

UEDA Daisuke. *Zen and Science.* A Treatise on Causality and Freedom. Tokyo, Risōsha, 1963. This is a treatise from the standpoint of a scientist.

Betty and Van Meter AMES. *Japan and Zen.* Cincinnati, University of Cincinnati, 1961. Prof. V. M. AMES is an American professorof philosophy.

Ingeborg Y. WENDT. *Zen, Japan und der Westen.* München, Paul List Verlag, 1961.

Philip KAPLEAU. *The Three Pillars of Zen. Teaching/Practice/ Enlightenment.* Tokyo, John Weatherhill, 1965.

H. DUMOULIN. Die Zen-Erleuchtung in neueren Erlebnisberichten, *Numen,* vol. 10, Fasc. 2, Aug. 1963. In this article present-day Zen is discussed.

H. DUMOULIN. Technique and Personal Devotion in the Zen Exercise. *Studies in Japanese Culture.* Tokyo, Sophia University, 1963, pp. 17–40.

k) Buddhist Thinkers of the Modern or Tokugawa Period

Hakuin's *Yasen Kanna* (夜船閑話 A Chat on a Boat in the Evening), translated by R. D. M. SHAW and Wilhelm SCHIFFER, *Monumenta Nipponica,* vol. 13, Nos. 1–2, 1957, pp. 101–127.

YANAGI Sōetsu. Mokujiki Gogyō Shōnin. Bonze und Bildschnitzer der Edozeit. *Monumenta Nipponica,* vol. 6, Nos. 1–2, 1943, pp. 202–218.

l) Bibliography

BANDO S., HANAYAMA S., SATO R., SAYEKI S., and SHIMA K. *A Bibliography on Japanese Buddhism.* Tokyo, CIIB Press, 1958.

HANAYAMA Shinsho. *A Bibliography of Buddhism.* Tokyo, Hokuseido (in press).

V   Shintoism

a) Outline

KATO Genchi. *A Study of Shintō, The Religion of the Japanese Nation.* Tokyo, The Zaidan-Hōjin-Meiji-Seitoku-Kinen-Gakkai (Meiji Japan Society), 1926. A very scholarly work, fully documented. Still worth while.

An Outline of Shinto Teachings. Compiled by Shinto Committee for the IXth International Congress for the History of Religions. Tokyo, 1958.

Shinto Shrines and Festivals. Tokyo, Kokugaku-in University, 1958.

Guide Book of Shinto Shrines. Tokyo, Kokugaku-in University, 1958.

Basic Terms of Shinto. Tokyo, Kokugakuin University, 1958.

KŌNO Shōzō. *Kannagara no Michi* (神ながらの道) (in Engl.). *Monumenta Nipponica,* vol. 3, No. 2, 1940, pp. 9–31.

D. C. HOLTOM. *The Meaning of Kami. Monumenta Nipponica,* vol. 3, 1940, p. 1 ff.; 392 ff.; vol. 4, 1941, pt. 2, pp. 25–68.

KATŌ Genchi's two books in Japanese are very valuable. They were fure fully appreciated by Heinrich DUMOULIN, *Monumenta Nipponica,* vol. 1, pt. 2, 1938, pp. 284–292 (in German).

b) Mediaeval Shintoism

Verfasst von KITABATAKE Chikafusa. Uversetzt, eingeleitet und erläutert von Hermann BOHNER. Tokyo, Japanisch-Deutsches Kulturinstitut, 1938. Reviewed by J. B. KRAUS, *Monumenta Nipponica,* vol. 1, 1938, pp. 285–286; by H. ZACHERT, *Monumenta Nipponica,* vol. 3, 1940, No. 2, pp. 311–312.

Saka's Diary of a Pilgrim to Ise. Translated by A. L. SADLER with an introduction by KATŌ Genchi. Edited by the Meiji Japan Society, Tokyo, 1940. Reviewed by R. H. VAN GULLIK, *Monumenta Nipponica,* vol. 4, 1941, pt. 2, pp. 297–298.

Yuiitsu-Shintō Myōbō-yōshū (唯一神道名法要集), probably written by YOSHIDA Kanetomo (吉田兼倶 1435–1511) was translated into German by ISHIBASHI T. and H. DUMOULIN, *Monumenta Nipponica,* vol. 3, 1940, No. 1, pp. 182–239.

KATŌ Genchi. The Theological System of Urabe no Kanetomo.

Transactions and Proceedings of the Japan Society, London, vol. 28.

c) Shintoism in the Modern or Tokugawa Period

MURAOKA Tsunetsugu. *Studies in Shinto Thought.* Translated by D. M. BROWN and James T. ARAKI. Tokyo, Japanese National Commission for UNESCO, 1964. Reviewed by Francisco Pérez RUIZ. *Monumenta Nipponica,* vol. 21, Nos. 1–2, 1966, pp. 212–214.

Heinrich DUMOULIN, H. STOLTE und W. SCHIFFER. Die Entwicklung der Kokugaku Dargestellt in ihren Hauptvertretern, *Monumenta Nipponica,* vol. 2, 1939, pp. 140–164.

AZUMAMARO Kada (1669–1736)'s *Sō-Gakkō-kei* (創學校啓 Gesuch um die Errichtung einer Kokugaku-Schule) was translated into German by H. DUMOULIN, *Monumenta Nipponica,* vol. 3, No. 2, 1940, pp. 230–249.

Two texts by MABUCHI Kamo (1697–1769) *Uta no Kokoro no Uchi* and *Niimanabi* (爾比末奈妣) were translated into German by H. DUMOULIN, *Monumenta Nipponica,* vol. 4, 1941, pt. 1, pp. 192–206; pt. 2, pp. 240–258. They are treatises on Japanese poetry.

MABUCHI Kamo's *Kokuikō* (国意考) was translated into German by H. DUMOULIN, *Monumenta Nipponica,* vol. 2, 1939, pp. 165–192.

MABUCHI Kamo's Commentary on the Norito of the Toshigoi-no-Matsuri (祈年祭) was translated into German by H. DUMOULIN, *Monumenta Nipponica,* vol. 12, Nos. 1–2, 1956, pp. 121–156. Nos. 3–4, pp. 101–130.

The innovation of the Way of Poetry by MABUCHI Kamo was discussed by H. DUMOULIN, *Monumenta Nipponica,* vol. 6, 1943, Nos. 1–2, pp. 110–145.

H. DUMOULIN. *Kamo Mabuchi.* Tokyo, Sophia University, 1943.

MOTOORI Norinaga's *Naobi no Mitama* (直毘零) was translated into German by Hans STOLTE, *Monumenta Nipponica,* vol. 2,

1939, pp. 193–211.

HIRATA Atsutane's *Taidō Wakumon* (大道或問) was translated into German by Wilhelm SCHIFFER, *Monumenta Nipponica,* vol. 2, 1939, pp. 212–236.

KADA AzumamaroKAMO Mabuchi KAMO Mabuchi KAMO Mabuchi KAMO Mabuchi KAMO Mabuchi KAMO Mabuchi

d) Sectarian Shintoism before the Meiji Restoration

Charles William HEPNER. *The Kurozumi Sect of Shintō.* Tokyo, Meiji Japan Society, 1935. Reviewed by H. DUMOULIN, *Monumenta Nipponica,* vol. 2, No. 2, 1939, pp. 322–324.

Delwin B. SCHNEIDER. *Konkokyo. A Japanese Religion.* Tokyo, International Institute for the Study of Religions, 1962.

VI Confucianism

Confucianism in Action. Ed. by Arthur F. WRIGHT and David S. VIVISON. Stanford University Press, 1959.

KITAMURA Sawakichi. *Grundriss der Ju-Lehre.* Tokyo, Maruzen, 1935. Reviewed ?y W. SCHIFFER, *Monumenta Nipponica,* vol. 2, 1939, pp. 320–322.

J. R. McEwan. *The Political Writings of Ogyū Sorai.* Cambridge, Cambridge University Press, 1962. Reviewed by Joseph PITTAU, *Monumenta Nipponica,* vol. 17, 1962, p. 341.

Onna Daigaku (女大學). Ein Frauenspiegel der Tokugawa-zeit. Translated into German by KOIKE Kenji, *Monumenta Nipponica,* vol. 2, No. 2, 1939, pp. 254–263.

Horst HAMMITZSCH. *Die Mito-Schule* und ihre programmatischen Schriften *Bairi Sensei Hiin, Kōdōkanki, Kōdōkangakusoku, Seiki no Uta* in Uebersetzung. Ein Beitrag zur Geistesgeschichte der Tokugawa-Zeit. Tokyo, Deutsche Gesellschaft für Natur- und Völkerkunde Ostasiens, 1939. Reviewed by H. DUMOULIN, *Monumenta Nipponica,* vol. 3, No. 2, 1940, pp. 327–329.

Horst HAMMITZSCH. *Aizawa Seishisai (1782–1863) und sein Werk Shinron. Monumenta Nipponica,* vol. 3, No. 1, 1940, pp. 61–74.

VII Shingaku School

The outline of Shingaku is set forth in the following article:—

Horst HAMMITZSCH. *Shingaku*. Eine Bewegung der Volksauf-
klärung und Volkserziehung in der Tokugawazeit, *Monumenta
Nipponica*, vol. 4, 1941, Pt. 1, pp. 1–32.

VIII Japanese Christianity

Christianity in Japan. *A Bibliography of Japanese and Chinese Sources.*
Pt. 1 (1543–1858). Tokyo, International Christian University,
1960.

Hubert CIESLIK. *Kirishitan-Literatur der Nachkriegszeit. Monumenta
Nipponica*, vol. 16, Nos. 3–4, 1960–61, pp. 187–213.

Charles W. IGLEHART. *Protestant Christianity in Japan*. Charles E.
Tuttle Co.

MASUTANI Fumio. *A Comparative Study of Buddhism and Christianity*.
Tokyo, CIIB Press ,1959.

T. N. CALLAWAY. *Japanese Buddhism and Christianity*. Tokyo,
Shinkyo Shuppansha, 1957.

Pierre HUMBERTCLAUDE. *Myōtei Mondō*. Une apologétique chré-
tienne japonaise de 1605. *Monumenta Nipponica,* vol. 1, Pt. 2.
1938, pp. 223–256; vol. 2, 1939, pp. 237–267.

HAYASHI Razan's Hai-Yaso (排耶蘇 Anti-Jesus) was translated into
German by Hans MÜLLER, *Monumenta Nipponica*, vol. 2, No. 1,
1939, pp. 268–275.

IX Mediaeval Thought

HIRAIZUMI H. Der Einfluss der Mappō-Lehre in der japanischen
Geschichte. *Monumenta Nipponica*, vol. 1, 1938, pp. 58–69.

The Honchō-Shinsen-Den was translated into German by Hermann BOHNER, *Monumenta Nipponica,* vol. 13, Nos. 1–2, pp.
129–152.

X The Thought of the Modern or Tokugawa Period

Robert N. BELLAH. *Tokugawa Religion*. The Values of Pre-Industrial Japan. Glencoe, Illinois, The Free Press, 1957. Reviewed by
P. BEONIO-BROCCHIERI, *Monumenta Nipponica*, vol. 12, Nos. 1–2,
1956, pp. 226–227.

Horst HAMMITZSCH. Kangaku und Kokugaku. Ein Bei'rag zur
Geistesgeschichte der Tokugawazeit. *Monumenta Nipponica*, vol.

2, 1939, pp. 1–23.

XI Independent Thinkers

Gino K. PIOVESANA. *A Bibliographical Note on Miura Baien. Monumenta Nipponica,* vol. 19, Nos. 3–4, 1964, pp. 232–234.

Other articles on independent thinkers are mentioned in the footnotes to Chapter VI.

XII Journals

Journal of Indian and Buddhist Studies, since 1952. The Japanese Association for Indian Studies, c/o The Department of Indian and Buddhist Philosophy, University of Tokyo.

Monumenta Nipponica. Tokyo, Sophia University.

Young Buddhists' Bulletin. Tokyo, CIIB Press, 1959.

The Young East, since 1952. The Young East Association.

The Eastern Buddhist. Kyoto, the Eastern Buddhist Society, c/o Otani University.

The American Buddhist, since 1957. The Buddhist Churches of America, San Francisco.

Articles on special problems are mentioned in the footnotes.

Abbreviations

CIIB Press: c/o Hongwanji-Temple, Tsukiji, Chuo-ku, Tokyo, Japan

HJAS: Harvard Journal of Asiatic Studies, Cambridge, Massachusetts

TASJ: Transactions of Asiatic Society of Japan, Yokohama and Tokyo.